THE
DIRECTOR'S CUT
ROY WARD BAKER

THE
DIRECTOR'S CUT

ROY WARD BAKER

Reynolds & Hearn Ltd
London

TO ALL THE CREWS

for their wholehearted support and brilliant craftsmanship in England, Ireland, Scotland and Wales, Hollywood, Spain, Italy, Sweden, Poland and France, The Belgian Congo, Kenya and Hong Kong.

NOTES AND ACKNOWLEDGMENTS

All descriptions in the male gender are assumed to
refer equally to the female gender where appropriate.

Extract from *Memo from Daryl F Zanuck* by Rudy
Behlmer, 1993, pp 205-6. Reproduced by courtesy of
the Grove Press.

The publishers wish to thank Andrew Pixley for his
advice in compiling the filmography. Special thanks
to Lofty Rice, John Herron and Charlie Baker at
Pinewood Studios.

First published in 2000 by
Reynolds & Hearn Ltd
61a Priory Road
Kew Gardens
Richmond
Surrey TW9 3DH

A CIP catalogue record for this book is available from
the British Library.

ISBN 1-903111-02-1

Designed by Paul Chamberlain.

Printed in Great Britain by MPG Books Ltd,
Bodmin, Cornwall.

CONTENTS

Photo: Peter Everard-Smith

FOREWORD

Roy Ward Baker personally came into my life in the sixties when I was making *The Saint* but I was very familiar with his work before then. The classic films *Morning Departure* and *The One That Got Away*, and then the epic *A Night to Remember*, were among his most famous.

It occurs to me that it has taken an awfully long time for Roy to put his experiences down on paper. He is famous for his anecdotes and rememberings of his early days of working with Alfred Hitchcock and his recollections always made fascinating listening.

In life we should learn from the people we work with and I am always grateful to Roy because I learnt a great deal from him, not only about acting but also directing.

I am immensely privileged to have been part of Roy's working life.

Roger Moore CBE
Monaco, 1999

APPRENTICE

A FINE START

My first visit to the flicks was to a fleapit in North End Road, Fulham. My father and mother took me there one night. Silent movies, of course, in the twenties.

The film was set in the eighteenth century, about a conjuror who travelled the courts of Europe demonstrating a mechanical chess player. It was in the form of a life-sized wax figure of a sinister-looking Chinese seated behind a large desk. It took on all comers at the game and always defeated them.

The magician freely demonstrated that the desk and the figure were completely empty. There was no machinery inside the thing, so how it operated was a mystery. It scared me to death. Worse was to come. The hero in the story had been hidden in the machine: now he was hiding in a room full of wax dummies and the villain came in with a huge sword and started decapitating the dummies! Not suitable fare for the little ones. I was taken out, screaming hysterically. No more film-going for me.

Many years later, reading the works of Edgar Allen Poe, I came across an article he wrote for the *Southern Daily Messenger* in April 1836 called 'Maelzel's Chess Player'. Maelzel was, among other things, the inventor of the metronome and a friend of Beethoven. He had built a chess-playing automaton and toured Europe and America with it, beating all challengers. Poe saw his display at Richmond, Virginia, and showed in his article how a French chess master called Schlumberger, who was a man of very small stature, could be concealed inside the dummy. When Maelzel was opening up the desk and the dummy to show there was nothing inside, he never exposed the whole contraption at once. He opened the left hand side of the desk, then closed it before showing the back of the dummy, then closed that before exposing the right hand side, and so on. To my great relief the ghost of the chess player was laid at last. As we shall see, it just goes to show that many mysteries are unravelled as the years roll by. As was said, Truth is the daughter of time. Such a relief – if you live long enough.

My mostly long-lived male line is composed entirely of Londoners. I was born in 1916 in Hornsey. My father, Horace John, was born in King's Cross in 1888. My grandfather was a cab driver, born in the same area in 1855. Unfortunately, my great-grandfather was a bit of a mystery. Nobody in the family had any knowledge of him – or said they hadn't. At long last my father explained that the reluctance to discuss him was because there was a rumour that he might have been deaf and dumb. However, my father gave me an address: 43 Primrose Street, Bishopsgate. And there they were, Charles Baker and his family, in the census of 1861.

Charles's age is given as 40, so he was born 1820/21. His place of birth was Finsbury, Middlesex. He was deaf and dumb and a French polisher by trade. He had a wife and two children, a boy and a girl. His marriage certificate shows his father was also named Charles and is described as a porter in the Bank of England, but there is no trace of him at the bank.

Failing a birth certificate, a parish register entry of a baptism is the alternative source. Only one has turned up of a Charles Baker which doesn't conflict with the few known facts. At St Pancras Old Church on 15 March 1821, a boy was brought for christening by his mother Sarah Baker. She gave him the name Charles. No name of a father is given. So he was illegitimate and the male line stops here. However, it can be pursued.

The records of St Pancras workhouse show that Sarah's child was born there 2 March 1821. She was later examined by the workhouse authorities. She declared on oath that the father of her child was Lord Frederick Beauclerk, who must have been about 13 years of age at the time of the conception. Such a precocious lad. She was 19, a yearly servant. He was the second son of the Ninth Duke of St Albans and he served with distinction in the Navy, retiring with the rank of Commander. His male line goes back to the first Duke, whose parents were King Charles II and Nell Gwyn. However amusing this may be, there is no direct link between my great-grandfather Charles and the child in the workhouse.

My mother, Florence Ward, also came from a London family. The Wards appear in Bermondsey early in the 1800s. They moved to Clerkenwell in 1872, where they established a bill-posting business which flourished, staffed almost completely by the founder, his son and three grandsons.

My father was a salesman in Billingsgate Fish Market, which was hard graft. Eventually he ran his own business. He'd only had an elementary education but as a result he was a firm believer in the basics of learning. As Miss Dora Bryan succinctly put it, 'It's always a comfort to know you've got your R's to fall back on.' He was deeply impressed by the historic atmosphere of the City of London and his dearest wish was that I should go to the City of London School. After a stay in France to learn the language and some heavy cramming at Marcy's, which was in a court at the back of the Cheshire Cheese in Fleet Street, I was accepted.

I derived nothing but benefit from my stay at CLS. They taught me how to learn – and that, to my mind, is the proper business of a school. The quality of the teaching was first class. Every one of the masters wore a gown; he had been properly educated himself and he had the gift of conveying that knowledge. Some of them may have enjoyed it.

This being 1928, we were now getting into the Depression, just at the time I was becoming more and more expensive to clothe and educate. As Bud Flanagan said: 'Things are so bad, even the people who never intended to pay have stopped ordering!' My father was an excellent salesman. He had charm, he had a great sense of humour and he could be persuasive. One of his maxims was: 'You don't try to sell anything to anyone – you create in them the desire to possess'. He got the orders, but he was under-capitalised and not very good at chasing debtors. One example was The Ambassador Restaurant, managed by one Peter Mazzina as a front for Maundy Gregory, the famous honours-peddler. Horace was stuck there for over £400. Nor did he get a gong.

During this period my father had become one of the regulars at a pub at the Seven Dials in St Martin's Lane. The head office of Metro-Goldwyn-Mayer was nearby, so he got to know a couple of the chaps who worked there who also used the pub. At that time the 'talkies' were coming shortly and MGM was rebuilding the Empire Theatre in Leicester Square, making it into one of the finest cinemas in Europe. There was some controversy at the time, with the usual moans about the destruction of the old Empire, one of the landmarks of London's musical theatre. It wasn't the only one to be remodelled. Warners was built on Daly's Theatre and the Odeon stands where the Alhambra did. But Theatreland is still full of musical shows. Some say too many.

The MGM men were full of excitement as they described the magnificent features of the new cinema: the grandeur of the marble entrance hall and – upstairs on the mezzanine floor – there was to be yet another large marble hall which would have a real pool complete with a fountain. More or less as a leg-pull father interrupted: 'You really must have some fish in that pool – goldfish, that sort of thing.'

Now, it was well-known to one and all that Father was a fish merchant and therefore to be accepted as an authority on fish, goldfish included. The MGM men were delighted with the idea – it was the one thing they hadn't thought of. Surely Horace would be the ideal man to arrange it. Would he do it?

Certainly he would. Be only too glad. Then he named his price: no charge for the fish but he would be very pleased to accept three tickets for the opening night.

I was now 12 and, after the disaster of *The Chess Player*, I had never been back to the movies, but it is not quite true to say I never saw any silent films at all. I vividly remember seeing *Easy Street* and other Charlie Chaplin two-reelers at a children's party. During a holiday at Folkestone I certainly recall a programme of cartoons, which we saw one rainy afternoon in the Pier Pavilion: *Felix the Cat*, and *Out of the Inkwell*, which combined live action with animation. But my experience of full-length feature films was nil, so I was in no way prepared for the excitements of the opening night of the new Empire, Leicester Square, on 9 November 1928.

The details of the occasion are a bit dim now; still, I remember a splendid symphony orchestra – a full complement of 90 players – and the mighty Wurlitzer, which rose majestically into view and had not one organist but two, and they were Sandy MacPherson and Reginald Foort, no less. The film was *Trelawney of the Wells*, with three great stars: Norma Shearer, Ralph Forbes and Owen Moore.

An opening of this importance at this time should have burst on the screen with a talkie but sadly *Trelawney* was silent, with a musical accompaniment by the orchestra. The All Talking, All Singing, All Dancing *Broadway Melody* didn't appear until the following May. However there was a Movietone programme bringing greetings from various notables, the first sound film I ever saw.

This time there were no hysterics from me, no carrying me out. I was rooted to my seat, movie-struck. I made up my mind then and there that I must get into films as soon as I could get out of school. In about five years time, that is.

Fortunate are the parents whose child knows what he wants to do; fortunate indeed is the child whose parents support his ambition. My parents did everything they could to help me. They always had. I was an only child and anything that was going, I got – and got thoroughly spoiled in the process.

My father was always intrigued by 'celebrities' and cultivated an acquaintance with theatre people which stood me in good stead later. One such friend was Billy Stewart, the manager of the Rialto Cinema in Coventry Street, which was showing *The Melody of Love*, Universal's answer to MGM's *Broadway Melody*. The stars were Tom Dugan, Walter Pidgeon – who had a good singing voice – and Mildred Harris. I was allowed to watch from the projection box and many a day I stood there, watching the programme round two or three times over.

The Rialto soon began to specialise in Continental films. Since my brief stay at the Lycée Corneille, at Rouen, I was of course accepted as fluent in French, so I was among those present at the London premiére of *Sous Les Toits de Paris*, in the capacity of interpreter. I met René Clair and Albert Préjean, and Annabella – who played the part of a ballerina in the film, most of the time dressed in a tutu. To me she was as magical as the fairy on the top of a Christmas tree. They all spoke English far better than I spoke French, but they never let on. I followed all Clair's subsequent pictures avidly: *Le Million, A Nous La Liberté, Le Dernier Milliardaire*. There were also some German pictures, *Three Men at a Petrol Station*; Leni Riefenstahl's *Blue Light*. They were all shown at the Rialto and there I was, up in the projection box.

One birthday my parents gave me a party at Lyons' Popular Café in Piccadilly and then took us all to the Rialto. The picture was *Check and Double Check*, with Amos 'n' Andy and Duke Ellington and his Cotton Club Orchestra. Children were really spoiled in those days. We had the best of everything. I pity the youngsters of today, fobbed off with third-rate noise masquerading as music, hideous clothes, junk food – and all disguised in trashy packaging.

I thoroughly enjoyed the jazz and the movies but I devoted most of my time to books. I was a very early reader and have been bookish all my life. To begin with, of course Stevenson and Dumas represented the better quality stuff, but my main interest was detective stories: Sexton Blake, Sherlock Holmes, Sapper and Edgar Wallace, Dorothy L Sayers and her anthologies.

At last I got to what you might call a proper grown-up novel: *All Quiet on the*

Western Front. This was the one that launched a flood of books about the First World War and I believe I read all of them, all from the public library. The only problem was that they all contained a lot of dialogue spoken by the brutal and licentious soldiery, which in those days was unprintable. Therefore the authors had to devise substitutes, like 'phurry' and 'blurry', which I found totally bewildering because I had no knowledge of the real words. I asked my father to explain and was fobbed off with the usual flumdummery which left me more confused than ever. I remember reading about the rape of Belgium and looking up the word in Nuttall's dictionary. The definition of rape was 'carnal knowledge of a woman without consent.' This appeared to be nonsense and again Dad fought shy of an explanation. So, as the habit of reading took a close hold on me, fired by my discovery of Aldous Huxley and Evelyn Waugh, I began to isolate myself and became a loner. I developed the habit of holding long conversations with myself.

It was clear to me that Father was finding it more and more difficult to maintain me, although nothing was said. For my part, I was simply anxious to leave school and start a job, start earning my own money. As long as it was in films.

Twelve months before this I had started writing letters to the film studios asking for a job. Soon another of my father's friends got to work on my behalf. This was one Cyril Percival, who worked for George Black, the great impresario of the Palladium, Moss Empires, and so on. Mr Black had a brother, Edward, who was studio manager at Gainsborough Studios in Islington. This connection got me an interview and, what's more, Mr Black took me on to the set, where Cicely Courtneidge was doing a musical number with a chorus of beautiful girls and a live orchestra. No playback in those days. That was a sight.

Edward Black was amused, and gently suggested that I wait until I had actually left school – another two whole years! – and then write to him again.

At last, in July 1933, the great day came: the end of the summer term and school was behind me. My immediate ambition was to collect my driving licence, obtainable on my 17th birthday at County Hall on payment of five shillings. Just for the asking. No test.

No longer a schoolboy, now fully mobile by borrowing Dad's car, I wrote again to Mr Black. Bad luck, there was no vacancy at the moment. I tried other studios without success. I had wantonly thrown myself on the labour market at the very moment when the unemployment figures had risen to three million, the highest ever. However, a pleasant surprise came in the form of a postcard from Mr Beeson, my former housemaster at CLS, telling me to apply to the Columbia Graphophone Company in Farringdon Road. They had a vacancy for a mail-room boy. I rushed off at once and got the job, at 25 shillings a week.

A mail-room boy doesn't sound at all grand but I was an instant success. A star overnight. Soon I was writing squibs for the Parlophone catalogue, which carried all the jazz records from America, as well as translating details from the French and German Odeon imports. Christmas was coming and a popular song demanded:

'Does Santa Claus Sleep with His Whiskers Over or Under the Sheet?' I wrote an answer to this, as from Father Christmas, in the form of a poem. Well, doggerel. It was sent to Henry Hall, a Columbia artiste, who read it out on his regular programme with the BBC Dance Orchestra on my 17th birthday. It is a mercy that I can't remember any of it, or I should be tempted to inflict my first published literary work on the present reader.

This was better than school, I can tell you. AND I could buy real jazz records, Louis Armstrong, Joe Venuti/Ed Lang, Duke Ellington, at staff prices. One and sevenpence ha'penny! Less than 10p of your money. Even more to the point, the Parlophone offices were right next to the mail-room and the manager there was dropping hints about a job for me in his department.

Why on earth did I ever leave that paradise?

One Thursday, early in February 1934, a voice from Gainsborough Studios telephoned. They now had a vacancy. Could I start work tomorrow morning?

Sorry, no, because I already have a job. For one thing, I would have to give notice. To make it tempting they said they were prepared to go to 25 shillings a week.

I was incredibly bold. I told them I was already getting that and I couldn't move for less than thirty. To my amazement they agreed to that and after explanations and regrets on both sides at Columbia, I started work at Gainsborough the following Monday.

IN THE THICK OF IT

The film in production at Islington was *Chu Chin Chow*, which was one of the longest running musical plays of all time with over 2200 performances. The play, by Oscar Asche, was based on *Ali Baba and the Forty Thieves*. It was first presented in 1916 and there was a silent film version but it had to wait for the talkies to be invented before it could be filmed properly. The cast was most distinguished: George Robey, Anna May Wong, Fritz Kortner and many more. The director was Walter Forde, a genial, good-natured man of long experience. Wherever he was shooting, on whatever stage, he commanded a grand piano to be brought and during the intervals of setting-up and lighting – which were long in those days – he played classics, ballads, show tunes; rather well, too, and pleasant to hear. He certainly got in a lot of practice. His wife, whose name was Culley, was always at his side. It seemed as if she was forever ordering trays of tea, to be fetched by me. Somehow I never quite took to Mrs Forde, but after all it was part of the job.

The art director was Oscar Werndorff, an eminent designer who had created some magnificent Oriental settings. Real fountains playing in cool courtyards, with real birds stalking about. The music wasn't the jazz that I preferred but it was a famous romantic score with several hit numbers. On top of all that, there was Anton Dolin directing a *corps de ballet* of gorgeous girls. The prima ballerina was Pearl

Argyle and she was the most exquisite creature of the lot. I had stepped straight into the glamorous world of the movies and then some.

Well, not quite.

I was a gofer, a production runner, as they are now known. In those days I don't think they were known as anything. 'Tea boy'? I disdain the description. After all, there was more to the job than that, as I soon found out. The first task I was put to was to help the wardrobe man sort out a lot of dirty, ragged old gowns that had been used for a crowd of beggars in a bazaar scene. The atmosphere was entirely convincing in that scene; you could almost smell it. Indeed, in the wardrobe you certainly could smell it. The wardrobe man was an ill-aspected type called Jack Worrock. He didn't like the job any more than I did and we didn't get on well.

That was Monday. On Tuesday, after the usual start at 8.00 am, we worked through until 10.30 pm. Next morning, all back to the studios at the usual time. That day we did even better: we worked until midnight. No overtime was paid, but for working after eight o'clock you got half a crown supper money and if the last tube had gone you'd probably find somebody to give you a lift home.

My mother thought I had entered a world of lunatics. The assistant director on the picture was Stanley Haynes – no lunatic he – one of the best in the business, who usually worked at the Shepherd's Bush Studios of Gaumont-British. Most of the time he was assistant to Victor Saville, who had a well-merited reputation for being rude and over-bearing but had made some good box-office successes. The deplorable manner was unnecessary. Some of this had rubbed off on Stanley but let me say at once that he was very nice to me.

I ventured to ask him if it was always like this. He gave me an oblique answer: 'After about six months in production, people make up their minds. Either to stay in or get out'. I never thought twice about it. I spent the next six years working at Gainsborough.

And how lucky I was. I worked on 38 pictures all told, and being on the set most of the time meant that I was working right alongside dozens of different actors, directors, cameramen and art directors, many of them really distinguished for their style and quality.

Make no mistake, a film studio revolves around the camera. Or in these days any production, be it entirely on location, still revolves around the camera. When you are starting out, the closer you can put yourself to the tripod, with your eyes and ears wide open and your mouth shut, the more you will unravel the mystery of how it's done. I am, though I have never been asked, a supporter of film schools and especially of acting schools. But, formal schooling or not, close contact at the centre, the camera, is indispensable. In the end your own professional pedigree will derive from the distinction and prowess of the people you have worked with. Bach overlapped with Haydn, who was a friend of Mozart and both of them shook hands with Beethoven and so on ... Anyway it's a good old principle – if you're hoping for an inheritance, make sure you inherit from the best people.

The studio in Poole Street Islington was originally an electricity power station for London Underground. It had been turned into a film studio in 1920 by the American company Famous Players Lasky, largely to make B pictures that would qualify with the quota demands of the impending Cinematograph Film Act. It had only two stages, a large one on the ground floor and a small one which was upstairs on the first floor. There was a huge lift by which large sections of sets were carried up to B Stage. The place was tiny and difficult to operate but it was compact and had all the necessary facilities.

On the top floor there were cutting rooms in which Alfred Roome and Terence Fisher slaved under the supervision of the sourest man I ever knew, Robert Dearing. Make-up, wardrobe and dressing-rooms and a minute stills department were next below that. On the ground floor, out at the back of the big stage, there were props' and carpenters' shops and a camera-room where between times we played pontoon for pennies.

There was a small restaurant, famous for its anchovy toast, which was managed by a briskly competent and attractive redhead called Miss Bertram. Down in the depths of the basement there was the electric power station, presumably left over from the Underground, which was run with loving care by a famous man called Stan Sargent. The other pillar of the electrical staff was Hugh Attwooll. In the cashier's department there lurked a forbidding character called Miss Munro, a dragon who breathed fire and smoke, capable of scorching the most genuine petty cash vouchers.

Gainsborough Pictures (1928) Limited was a subsidiary of the Gaumont-British Picture Corporation. G-B operated at the larger – and posher – studios at Lime Grove, Shepherd's Bush. These studios were the first to be built since the advent of sound, so they were purpose-built. All the other film studios around London were glorified factories or country houses which had been sound-proofed as effectively as was possible. G-B also had a circuit of about 300 cinemas, they manufactured Bush radio sets and among many other things they owned a newspaper, the *Sunday Referee*. The whole conglomeration was owned by the Ostrer Brothers: Isadore, Mark, Maurice, David and Harry; and ME Balcon was the managing director.

The Islington regime could never exist today. There were no regular hours. At the beginning of my time there we worked Saturday mornings but that didn't last long. When there was work to be done you were expected to do it and you did not leave for home until all your current tasks had been completed. You got a lot of buckshee time off, however, when there was nothing to do between pictures. Pay was no higher than the going rate, but it was paid 52 weeks a year, which included a two-week holiday. There were trade unions, but there were only two: NATKE for the craftsmen and ETU for the electricians. ETU were the only ones who ever seemed to make any trouble, and when they did for some reason they always did it at British International Pictures at Elstree. So we led a tranquil life, blissful in our ignorance. The Association of Ciné-Technicians was formed about this time, encouraged by Michael Balcon and Freddie Young among others, but it had little impact.

The best part of my luck was to have been put in the production department. In sound, or editing or any other, one is restricted to one's own discipline. As an assistant director of however lowly a grade one could poke one's nose into everyone else's business, until – sometimes – told to bugger off. I could turn my hand to almost any job that needed doing: I was at various times location manager, assistant editor, even second unit director, and had all the jobs in the production department from tea-boy to production manager. I lived for the job, enjoying myself no end. I was efficient, hard-working and conscientious to a fault. A paragon. Horrible to contemplate, but it's many years ago now.

Well, yes – of course there were some mistakes. The one I remember most was the day I called Kathleen Harrison when she wasn't needed. Now, there was a real lady. This could have been an expensive error, but she dismissed any question of compensation, merely suggesting that the company might pay the cost of her hire car. She died, greatly lamented, in 1995 at almost 104 years of age.

The main drawbacks to this idyll were the personal ones natural to my tender years. For instance, promotion was never fast enough. Yet I had nothing to grumble about, mainly because the man who was production manager during all my time at Gainsborough was like a benevolent uncle to me. His help and encouragement were beyond value. He was utterly loyal if I made a mistake and when I managed something well, he saw that I got the credit. His name was Fred Gunn.

When he was my age he was serving in the Royal Tank Corps in France in the First World War. He had a synoptic repertoire of soldiers' songs, all parodies of well-known hymn tunes to which exuberantly ribald lyrics had been fitted. All were very funny and some were quite poignant in an unselfconscious way. A lot of these numbers were among those that were later staged as *Oh What a Lovely War!*

Fred was a true friend, always practical, often blunt. It seems I was like all young men: I couldn't get up in the morning. I never arrived too early for work. Often a little bit late. I remember one occasion when I arrived in surprisingly good time: 'Hullo' said Fred, 'what happened to you this morning – d'you shit the bed?'

All the films we made at Gainsborough were for entertainment only. There were a lot of comedies, several musicals, some dramas and a few thrillers. As far as the people at Gaumont-British were concerned we were definitely the poor relations. Conversely we bemoaned the fact that we were turning out money-making pictures and they were squandering all the profits on prestigious epics. Still, in the early thirties the Gaumont-British Picture Corporation was an established business, a going concern. ME Balcon tried to recruit the best talent. He was the first to attempt to develop an Empire market by shooting pictures on location in Canada, Australia and South Africa; a risky and expensive proceeding with everyone travelling there and back by steamship. He brought in a great deal of the refugee talent from Europe: Ernö Metzner, Oscar Werndorff, Fritz Kortner, Berthold Viertel, the Siodmaks, Conrad Veidt. It should be stated that there was a grumbling undercurrent of resentment about this among the natives, but it was never serious and it was generally admitted that some of the newcomers had more experience in a bigger world – Vienna, Berlin and Paris – and a lot could be learned from them. The Ostrers and ME came near to establishing the core of a valid British/International film industry, and precious little thanks did they get for it.

However, the Ostrers made the mistake of pursuing that will-o'-the-wisp, that perennial curse of the British film industry which persists to this day: they made serious efforts to establish a foothold in the American market. To that end American stars, directors and cameramen were imported, all to no avail. Any attempt in this direction is misguided. The Americans simply don't need anybody else's movies; they have more than enough of their own. Even when they do venture into something exotic, it should be enough to point out that most of the major 'British' films of the last 20 years or so have been financed by American companies, which have rightly taken the profits.

As to the other production companies, the many and varied outfits at Elstree, led by BIP, had been going as long as G-B, but they were all firmly tied in to the domestic market with limited ambitions. As Earl St John sharply remarked, 'the British could only make two pictures: a war story based on fact and a seaside postcard comedy.' It was either *The Flag Lieutenant* or *Getting Gertie's Garter*.

During the twenties and thirties the politicians tried to encourage the native industry. In 1927 they gave it a small measure of protection against foreign competition by the Cinematograph Film Act, under which cinema owners were obliged to show a percentage of British films annually. Five per cent. The picture palaces were open six days a week, 52 weeks a year, so the obligation was two weeks. It is regrettable that numbers of cinema owners would have been happy to rely exclusively on imports, which were cheaper and offered bigger star names.

Still, by the middle of the thirties, film production was certainly thriving. It is surprising but true that in the year 1935 Mr Boot started to build Pinewood Studios, Mr Soskin started to build Amalgamated Studios at Elstree, and Mr Korda was building Denham Studios – which included a processing laboratory which soon became one of the finest in Europe. In addition, five new stages were built at Sound City, Shepperton. All of these were direct-sound studios, designed and built for the purpose.

Alexander Korda was in a class of his own. A lot of his strength as a producer came from the fact that he had directed pictures himself and had found out how they are made. Too many producers haven't the foggiest, despite years in the industry. Korda assembled more superior talent in Britain than anyone had hitherto managed. He was good with the press and generally speaking he always had good support from the journalists and critics. The importance of this cannot be over-estimated and nowadays relations with the media are carefully nurtured. In the thirties and right up until the sixties a lot of people neglected this obligation, much to their disadvantage.

Korda was an artist at bamboozling the money-men, so they thought it worthwhile to make a bob or two while the going was good, but they stood ever ready to pull the cushion out just when the ride was getting bumpier. During the sixties one of the Great Ironies of All Time came about when the original investors decided to flog the Korda backlog. They never had any appreciation of its value, so they let it go for a song, which blossomed into a full scale opera when the buyers represented it on TV and video.

Korda was no mean operator. In 1937, in partnership with the great Samuel Goldwyn, he reached the point of trying to buy United Artists from the then owners: Mary Pickford, Charles Chaplin, Douglas Fairbanks and David O Selznick. The deal fell through. If it had worked out, two individuals like Goldwyn and Korda might not have been able to operate together successfully, as a lot of people predicted at the time. But what if they had? With a war which everyone could see coming in 18 months or so, they might have found themselves obliged to make a go of it and the effect on the British industry would have been profound and beneficial.

But, looking at it strictly from the point of view of one who actually makes films, consider for a moment the position nowadays of the people who work in the Irish, French, Italian and German industries. They make many good films, good in the general sense, because they are true to the culture from which they derive. They are heavily supported by their governments, it is true. It must be admitted that financial support from the state tends to encourage self-indulgence; their own home audiences often find the native product boring and prefer the American films. Given adequate discretion and self-control it is notable that, during the last ten years or so, several small-scale, truly British pictures have achieved great international success. And all of them derive from their own culture.

I must learn not to raise my voice. I am getting ahead of myself. And above myself too. I am still carrying cups of tea at Gainsborough.

DOWN TO EARTH

The second film I worked on was *My Old Dutch*, directed by Sinclair Hill. He was an amiable person who conveyed a general air of absent-mindedness. He was forever losing his pipe and it fell to me to find it. Up to this time he had directed 68 films, so he wasn't a new boy. This was a sentimental comedy with music, the story based on the old song: 'We've bin tergevver nah fer 40 years...' Gordon Harker and Betty Balfour were the stars. She was a great star of the silent days and was attended by her French maid, who was in fact Belgian. The maid admired my red hair and offered to put waves in it. Sad to say, I refused. It's no wonder the dancing girls on *Chu Chin Chow* had nicknamed me 'Dismal Desmond'.

There were a number of old time music-hall stars in the supporting cast, including Lily Morris ('Why Am I Always A Bridesmaid?') and the great Florrie Forde, who delivered 'Down At The Old Bull and Bush' in a voice like a foghorn with a vox humana stop. She was a terrific character.

Following this, *The Camels Are Coming* returned from location shooting in Egypt. Nowadays one can't imagine sending a movie unit on such a trip under similar conditions. For one thing, it took three weeks to get there. And when they got back there were ten weeks shooting in the studio. The story was a spoof on *Beau Geste* starring Jack Hulbert. The director was an American, Tim Whelan. All I can remember of it is Anna Lee's cut-glass accent. When the Arabs were storming the desert fortress she had to shout: 'Jack! Jack! They're coming over the wall!' It came out as: 'Jeck! Jeck! Theah co'in eo'th'waw!'

This triviality has stuck in my mind because it is a persistent problem with so many actors. Everybody has a basic accent, but whatever it may be, diction and intelligibility must be impeccable. There is nothing more irritating to an audience than dialogue they can't follow. There are many stars whose first language is not English yet they can be perfectly understood, without any loss of the exotic attraction of their personalities. For instance, Ingrid Bergman, Charles Boyer and many more. Mumbling is sheer affectation and the cult of clinging to a regional accent which is meaningless outside its own parish is inverted snobbery.

This dictum must also be observed when the actor is assuming a foreign accent. For example, Albert Finney in *A Man Of No Importance* played with an almost convincing Dublin accent and could be understood throughout, while some of the genuine Irish actors around him were difficult to follow. It also applies when the character is dying in agony or is in floods of tears: if at the same time they have lines to deliver, they must still be intelligible while groaning or sobbing. Consider Dame Thora Hird's superb work with Alan Bennett, or the plight of the unfortunate Violetta in *La Traviata,* who has to sing an aria as she dies of consumption. If there is a foreign character in your story, the most satisfactory way to play it is to cast an actor native to that country who can speak English intelligibly. His own native accent will come through, lending versimilitude to the character.

At the end of shooting the Hulbert picture, production came to a temporary halt. So I asked if I could go into the cutting rooms for a spell, to see what was what. Charles Frend was over at the Bush editing a Leslie Henson and Frances Day musical called *Oh! Daddy,* and he was good enough to take me on as an assistant. He showed me how to file the trims and I began to get the hang of the general cutting room routine. I saw how picture and sound are kept separate until the final laboratory stage – elementary, but it helps one's understanding to see and handle the process in action. Some appreciation of the value of dubbing may emerge.

I suppose I was of some use to Charles, but I never achieved a full mastery of the joining machine. There is no point in describing the good old Bell and Howell here; it fell out of use many years ago, superseded by the Steenbeck. Nowadays by computers. The day came when the director of the film, Graham Cutts, came to the studio to see the rough cut. My joins let me down and every so often the film broke. Finally they had to give up the showing. As soon as production resumed at Islington

I scuttled back to the production department. I had gleaned some useful wrinkles about the editing process and was ever grateful to Charles, but I saw no future for myself as a film editor.

So in September 1934 we embarked on a musical comedy called *Heat Wave*. This was to star Les Allen, the singer with Henry Hall's Dance Orchestra. He had gone solo. He should have called *misère*. The plot was about an English fruit and veg dealer who goes on a business trip to South America. His notes about bananas and oranges are mistaken for a code, he is arrested as a spy and accused of attempting the life of the president. This was the plot.

Well you may laugh, but I had a special interest here. *Heat Wave* came at a time in my life when, like many another man who is 30 years ahead of his time, I was trying to teach myself to play the guitar. Ed Lang and Django Rheinhardt were about the only two going; these days it is hard to imagine a world with only two guitarists ... both good ones. It might be more peaceful. Anyway, at that time rhumba bands were just coming into popularity and one of the best was playing in Paris. Some bright chap had the wit to bring them over – the Lecuona Cuban Boys. Ernesto Lecuona was alive and well in Islington and I was having tuition from the great man himself.

This farrago was typical of the parasitism on another medium of which the movies are persistently guilty – in those days, the radio. In those days, the wireless. The BBC made many great stars, as they still do, but the public was dying to see what their idols actually looked like and the movies hastened to oblige. The snag was that the radio stars were asked to do roughly what they did on the wireless. It could be said that the film has some affinity with the theatre and the novel, but borrowing from the wireless is going too near the bottom of the barrel. In any case, translation from one medium to another demands careful consideration of the style and technique of the one, followed by a re-interpretation of the matter in terms of the style and technique of the other. The script, settings, characters and all require a complete re-think.

The next picture turned out to be an introduction to yet another world: Aldwych farce. Tom Walls, Ralph Lynn and J Robertson Hare in *Fighting Stock,* with a screenplay by Ben Travers. We made four of these films all told and they were absolute pie, the guaranteed rest-cure for overworked assistant directors. First thing in the morning, TW exercised his horses on the Downs at Epsom – a pursuit not to be despised: he had an entry in the Derby with one of those horses, called 'April the Fifth'. We were all on it of course, especially me, because I had an additional interest: my Uncle Ted's birthday fell on April 6th. What better reasons could there be for backing a horse? It WON.

After the exercise TW would appear at the studio around elevenish. He then rehearsed a three or four page dialogue scene and set up the camera on an all-embracing shot to include all the actors and most of the set – a set-up still known to some of us as a Tom Walls tight 15. By then it was time for lunch.

For TW this took the form of a elaborate picnic in his dressing-room, during which – it was rumoured – he might go over some of the finer points with a certain lady of the cast. When adequately refreshed he came down to the set and shot the scene. There might then be a mid-shot and a few close-ups but by about five o'clock Maslin the chauffeur would be standing by the Rolls, ready to go home.

The playing of these farces was rather special and very skilled indeed. The actors had played together many times before and they made it look so easy, which is a most admirable quality. Of course it was merely photographed theatre and, true, their biggest successes like *Thark* and *Rookery Nook* were behind them, but these were still funny pictures and they gave pleasure to a lot of people.

The cinema had offered photographed stageplays from the early silent days, but once the talkies arrived the theatre was plundered for material. Sound had come in little more than five years previously. Obviously it caused an upheaval and a lot of fresh thinking. One school of diehards maintained that sound had ruined The Art of the Film. Quite correct. They went on trying to make silent films with an accompanying sound track but it was clearly a lost cause. Two examples are Charles Chaplin and Robert Flaherty. Incidentally, Flaherty's famous *Man of Aran* was a Gainsborough picture, made entirely on location.

Others took the opposite view, that sound was a blessing that had enabled cinema to come to fruition at last as a synthesis of all the arts. Their ideal film might include elements of theatre, ballet, cartoon, music, poetry, opera and high-wire walking. Some of René Clair's work was on these lines, a mixture of film and operetta.

The moment it became possible to convey information to the audience by means of dialogue it was all too easy for the screenwriter and the director to present a story which depended almost entirely on the spoken word. Some say that there is no harm in this, especially if the film is based on a play in the first place. If the camera is used as a recording instrument, the virtue of the original is left more or less intact. It can be used as a method of preserving a great actor's Hamlet or simply to show the play itself to people who will never live within a thousand miles of a theatre. Indeed, there are many examples of good plays which have suffered from being 'opened out' on to the big screen.

The ideal material for a proper motion picture is an original script, or at worst it should be based on a novel. Writers have discovered that the most profitable way to offer a script for filming is to present it in the form of a novel, especially if it has sold well. So the canny ones don't write screenplays.

I must admit that the ability of film to incorporate every conceivable dramatic element with limitless scope in picture and sound can lead to disaster. If there are no restrictions, no ground rules, therefore there will be no discipline. And therefore no art. There is only form, no content, and the art lies in the content. It is amusing that shortage of money is sometimes a healthy restriction and low budget films are sometimes so good. An open purse can lead to a glorified pop video. Wonderful package, with nothing inside it.

Still, in the course of guiding a play on to the screen, there is much to be learned from an association with the theatre, even if it be an uneasy one. In the theatre there are rules and disciplines. First you have to persuade the audience willingly to suspend their disbelief and then you can make enormous capital out of the restrictions that are part and parcel of the medium. For instance, the wooden O itself; or playing to the fourth wall; or not playing to the fourth wall; or playing in the round. Believe me, I envy theatre directors. They can offer illusions which are deliberately presented as illusions and yet their effect on the audience is hugely increased. It is for these reasons that live theatre will remain for ever the Pierian spring of dramatic inspiration. It has in addition the flesh-and-blood connection, which is priceless. All actors must start there and make periodic return visits for refreshment. That's where it's at – in the theatre.

CLAUDE RAINS, FAY WRAY – AND A RAISE

The essential characteristic of the motion picture is that it offers complete control of time and space. It is obvious that there are no unities, but little use was made of this facility until recently. Some of the most concentrated, triple-distilled presentations of situation, character, atmosphere and action are to be seen on television, in some of the one-minute commercials. It is amazing that so much information can be put over in such a short space of time. This has had its effect on films and they are a lot livelier and brisker than they used to be.

The next picture would have lent itself to bold treatment on those lines. This was *The Clairvoyant*, about a man doing a thought-reading act on the halls who suddenly discovers that he really can read people's minds and see into the future. At that moment he happens to be travelling on an express train and he knows it is going to crash... Great stuff. Claude Rains was the star, with Fay Wray, straight from the hairy hand of King Kong.

Quick on our feet as always, we returned to comedy for *Boys Will Be Boys*, which was the first of nine pictures we made with Will Hay. I had seen his act many times at the Palladium and the Holborn Empire. He played a seedy schoolmaster at a broken-down private school, waging a constant battle of wits with the boys, who baited him mercilessly. Somehow by ruthless cunning he always beat them in the end.

The story was based on Beachcomber's *Narkover* and Will Hay was Doctor Smart-Allick, with Gordon Harker, Claude Dampier, Davy Burnaby – he was one of the original *Co-Optimists* – and Jimmy Hanley. Will Hay had already made several pictures, mostly at Elstree; among them were two plays by Pinero: *The Magistrate* and *Dandy Dick*. He was well cast in those parts, so he was an actor as well as a music hall comedian.

The director was a tall, amiable American named William Beaudine, who had directed *Dandy Dick*. He started with two-reelers in the silent days in Hollywood and with his vast experience and boundless energy he really perked the place up. At the end of a good take he would shout: 'Cut! Prinnit! Over here with a fifty!'. This great-ly impressed the producers when they saw the rushes the following morning. They could hear all this showmanship as the take ran out. They thought, this director real-ly knows what he wants; he's got the next set-up all worked out. Of course nobody ever checked whether the next up-set was in fact over there with a 50mm lens.

Some time ago I was directing a lot of TV episodes where celerity and dispatch are the order of the day and I used the 'Cut! Prinnit! Over here with a fifty!' gag, with gratifying results. I am told that some other directors have adopted it since. Now they know where it comes from.

There is no doubt that the actors and crew take their tone from the director and his bearing governs the speed of shooting. But too many directors these days seem to be shooting the schedule and forgetting the script. They don't use the camera to its full effect; they don't get the best performances that the cast may be capable of giving and they don't realise the full potential of the script. There are producers who encourage this attitude. They don't care if the film is good – they want it Friday. They don't realise that they haven't got a director at all, but a glorified production manager.

An additional danger is that if such a director gets hold of a fireproof script – very rare – and a good cast, he may look good on the credits. The critics often fall for this one. It takes caution, an experienced eye and a tiny bit of *reliable* inside infor-mation to make a proper assessment of a credit. Of course, as Julian Wintle used to say, the high ideal is to deliver it good – and Friday.

Like most comedians Will Hay was irascible, morose and hypochondriacal. You never said, 'Good morning Bill, how are you?' because he'd tell you how he was, at great length and in clinical detail. I once saw him signing autographs. He wrote his sig-nature in a curious way. He wrote W and then he left a gap, over which he continued the line to the H, a, y. Then he'd go back and fill in the gap with the missing 'ill'.

He could produce a charming smile when he wanted, he was a dyed-in-the-wool pro and a very hard worker. He was intelligent and if you met him socially you would never have taken him for a music hall comedian. In the 1920s he flew his own air-craft. He had an astronomical observatory at the bottom of his garden and he made occasional contributions to scientific journals. At one time he discovered a comet, or some heavenly body – at any rate he made an observation of some scientific value. He could be snobby about people who were apparently not as bright as he. For instance, he never got on with Graham Moffat, who played Albert, the Fat Boy.

Graham started as a page boy at Gaumont-British. Indeed they were posh at the Bush. They had a Sergeant of the Corps of Commissionaires who was in charge of six page boys, all smartly turned out in the traditional bumfreezer with a row of lit-tle brass buttons down the front and a pillbox hat.

Graham was noticed because he was a fat boy with a cheeky manner and some-body put him in a picture. It was just a one line appearance but he got a laugh, so he was cast in this Will Hay picture, this time with a few more lines, but not yet as Albert. It built up from there. I don't believe he ever had an acting lesson in his life and he was really good. So much so that people used to shout at him if he fluffed or did something clumsily, because they expected him to be fully professional. He was only 15 when all this started, and anyway the clumsiness was all part of the character.

There followed another rest period with Tom Walls called *Stormy Weather*, after which Jack Hulbert reappeared with *Jack Of All Trades,* which was to be directed by Hulbert with Robert Stevenson as co-director. This was not a rest period. Hulbert was in his element on this one. It included an elaborate dance routine which was staged on an enormous street set – at night.

G-B had a big exterior lot at Northolt, sited on a slope, now a housing estate, overlooking the airfield. Hitchcock had lately caused a splendid street set to arise here, complete with a working tramcar. This set was revamped and night after night the unit trooped out there to shoot Hulbert's dance.

Fortunately Tom Walls gave us a welcome breather with *Foreign Affairs*. Then came a really odd one. At least, the film wasn't odd. Indeed it was a simple gangster picture. It was the manner of making it that was unusual. The film had already been made in France. The nifty notion was to bring the principal cast over from France, except the leading man who would be an English star for box-office reasons. Since these French *comediens* could all speak English – or said they could – all one had to do was to retake all the close-ups in the French version against small matching sets and cut them into the original medium and long-shots. *Voilà tout!* – a brand new English film on the cheap.

The English star thrown into this maelström of French muggers was John Mills as he then was, so that was all right. As he then was, disregarding many later triumphs, he had already established himself on the stage, mostly in musicals and had a big success in a film called *Brown On Resolution*, so he was able to take care of himself.

The director was Herbert Mason and a miserable task he had. Previously a producer, it was his first picture as director. Obviously the original scheme didn't work out and he finished up re-making nearly all the film. Half the French actors couldn't play in English and had lost most of the wardrobe they'd worn in the original. We went up to Brandon and Mildenhall in Suffolk for night locations, because the only long straight roads lined with poplar trees, like they have in France, are there. Since we were not supposed to need any sets, no space had been allocated at the studios. When it turned out they would be needed after all, the art director Walter Murton had to build them in an empty factory on Western Avenue, which wasn't sound proof.

Nobody appreciated it at the time, but there was one bonus in all this muddle. The leading lady was Lilli Palmer. She had just arrived from Vienna via Paris. She was about 16 and we'll all go a long way before we see anyone lovelier or more talented. She had quite a temper and was not popular, but on that saga, if you didn't have a temper you must have been under gas.

The title of this epic – it was one of those turkeys that has about a dozen titles along the way – was *First Offence*. Poor Mason. I hope they dealt with him leniently. He went on to direct a couple of films with George Arliss and also with Jack

Hulbert and Cicely Courtneidge.

I had by now become officially acknowledged as second assistant and it was about this time that we got a new recruit, in the elegant form of Bertie Ostrer. Not long down from Oxford where he was a member of the university ski team, he announced himself as willing to help in any way and anxious to learn how the whole thing worked. The Guv'nor's nephew had arrived.

He was genuine. He turned out to be one of the best assistants I ever had. We got on famously. After a week or two he asked me, 'How much do they pay you for doing all this?' I had by now had a raise of a pound, so I told him, 'Two pound ten'.

'Really', said he.

The following Monday I was told that my wages had been increased to five pounds a week. In those days this was good pay for a working man with a family. I was 18, with no responsibilities. I could afford a car, I could take girls out ... I wonder what Bertie's uncle thought. You bring in your nephew to learn the business, maybe he'll take some responsibility some day, and the first thing he wants to do is to double everyone's pay.

CLASS DISTINCTION

I could already see that one of the attractions of this life was its constant variety. Never a dull moment. Once again we came into a complete change of atmosphere. Robert Stevenson, after all that co-directing with Jack Hulbert, wrote a script about Lady Jane Grey. He now directed a first class film, which was titled *Tudor Rose*.

Henry VIII dies and his son Edward VI accedes – a very sick young man, unlikely to have issue. The Dudley family, with Edward's agreement, plan to substitute Dudleys for Tudors at Edward's death. Their candidate for the throne, instead of Mary Tudor or Elizabeth – both of whom had a better right – is Henry's niece Lady Jane Grey, who is not yet 16. They marry her against her will to Guilford Dudley. Edward dies and the Council approve Jane as his successor. She is proclaimed Queen, but nine days later Mary Tudor's supporters put Jane in the Tower. Later, partly because of her father's foolhardy involvement in Wyatt's rebellion, Jane and her husband are beheaded.

Well, this was all about something. Real people. Remote in time, in strange, rather beautiful costume, but they had lived and breathed and done these things, made these decisions and faced the consequences. As far as I was concerned this was another cup of tea altogether. Nova Pilbeam was Jane, with Desmond Tester, Sir Cedric Hardwicke, Sybil Thorndyke, Felix Aylmer, John Mills, Gwen Ffrangcon-Davies, John Laurie and many more of the Quality.

It was fascinating to watch these actors at work. I was completely bowled over by this production and Robert Stevenson became my hero. This was when I began to nurture a tiny ambition to be a director. It was also the planting of a seed which will bloom later as a hard luck story.

Production was booming. Since we started *The Clairvoyant* in January 1935 to the completion of *Tudor Rose* in January 1936 we had turned out seven films. Not bad for a small studio. The current Tom Walls effort, *Pot Luck*, had started shooting at the Bush because there was no space at Islington, but came to us for a few weeks. Bill Beaudine brought in *Where There's A Will* with Will Hay as a solicitor. We took off into science-fiction with Boris Karloff in *The Man Who Changed His Mind*, possibly one of the first brain transplants ever to be screened. It was directed by Robert Stevenson and photographed by Jack Cox.

So far, as lighting men we'd had Mutz Greenbaum on *Chu Chin Chow* and *Tudor Rose*: he was usually given the glamourous costume productions. Leslie Rowson did *My Old Dutch* and Roy Kellino two of the Tom Walls pictures. Arthur Crabtree remained totally calm while lighting the disorganised *First Offence*. Otherwise our cameramen were three Americans: Glen MacWilliams, Phil Tannura and Charles van Enger.

MacWilliams had high standards and shot some of the bigger pictures at the Bush. He came to Islington only once, I think, to photograph *The Clairvoyant*. Tannura had mostly done Tom Walls pictures; van Enger usually put two large cans on each side of the camera and was therefore known disrespectfully as Flat Light Charlie. This is now common practice for colour film, but in the days of black and white every kind of crosslight and backlight was used to give the picture a stereoscopic appearance.

Jack Cox also had experience of silent pictures. He had a high reputation for photographing dramas and was Hitchcock's cameraman on *Blackmail* and others. He was noted for a complete lack of pretence and a sardonic wit.

The cast of *The Man Who Changed His Mind* with Boris Karloff included Anna Lee, Frank Cellier, John Loder, Donald Calthrop and Cecil Parker, so there was some good dramatic acting going on. Karloff turned out to be utterly charming and like the other actors from Hollywood he had a special quality of professionalism about making movies.

This was an excellent cast, but generally speaking our pre-war world was full of actors who fluffed their lines and missed their marks, were hopelessly inefficient about their wardrobe, make-up, props, etc., and spent most of their time wandering off the set. This behaviour was quite common and to a certain extent was tolerated.

We were dealing with two different kinds of actor. One sort came from the music hall and the theatre. With slight modifications of projection, barely adequate in some cases, they more or less carried on doing what they were doing in their original environment. The second group were newcomers and training for film acting was almost non-existent. The schools concentrated on the theatre. In some quarters training for the cinema was frowned upon as being too restricting of the free expression of the *artiste* with an 'e'.

Anybody, working in whatever medium, who believes that technique can be disregarded, is simply not an artist. Work of some interest may be produced by dogged persistence or by a fluke, but the result will be a happy accident rather than an artistic endeavour. It is unlikely that it will be repeated. True, a work may be dashed off in the heat of the moment or the circumstances of the production process may not be ideal, but the resultant piece will be the outcome of a positive, deliberate act of conviction, employing all the technical resources of the medium. What's more, the performer in film and in the theatre must be able to repeat the act accurately, some-times against the most adverse conditions.

People like Claude Rains, Boris Karloff and Fay Wray were eye-openers to us. They had an instinct for the camera and they weren't afraid of it. They always knew where it was and what it was doing without having to look. More importantly, they had an elementary understanding of editing, sensing how the set-ups would cut together.

Some of the actors from the theatre, particularly the longer established ones whose theatrical habits had become ingrained, failed to make their proper impact on the film audience. They were sometimes effective and got a laugh or a tear in the right place but they never realised their full potential on the screen, because they just did-n't have the knack. It was rarely that a director had the time to nurse an actor through the ABC of film technique. For lack of an elementary grasp of the simpler principles, many an actor's finest moments finished up on the cutting room floor.

Once the shooting is completed, freedom of action in the editing room is limited by the material available. Barring re-takes or a well-timed fire the film is the film as it is in the cans on the racks. If by chance the actor has landed the director and the conti-nuity girl with an unavoidable lapse in continuity, there may be a range of alternatives available to the director. You see, dear boy, he may stay back in the two-shot, where your performance was not so sparkling and you are sharing the screen with another actor, who has a prettier nose; worse still, he may cut to the other feller's close-up – and you won't be seen at all. Be warned. And you may not be asked again.

Another thing, while all this free advice is being handed out: you disregard your marks at your peril. If you don't quite hit them the focus-puller will use his experi-ence and keep you sharp, but the lighting will have been set for you on those marks... Think about it. You may have deepset eyes or a long nose... Of course, if it's true to the character and you fear to compromise your artistic integrity...

Great delicacy of touch is required on the part of the director in handling an actor who genuinely has problems with technique. I say genuinely, because there are a few around who reject such petty concerns as beneath their dignity, something to be left to the servants. With those who merit the time and trouble, how far should one go in insisting on points of continuity? How many can you let slip? Can you print several takes, or cover yourself with an extra angle on some other character? How many tricks have you got up your sleeve and which of them will work when you encounter someone like Marilyn Monroe? – of whom more later.

For different reasons one may run into similar problems with experienced actors. Is this poor devil always drunk after lunch? Can I get the bulk of his work covered before 1.00 pm? All without engendering resentment among the other actors because special accomodation is being made for one man's weakness, which will make additional demands on their strength. And one's own strength.

Delicacy of touch – or strong arm methods? Carol Reed believed that there is always danger in pressing an actor too hard; whatever quality he has may be spoiled altogether. Except for the odd one who responds to being bullied the vast majority of actors are fragile creatures who need to be handled with nicety of judgment. One dictum can be laid down without question: if there is a conflict between performance and technique, the director must go all out for performance.

In some ways the pendulum has swung too far in the opposite direction. Some actors now have an only too well developed technique. I have actually discovered them working out how they're going to handle a scene, making private deals with each other: 'So I'll go dee dah dee dah with that line and then I'll turn away to the door; then you do your bit about the McGuffin and I'll swing back into it on my last line. OK sweetie?' My word, some of the face-makers do get above their station at times. True, I have heard of cases where the director wasn't offering much help, simply letting them get on with it. Once they get to know you or if they don't, they may have the wit to look you up in the big fat book, they may discover you've made a few pictures before. Then matters will settle down and the work may proceed in an orderly fashion. By Gad, Sir, we can't have this anarchy.

Even worse – and you'll hardly credit this – I once caught an actor making a private arrangement with my camera operator. If there is one thing I absolutely bar on my set, it is technicians giving direct instructions to the actors. The result is ALWAYS fatal to the performance. The director can easily drop in the little technical notes while setting-up and rehearsing, so that the actor will absorb it all quite naturally as part of the playing of the scene. If the director knows enough of the technique himself – and he better had – he can leave out a lot of the pettifogging detail which will unnecessarily confuse the actor. I give myself an awful lot of extra work and I spend a lot more time on my feet than I would wish, but nevertheless it must be done.

One day, starting an episode of the television series *Minder*, I was most amused when I heard Dennis Waterman quoting one of my catchphrases: 'Here he comes again! Watch it lads ... no private deals!'.

The director alone knows *completely* what the essentials are and how the performance and the technique at any one moment must fit into the scene, the scene into the sequence and the sequence into the film, always with reference to the context of each moment – what came before and what is to come. All these decisions must be worked out in the director's mind before main photography starts, with the final details to be settled on the floor, during the shooting. Equally important, the director alone knows what can be left out. The two OK words for this process are: selection and emphasis. Any director must have a full understanding of the enormous importance of these signposts and the power and influence they have. But beware – it is all too easy to ruin a performance by over-directing it. Some directors are too anxious to show that they are directing. And some directors are underestimated because they don't intervene unnecessarily.

OUT AND ABOUT

The next batch of pictures included much more location work, so Fred Gunn pushed me out to find suitable sites. Born and bred in the Smoke I soon discovered the pleasures of touring around the countryside. I became quite an adept with a still camera. When I had found some possible places I was able to show the stills of them to the director himself and discuss with him the different possiblilities each one offered. Up until now I had little personal contact with these great men. Now I began to see things from the director's point of view: why one setting was right for the scene and another would be wrong.

Everybody Dance was a Cicely Courtneidge musical comedy. Jack wasn't in it. The cast included Ernest Truex, Alma Taylor – a big star of the silents – and Kathleen Harrison. The songs were by Mack Gordon and Harry Revel. For this one I found a lovely Tudor timbered farmhouse near Ongar, in Essex. One day during the shoot at the farm the director, Charles Reisner, had a last minute inspiration. He must have a pony and trap driving by in the background of the scene. I was sent off to raise one, at once.

I went to the obvious place, the local pub, ordered a half of bitter and asked the attractive young barmaid where I could get a pony and trap. She surprised me a bit by looking startled and saying, 'What?'

I repeated, I was looking for a pony and trap, for the filming. Did she know of one that might be hired? She surprised me again by bursting into shrieks of laughter. I thought she was having a fit. However she put me on my way to finding one. It was only when I left the pub that I understood her reaction. Since I come from a long line of people born within the sound of Bow Bells – although I was the first one to get the ringing noise out of my head – I should have remembered my rhyming slang.

Next production: Will Hay was to be the captain of a rusty old tramp steamer. The original story came unexpectedly from Robert Stevenson, who called it *Windbag the Sailor.* The screenplay was by Val Guest and Marriott Edgar – he who wrote *Sam, Pick Up Thy Musket* and many more monologues. The director was Bill Beaudine and the cameraman Jack Cox. A lot of the shooting had to be done at sea. There was a sequence in a harbour where the ship had to demolish a jetty and another on a desert island, where the heroes are shipwrecked. I managed to convince Fred Gunn that the only way we could be sure to find the best place for these locations would be to inspect every harbour on the south coast of England.

I had talked myself into a pleasant two week tour from Dover to Penzance. I finally decided on Falmouth, interviewed the harbour authorities and found a spot to build a false jetty to be knocked down. I selected a beach in Cornwall for the desert island. The script specified a desert island so I started looking for an island, until it dawned on me that all I needed was a long sandy beach with no human habitation.

I had begun to grasp one of the basic truths about movies: the only thing that matters is what is on the screen. Anything outside the frame-line doesn't count. This provides two traps for the unwary. You may include something that shouldn't be seen, or you might leave out something that should be in. It sounds absolutely simple and platitudinous to mention, but there are plenty of examples of neglect of this obvious principle to be seen every day. Just switch on the television. Too many of the practitioners of that art don't realise that because an actor's lines can be heard clearly, there is no guarantee that he is on screen at the time. Or if he is, that the audience can see his face. So often one hears important plot lines being played on the back of the actor's head. Or on his feet. Just because they have read it in the script they will swear it is on the screen. As Kay Walsh said – and believe me she's a good judge – it may be in your head or even on the paper, but you've got to be sure it's also on the screen, where the audience can appreciate it.

On the other hand, the art of including things out is most useful at times. One of the essentials of the close-up is that it contains only one head, one gun, or whatever – and nothing else. It excludes all the other characters in the scene and most of the setting.

Another admonition that may be mentioned here is, what does the director do with himself while the take is in progress? I recommend a discreet withdrawal behind the camera. During first rehearsals, setting up, lighting and final rehearsals the director spends all his time in front of the camera. Now is the time to stand back, to see if the effort that he and the screenwriter and the actors are putting into the scene is coming back to the camera.

A director who plants himself in a canvas chair directly under the camera is guaranteed to put any actor off his stroke. It can be dangerous too. I remember Marcel Varnel, whose habit this was until one day he jumped up suddenly, shouting 'Cut!' and gave his head a nasty gash on the matte box.

While we are on the subject of takes, please allow long overlaps, in spite of possible disapproval in the production department. When you are covering a section of a longer scene, don't start the take at the very point you want to use it. It is a tremendous help to the actors to give them a run in to the scene and don't shout out 'Cut!' immediately they reach the end of the section. They will switch off at once and so will camera and sound. When you are editing you may want to hold on them for a beat. At the shooting stage it is impossible to tell precisely which frame will be the one at which to make the cut.

I presented the stills of Falmouth to Bill Beaudine and Fred Gunn. They approved. We now had to find the steamer. Fred pushed me out once more and I discovered the Baltic Exchange, which is the place to go if you want to charter a ship. Especially if you're going to alter its appearance with modifications to the superstructure and demolish a jetty with it. The people there were highly amused. Will Hay's name was a help of course and they were willing to co-operate. They must have found it odd to be dealing with a teenager. When the transaction reached board level for final sanction, Fred insisted that I go alone. I would be the spokesman anyway. However he finally agreed to come along and back me up. Where ignorance is bliss ... all this was a breeze to a 19-year-old.

The breeze blew stronger when I set about the next part of the operation. Accomodation had to be found for a unit and actors of 82 people – and they arrived on August Bank Holiday. On top of that, six of the actors for the desert island scenes were black. In 1936. Let me see you get out of that. With a lot of help from Fred Lawrence, our resident casting director – a true veteran – they were all settled in eventually. I raise my glass to the hotel managers and landladies of Falmouth.

This was the picture that introduced the third character into the Will Hay scheme: the old man, Harbottle. It was played by Moore Marriott, a delightful, modest person who had specialised in playing old men while still in his forties. Apart from work in the theatre he had been making films since 1908. He said he had lost most of his hair early on, so all he had to do was to take his false teeth out and he'd got a character. There was a lot more to it than that.

Will Hay followed straight on with *Good Morning Boys,* returning to his schoolmaster character. A new director appeared, Marcel Varnel, a stocky, boundlessly energetic character with long experience in the theatre and films in France. The cast included Will Hay Junior and Lilli Palmer.

Then the Crazy Gang came busting in. They had built up enormous popularity in long runs at the Palladium with a music hall programme in which the acts were all mixed together, they interrupted each other, and there were interruptions from plants in the audience. All of which gave a non-stop show, continually surprising the audience with the speed of the jokes. It certainly gave new life to the music hall. They continued the format for many years after the War, at the Victoria Palace.

Bud Flanagan was the ringleader, with Chesney Allen, the last of the great straight men. The second pair of the Gang, Nervo and Knox, were both comics. The third pair, Naughton and Gold, were in the older tradition. They were all great to work with and the jokes never stopped, in front of the camera or in the green room. Smoking was prohibited on the set and so everybody nipped off the stage at some time or another for a quick drag in the green room.

The Gang used to mock each other unmercifully. Jimmy Gold was supposed to be a miser. Probably true. Charlie Naughton was supposed to be much older than any of the others, older than Methuselah. He was also the shortest and known as Mr Shorthouse. He was generally the butt of the others' japes. Bud Flanagan declared that he wished to be addressed as The Star, which got the expected reception. Teddy Knox could talk posh and had some great unprintable songs. Well, they're no good unless they're sung. There was never a shortage of entertainment with this lot. Despite all these diversions a film was made, which had the Crazy Gang running wild in a film studio.

It was called *Okay For Sound.* It wasn't very funny. The *Hellzapoppin'* style doesn't transfer from the theatre to the cinema. It is true that any film should appear to happen on the spur of the moment, but the spontaneity of a Crazy Gang show absolutely depended on the responses of the audience and the Gang's reactions to them. Film cannot do that.

We had now reached the end of 1936 and after the boom time there came the first signs of financial trouble at Gaumont-British. Early in 1937 Michael Balcon suddenly left the Bush and soon afterward emerged as head of production for MGM-British at Denham. The Ostrer brothers were decidedly put out about this. In April the Bush was closed down and future G-B production was transferred to Pinewood. Gainsborough too was slipping, reporting a loss of £98,000 for 1936. After a lot of re-organising Maurice Ostrer was made responsible for Gainsborough, with Edward Black as producer in charge and a nice man called Frank Coven came in as studio manager. None of these crises had any effect on us at Islington. We went blithely on to the next picture.

Said O'Reilly to MacNab was an anthology of those jokes which begin 'There was an Irishman and a Scotsman' with an American comedian called Will Mahoney and the leading Scottish comedian Will Fyffe. As part of his act Mahoney played the xylophone by tying the sticks on to his shoes and dancing on the thing. That's something Teddy Brown could never do. Those who remember him with affection will recall his music hall act. He too played the xylophone but he weighed about 20 stone. Bill Beaudine got this one.

The next scene for my location spotting was Rye, in Sussex. The subject was a famous novel by Russell Thorndike called *Dr Syn* and it was a vehicle for George Arliss. The story takes place in and around Rye in the 18th Century. One important sequence shows the local smugglers, who know every bit of the territory, luring the excise men into the most treacherous parts of the marshes. The excise men sink helplessly into the bogs and the smugglers get away with the duty-free. I was warned to look for really muddy marshes where a man might sink to his waist. I found the very thing and took some good stills of tall reeds growing in several feet of black mud.

Roy William Neill was co-directing with Maude Howell, who wrote most of Arliss' scripts. Neill was a difficult man to please; I don't think he liked the job anyway, but he okayed the stills. These marsh scenes were at the end of the schedule and when the unit arrived at the end of a warm, dry spring, the marsh had dried out as hard as a rock. Thus I was handed another useful bit of experience: always double-check locations just before shooting. Indeed it is unwise to resolve a final plan of shooting for any location until the day you are shooting it, because the natural conditions vary constantly. The lighting cameraman will play his cards according to the state of the weather and so should the director. Shooting strictly to continuity of script is inadvisable and should not be attempted. Since most pictures have been shot on location for years now, the crews have developed a great sense of flexibility. It applies to everybody, wardrobe, make-up and all, especially the actors, leaping into and out of and back into several different costumes during the day.

This certainly does not mean that every decision can be left to the last moment, but a thorough appraisal of all the possible permutations of a location should be made. A general scheme is essential – otherwise one would never decide on any particular place – but last-minute adaptability and improvisation are vital. If there are interior scenes that can be staged in the same place, giving weather cover, that is a bonus. The location manager – usually known as 'tea 'n' toilets' – will want to know what the director's general plans are, so that he can site the circus: the woefully extended train of vehicles that must be placed accessibly but out of sight. Honey wagon, props van, generator, cable run – but the first assistant director, being inside the director's mind at all times, will take care of these mundane problems.

George Arliss was rather distant, dignified but always courteous. He specialised in potted biographies of historical characters like Wellington, Disraeli, etc. In the 1920s he had a string of successful plays about them on Broadway and some of them had been filmed in Hollywood as silents. When sound came in he went back to Hollywood and made some of them again, for Warner Bros. Once again we had the chance to watch somebody who knew what he was doing.

He had a strict routine: 9.00 am on set, made up, dressed and word perfect. 1.00 pm to 2.00 pm, lunch. At 4.30 pm his butler, the famous Jenner, appears on set to tell him tea is ready and that is the end of the day for Mr Arliss. This went on five days a week, for four weeks only. Our schedules were usually six or seven weeks, so there was some time to cover scenes in which Mr Arliss didn't appear. These schedules were really quite comfortable because feature films in those days ran only about eighty minutes, giving an average screen time of two minutes a day. You may well hear some of us speak of The Good Old Days. They were.

The leading lady in *Dr Syn* was Margaret Lockwood, who had just had a big success in a film of *Lorna Doone*. Still in her teens, beautiful and with a figure to match, she was being heavily tipped as the next big star. For once the tipsters got it right – not that much prescience was required.

Vetchinsky was the art director and I remember trying to pull his leg about one of the sets. It was a village street and he'd designed it in an *olde worlde* shape, with the houses at all angles. Surely, I said, the action of this picture takes place in the 18th Century, so the houses should be straight, as they were originally built. Vetch never used bad language but he was tempted this time.

Will Hay was now to be a railway stationmaster, in *Oh! Mr Porter*. Off I went, to find a railway line, a wayside station and a train. After a lot of map-reading sessions and some pleasant journeys, combined with a lot of help from the Southern Railway, a disused line was found. It was conveniently close to the Swan at Alton in Hampshire, which I designated unit HQ, thus showing promise as a budding location manager.

I think it was during the making of this film that Will Hay began to find that too many of the laughs were going to Harbottle and Albert and he was stooging for them. He was right, too. Long discussions ensued with Marcel Varnel, who was again directing. I was able to listen in to some of it, by hanging about close to the debate. It is curious how the central figure in a series of stories can so easily become a coathanger for the story and all the interest go to the subsidiary characters. The writers don't do this deliberately. Part of the problem is that they are trying to fit a story to an already clearly defined character, rather than the other way round. Also, the established central character is always doing the same things in all the stories, whereas the other people are mostly new to each story.

It was at Alton that I achieved that common ambition: once or twice I was allowed to drive the train.

My next location took me back to the west country, to Exmoor, for *Owd Bob*, a sheepdog story. It was later re-made by Disney. Robert Stevenson directed Will Fyffe, Margaret Lockwood and John Loder and some marvellous sheepdogs. There were many quiet summer days filming the dogs working the sheep.

Bank Holiday was a 'Grand Hotel', or portmanteau, story. Several different plot lines are interwoven to coincide in a common time and place, with a large cast of characters. This is good film material because it provides variety of character and change of scene and parallel action. There is always something to cut to, including a laughing Chinaman if you like. However, if the construction is too ingenious the plots may appear contrived and the *dénouements* too pat. Life is not like that. Not an easy style to bring off. Margaret Lockwood, John Lodge, Hugh Williams and Rene Ray starred, with many others.

The script was by the eminent playwright Rodney Ackland, with Hans Wilhelm. The director, Carol Reed, was new to us. He was 29, one of the new school like Stevenson. It was fascinating to watch the infinite pains Carol took over the playing of every character in every scene. There was clearly a great deal to be learned here. One of his great strengths was his judgement in handling actors.

He had started work in the theatre, with Basil Dean, who was the dominant figure in the London theatre all through the 1920s and early 30s. Soon after the introduction of sound, Edgar Wallace decided to become a film director to make his plays and books into films. Dean was involved in this and Carol Reed was the assistant director. These experiences had given him a better understanding of actors than most directors and he also knew about film. This was where I first saw the technique of not pushing an actor farther than he can go. Carol Reed had an uncanny sense of knowing when he had reached the limit of expression with an actor and never pressed him further. From that moment he used every trick in the book to support the effectiveness of that character in the story, without the actor realising. There is never a bad performance in a Carol Reed picture.

I had by now worked on 25 pictures and was sickening badly for promotion. *Bank Holiday* opened with a sequence showing people knocking off work prior to the holiday. It was an unrelated series of odd shots and I was sent out with a small camera unit to shoot some of them. My cup ran over that day, I can tell you.

Next day, it was back to second assistant in the bargain basement with the Crazy Gang. This was an adaptation of WA Darlington's farce *Alf's Button* which was based on the story of 'Aladdin and the Magic Lamp'. It had already been staged three times and filmed twice. Scripted by Val Guest and Marriott Edgar it was called *Alf's Button Afloat*. It put Alf – Bud Flanagan – in the Royal Marines, just to make it different. To make it even more different, all six of the Gang had to sing the quartet from *Rigoletto* – 'Bella figlia dell' amore'. I was given the job of teaching them the Italian words so that they could mime to a playback, which was recorded by genuine opera singers. They never mastered it but in the course of the tuition they saw to it that I did. I can still sing bits of it.

Every time Alf polished his button the genie, played by the great Alastair Sim, had to appear. This was done by the Pepper's Ghost method, which originated in the theatre.

The camera shoots toward the set as normal. At right angles to this set a false set is built. This is lined throughout with black velvet: walls, floor and ceiling. A thin sheet of glass is placed in front of the camera at an angle of 45 degrees. Alf is in the real set and the genie stands in the black velvet set. When lights are dimmed up on him his reflection appears in the glass and he seems to be standing in the real set, talking to Alf. They must both be in focus, the eyelines must be correct and the lighting on both actors must balance.

Once set up, which took less than 20 minutes, there were some changes to be rung. One was to put the genie on a black-painted trolley and wheel him in from a tiny figure to a giant who towered over Alf. Or contrariwise, diminish him. And many other wrinkles.

Pepper's Ghost is never used these days, but I have described it at length to explain my devotion to the principle of practical special effects. I like to have some trusty special effects man on the set, pulling a string on cue. It works every time and if it doesn't, you know it hasn't right then and there. It certainly worked a treat for *Dracula*.

Nowadays, real effects are demanded by colour and widescreen. If the script calls for a car crash, you have to crash a car. This is as true today for purely physical effects as ever it was, but the use of computers and television techniques has enormously improved the scope and quality of special effects. There is one snag however: they are very expensive. Some other doubts have been expressed. A few pictures have been shown containing little else beside the effects, with poor results; the audiences don't take them seriously. There are also reports of slackness in the shooting units. If a take is not 100 per cent okay. they are content to leave it to be corrected by the computers, instead of going for another take.

After the great successes of *Windbag the Sailor* and *Oh! Mr Porter*, which are still very funny films, the trio of Will Hay, Moore Marriott and Graham Moffat was firmly established and lasted for another four pictures at Gainsborough. The next one was *Convict 99*, with Will Hay as the Governor of the prison. I seem to remember Moore Marriott as one of the convicts. He spent ages and ages digging an escape tunnel and finally broke through – into the Governor's office.

I had learned a little something from all the directors I had worked for and certainly from two of them, Robert Stevenson and Carol Reed, who might be described as eye-openers. A third eye-opener was about to appear.

HITCH

Alfred Hitchcock was by a long way the eminent British director. He had started his career at Islington in the silent days as a writer of sub-titles. 'Came the dawn' – that sort of thing. Now he was coming back to Islington to make *The Lady Vanishes*.

At Elstree, at the time sound arrived, he made two famous pictures: *Blackmail* and *Murder*. He followed with a string of successes at Gaumont-British: *Sabotage*, *The Man Who Knew Too Much*, *The 39 Steps*. He was the first English director to be his own best publicist; he was the first to make his name well known to the general public. His professional reputation was also high and the personal reputation that came ahead of him was also formidable. He was a practical joker and some of the jokes were hilariously funny, but on other occasions the victim had not joined in the laughter. I heard, like most people, blow by blow accounts of these pranks but I was never a witness to one. The nearest I ever got to a first hand account was from Dicky Bevill, a production manager who worked a lot for Hitchcock.

Hitch, like Dvorák, was a student of timetables and was proud of his ability to give authoritative travel information. At this time he had a country house at Shamley Green in Surrey and he invited Bevill to drive down for lunch on Sunday. 'But Hitch, my car is in dock.'

'Then come by Green Line bus. No trouble, it passes your door.'

Bevill was doubtful. 'I've never seen a bus running down Elgin Avenue.'

'Now don't argue. The 11.10 will suit you. Take that and you'll be in good time.'

'But Hitch – '

'Just do as I say.'

Only to be certain that Hitchcock was wrong, Bevill stood outside his flat in Elgin Avenue at 11.10 on Sunday morning. Right on time a Green Line bus appeared, stopped alongside him and the conductor opened the door. 'Shamley Green?' asked Bevill. 'That's right, sir.'

Of course Hitchcock had hired the bus and honour was satisfied. A harmless joke; personal publicity may be misleading. Still, we were all a bit frightened of the man before he ever set foot in the studios. As it turned out, he was a strict disciplinarian. There was no larking about on his set. He was by no means a monster but he would not tolerate any variation of his instructions.

I vividly remember a considerable fuss when Linden Travers, a beautiful girl, was placed by Hitchcock in the window seat of a railway carriage, with Paul Lukas in the seat opposite. This was an even-Stephen two-shot, two profiles, shooting across the compartment. Miss Travers was on the left of camera, which meant that the right side of her face was toward camera. She believed, perhaps rightly, that her left profile was better and she managed to persuade the cameraman, Jack Cox – albeit with some doubt – to allow her to change places with Paul Lukas.

Miss Travers was probably right. Most people's faces are more attractive on the left side than on the right. Some say, as for instance Osbert Sitwell in *Left Hand, Right Hand*, that our left side shows our original nature and the right side shows what we have subsequently made of it. Be that as it may I shall now offer another piece of Advice to Young Men: don't play people in profile except for special reasons; always show both eyes but favour the left side and above all, always set the height of the camera above the chin, especially with women. The eye-line should be close to the left side of the matte-box. This advice is elementary, so why waste the reader's time on it ? Because it is so often wantonly ignored, after 100 years of cinema and umpteen years of television. The mere sight of these misdemeanours is most upsetting. I am not a couch potato, but sometimes the sofa is useful: I can hide behind it.

We were on the set with Hitchcock, shooting across a train compartment.

When setting-up and lighting were completed Hitch was called back on the set. He took one look from left to right, expecting to see Miss Travers and Mr Lukas, in that order. Instead, he saw Mr Lukas and Miss Travers. He decided to pretend to be baffled. Something appeared to be wrong with the set-up as he had planned it and for the life of him he couldn't figure out what it could be. The railway compartment had to be raised above the studio floor because it was built on rockers to allow movement. Therefore the camera was also on a rostrum and Hitch was not inclined to clamber up and down to look through the lens. Hitch had started life as a caricaturist and in a case like this his method was to give Jack Cox a small drawing of the set-up. He demanded to see the original sketch. Light dawned and after stringing the poor girl along a bit more, she suddenly found herself back where she had been put. Maybe Paul Lukas's left profile was the better. Maybe it was a matter of principle. More likely, the man was indulging himself at the poor girl's expense. I am sure that Hitchcock hated actors.

I doubt he ever treated Cary Grant, Ingrid Bergman or other stars in this way. He might have retorted, it wouldn't be necessary anyway. The man's manner was of no consequence beside his abilities as a first-class picture-maker.

During that ten weeks shoot in the studio I reckon I learned as much about film direction as I did in all the rest of my time at Gainsborough. This is not to belittle the qualities of the other directors. It's just that those ten weeks were a sort of crash course in how to do it.

To start with, Hitchcock's methodical approach. He boasted that he always had the film fully worked out in his mind's eye before he started shooting. I was now second assistant and as we came to each set, one of my duties was to obtain from the art department a number of copies of a small-scale outline plan of the set. I put them in Hitchcock's office each day before lunch. Incidentally, he was another devotee of the Fortnum's hamper. One day we were shooting on the dining car set. Hitch invited his small daughter to have lunch with him in the make-believe wagon restaurant, complete with mock Champagne and all the trimmings. There the two of them were, in the half dark of the empty stage, with a couple of working lights and the practicals in the diner.

After lunch each day I collected the plans from the office. Hitch had drawn each set-up on them as he intended to shoot it the following day, in some cases specifying the lens. This left no doubt in my mind about the next day's requirements as to characters, props, costumes, etcetera, and no excuse for failure. With such full and accurate information you couldn't fail and he never double-crossed you by changing his mind. The system was a blessing on a film like *The Lady Vanishes*, because most of the action takes place on a long train journey. Shooting in cramped train compartments with back or front projection, travelling matte or revolving drums is difficult enough. The organisation of the schedule is extremely complicated and must be worked out to the last detail. I have seen people come badly unstuck with trains, even with short sequences. I blessed my stars for this experience when I later shot a long train sequence in *The One That Got Away*.

It must have been great for Jack Cox to be back with Hitchcock. The art director was Vetchinsky, who had been working for some years at Islington. A connoisseur of cigars, food and wine, he was tall and decidedly overweight and reputedly stone deaf. I don't believe he was as deaf as he made out. Selective hearing, possibly, like my dog. He had a high-pitched, adenoidal voice which was easy to imitate. Everybody could and did give their impression of Vetch, often with affection. Not always though. Some of his assistants were heard to grumble that they did all the work while Vetch swanned around schmoozing to the producers. Some years later it was interesting to work with some of these chaps who had now become art directors in their own right. It was amusing to speculate about the effect on them of the training they had received from Vetch.

Vetch built one of the sets in false perspective. This was the platform of a small country railway station, which was made to look much longer than it was, by foreshortening each end of the platform to a false vanishing point. We called some small children and dressed them as adults. With full-size people and buildings in the foreground and the children in the two rapidly diminishing ends of the platform, it looked absolutely convincing. Of course it is restricting. You can shoot only one angle on the perspective and the main action must be played across the set, on the full-size section. The director has to commit himself to shooting the scene in a certain way and a lot of directors won't – can't – do this.

For my part I have thankfully inherited the Hitchcock method of pre-planning. I have no desire to leave everything to the inspiration of the last moment. I don't see how anyone can build a set until all the scenes in that set have been carefully analysed and visualised as they will appear in the finished film. Only then can one see where the various physical requirements must be placed and their relationships to each other. Joseph Losey did this brilliantly with his art director Richard Macdonald on *The Servant*. They worked out the action of the scenes and then constructed the sets around them.

Once the shape of the staging, the character moves, is blocked in, the art director will see straight away where to place his important atmospheric detail, which will be seen and absorbed naturally by the audience as the scene unfolds. You won't have to throw in an insert of the kitchen sink to show the audience that the scene is taking place in a kitchen and not in the ballroom at Buckingham Palace as they may have supposed. The dressing of the set can sometimes be more important than the set itself. The set takes its shape from the action to be played within it and the dressing conveys the sense of place and atmosphere.

A different school of thought leaves the art director free to design a set into which the director has to fit the action. This was the old Hollywood method, in the days when the staging was almost routine: long shot, mid shot, close-ups. On the other hand there are the rare occasions when an art director who is sickening for an Oscar gets the bit between his teeth and no one can control him. Then the director is in real trouble because the sets will probably have been designed for one long shot only.

It is fair to add that art directors are sometimes driven crazy by directors who have a mania for putting the actors up against the back wall of a set, thus wasting three-quarters of it. It is surprising how often this happens. Why they do it, nobody knows. Lesson one is, the action of the scene must be brought right down into the foreground of the set, giving all the depth available behind the actors. Reverses can be covered against a small section of set, usually borrowed from the main set.

The Lady Vanishes had a high-powered cast. It was Paul Lukas' first appearance in an English language film, when he was still lighting cigarettes one at a time; Margaret Lockwood and Michael Redgrave; Dame May Whitty; Mary Clare; Catherine Lacey and Googie Withers. It was based on the book *The Wheel Spins* by Ethel Lina White and the script was by Frank Launder and Sydney Gilliat. They introduced two new characters, Charters and Caldicott, cricket-mad Englishmen whose only concern – despite the imminence of a major European war – is to get the latest news of the current test match. These two were beautifully played by Basil Radford and Naunton Wayne.

The picture was made in 1938 and the writers took every opportunity to throw telling sidelights on the political situation in Europe. This was one reason for its enormous success. When the story was re-made in the late seventies, those reflections didn't apply and so it failed.

Back to earth with a bump for the next picture, *Hey! Hey! USA!*, which had Will Hay teamed with a famous American comedian, Edgar Kennedy. Kennedy had perfected the double-take, slowed it down and called it the slow burn. He was experienced and funny and pleasant to work with, but all I clearly remember about this picture concerns another American actor called David Burns. Burns had the greatest command of foul language and blasphemy I had ever heard and he used it to describe his sexual adventures in disgusting detail. These adventures may have been real – or imaginary.

Will Hay and co followed on with *Old Bones of the River*, based on Edgar Wallace's *Sanders of the River*. It was a funny script and it took us away from Islington for a spell to Sound City, Shepperton. There was an African village on the back lot which had been built for Korda's film of *Sanders*. Just about the end of shooting we were losing interest in the task at hand and beginning to realise that things of moment were going on in the real world. It was now September 1938 and the Munich crisis was on.

Generally speaking everyone breathed a sigh of relief when Mr Chamberlain waved his piece of paper. With any luck, that would be the end of the threat of war. Many wiser – and older – folk guessed that we were only buying time or, if you prefer, putting off the evil day.

I remembered all those books about the Great War which I had read only ten years previously. *All Quiet, Goodbye To All That, Her Privates We, Bretherton, Memoirs of George Sherston, Journey's End*, etcetera: a long, long list which left a deep and lasting impression. In view of all the evidence of these eye-witness accounts it seemed impossible that such a calamity could ever happen again. It was all such a ghastly folly. There was no rhyme or reason to it. Surely nobody could ever again take seriously the idea that three half-dotty and degenerate cousins could drown the world in a blood-bath, slaughtering millions of men in utter futility. Maybe it was simply because they had enormous armies and navies and were bursting to use them. It was said to be a war to end wars and we believed it. Surely there could never be another one. This left out of account the possibility that although there might never be another war like that one, there might still be another war.

Carol Reed came in and cheered us up with *A Girl Must Live*. The girls were gorgeous: Margaret Lockwood, Lilli Palmer and Renée Houston. There was also George Robey, Hugh Sinclair, and Naunton Wayne. The dreadful David Burns was also in it.

Will Hay was now going to be a copper, in *Ask A Policeman*, dear to me because it gave me my only chance to drive round Brooklands race track. Not everyone can say that, you know. For reasons best known to the scriptwriters PC Hay commandeers an omnibus to chase the villains and they all blunder into a motor race at Brooklands. It was still in working order and you bet I took the first opportunity to dash round the circuit in my silver Singer Le Mans. The car wasn't fast enough to push up the famous banking but I did at least one lap. With the windscreen folded down, of course. I probably turned my cap back to front, as well.

Around this time I remember one Sunday afternoon at Will's house, where we watched a live television broadcast of *Private Lives*. The television screen was about seven inches by five, black and white, from Ally Pally. It was remarkable but I thought no more about it and it was all switched off in September '39 for six years.

Will followed on again with *Where's That Fire?*; now he's a fireman.

Coincidentally with the end of shooting early in March – this is now 1939 – we all went to the Gaumont-British Ball at the Albert Hall. This had been an annual event for some time. This will sound really corny but I must tell of walking round one of the upper corridors in the early hours of the morning. The floor was strewn with burst balloons, bottles, torn streamers and so on. In amongst the debris there were one or two discarded copies of the early editions of the morning papers. *The Daily Mirror* headlined

CZECHOSLOVAKIA INVADED

Suddenly, all the fun of the ball had evaporated. Definitely corny. But true.

The revised Cinematograph Film Act was now having its effect. Several of the American majors were buying interests in British studios and 20th Century-Fox came to Islington. Their first picture was *Shipyard Sally*, a vehicle for Gracie Fields directed by Monty Banks. This was the one in which the shipyard workers all go out on strike and Gracie sings a rousing song to them and they all go back to work.

Frozen Limits was the last of the Crazy Gang pictures. My recollection of both these pictures is hazy. We are now in August 1939 and my mind was on other things. During the summer I had registered for national service, along with thousands of others in my age group. Some of the more public spirited men like Hugh Attwooll were busy in the Territorial Army. He suggested I should join too, but I decided against the idea. I believe now that he was right. It might have been better for me if I had followed his advice, but what's the use of second thoughts?

At the very end of August we started shooting another radio spin-off, *Band Waggon*, the famous Arthur Askey/Richard Murdoch radio show. On Friday at the end of the first week Edward Black called everybody together and announced that Islington Studios was now to be closed down. The production would be moved to Shepherd's Bush over the weekend. The Bush had been dark for the last two-and-a-half years, so the prospect of re-activating it was not inviting. On the other hand we should have the place to ourselves. Incidentally the move was a good one in one way because it provided an excellent location for the film. The two heroes in the comedy series were supposed to be living – unbeknown to the Director-General – in a flat on the roof of the BBC in Portland Place. The flat roof of Lime Grove made an ideal setting.

These minor consolations did little to dispel the prevailing gloom as the unit broke up and went their various ways to spend their weekend at home. The Sunday of that weekend was 3 September 1939.

WAR AND PEACE

'THE DAY WAR BROKE OUT...'

The phrase lives on and so does the man who wrote it. Robb Wilton was another of my father's theatrical friends all through the thirties and I knew him well. He lived near us and we often met in the local. I had seen him many times in the halls. He was another example of a comedian who was also an actor, so his delivery was all the more telling. Indeed his first years in the theatre were spent in straight parts, until Florence his wife, prompted him to try a comedy act. His timing was faultless.

He is also a prime example of a comedian who creates a whole world around his character. Not a fantasy world, either. A real world seen with a squint, touchingly resigned to its quirks and so, nearly real. When one compares this sort of work to the contrived, meretricious triviality that is accepted today, full of cheap one-liners and faintly kinky sexual innuendo ... well, I don't know I'm sure. For one thing, it would be a giant leap for mankind if the telly would stop putting all their comedians into women's clothes. Make-up, hairdressing and costuming have all improved so much that they have lost the point of the original idea. Norman Wisdom had a tremendous success in the theatre with *Charley's Aunt* because he played it as a man dressed up as a woman, not as a transvestite. And the audience got a lot of fun in watching the other characters in the play as they blithely accepted him as Charley's aunt.

The 'phoney' war began and the expected air raids didn't materialise. Carol Reed came to the Bush to make a proper film, *Night Train to Munich*, written by Launder and Gilliat in continuation of the themes of their *Lady Vanishes*. The stars were Margaret Lockwood, Rex Harrison, Paul Henreid, etc. Meanwhile, my call-up would come soon and I admit I rather fancied the gallant fighter pilot role. On 15 February 1940, six years to the day after I joined Gainsborough, I said a fond farewell to my mother and father and joined the Army. 3966537 Pte Baker RH, The Verne, Portland Bill – originally built as a prison and it felt like it. No Spitfire for me. Like many other men and women I went where I was sent and did what I was told to do.

When I was at school, the OTC was looked upon as a tiresome chore but I had learned to form fours, salute, fire a rifle, read a map and had done some field exercises on Wimbledon Common. All I now had to do was to learn to form threes instead of fours. All these meagre qualifications didn't add up to much but nevertheless, after a year as Acting/Unpaid/Lance-Corporal, they led to a posting to 163 OCTU at Pwllheli in North Wales.

Twelve weeks later I arrived home in London with my first pip on my shoulder, and after a week's leave I presented myself to the adjutant at the headquarters of the Bedfordshire and Hertfordshire Regiment at Bedford. I mentioned a War Office message which had just been circulated, asking for people who had experience of film production to report the fact. They were increasing the production of training films. At that time I had no deep desire to go back to films but I certainly had the experience they wanted and thought it right to mention it. On the other hand, the adjutant needed bods to bring the battalions up to strength. A posting to the 9th Battalion at Cromer was on offer and I took it. Apart from field exercises we spent a lot of time putting up barbed-wire defences on the coast.

After a year or so of this the War Office repeated its demand for film people. This time I sent my name in and I soon found myself at the old Fox-British Studios at Wembley Park, which had been taken over by AKS – the Army Kinematograph Service Film Production Unit RAOC – dedicated to producing technical training films. It had exclusive use of a fully-equipped film studio and, having started with animated blackboard diagrams, was already broadening its scope, moving into dialogue scenes played by actors in studio sets and on locations.

The personnel were all experienced filmmakers. The doyen and most prestigious was Freddie Young, the lighting cameraman who later won all those Oscars photographing David Lean's pictures. Carol Reed was a member, although it appeared that he did most of his work at the Ritz.

The man who got the AKS production unit together in the first place was Thorold Dickenson, a supervising editor and director who worked at Ealing. He had recruited a talented group of editors (Reginald Mills, Ray Pitt, Geoffrey Foot, Derek Hyde-Chambers, Ted Hunter), cameramen (Bunny Francke, Tubby Englander, Freddie Francis), top class continuity girls (Angela Martelli, Phyllis Crocker), and many more besides. The sound supervisor at Wembley was John Cox.

A most intriguing man was George Ashworth, the camera engineer. He it was who enabled the blackboard diagrams to move, by building what would now be an elaborate rostrum camera. Out of whatever bits and pieces were to hand he made a mechanism which operated the camera one frame at a time. You moved the arrow or the gun or the tank – all cut out of cartridge paper – an inch or so across the blackboard. Then you pulled a string hanging by the tripod and the camera obediently exposed one frame. It worked perfectly.

My first job was as production manager on a picture being directed by one Jay Lewis, who had some experience in documentary. Otherwise I don't remember anything about it. I didn't take a lot of notice of Jay Lewis at the time; some years later he became a major influence in my life.

The move back to London had taken me away from the shelter of Cromer and into the air-raids. They were a constant nuisance and sometimes frightening indeed.

I do not wish to remind myself of any bomb stories.

One Sunday, in the general interest of good order and military discipline, a church parade was ordered at Wembley Park. It was to include the entire unit, ie, all the C of Es, even including the presence of the personnel from HQ who worked in a block of offices in Curzon Street. This is how I came to meet Eric Ambler, another profound influence in my life, this time benign.

I was entering on a most formative stage, making many good friends and learning from some excellent technicians. There were some good writers working at Wembley, among them Jack House, the eminent Glasgow journalist and, later, the brilliant Round Britain quizzer.

It was not long before I noticed there was a shortage of directors at AKS. One of the next productions in the planning stage was *Home Guard Town Fighting Series* and no director was assigned to it. Step forward one plucky little chap – me. Presumably on the principle of 'one volunteer is better than ten pressed men' the powers that were accepted my proposal.

The series was designed in eight parts, adding up to 80 minutes running time – about the length of a feature film of those days. The purpose of it was to instruct the Home Guard how to clear a town which had been occupied by the enemy: how to proceed methodically, street by street, house by house, with hints on discovering and dealing with booby traps, snipers and so on. It was all to be shot silent. The commentary, background noises and music were to be fitted when the visuals were finally edited. For me, it was a golden opportunity: it was all action. The story had to be told in moving pictures – what more could a first-time director want?

In this position at the unripe age of 26 there was a lot I could want, although I wasn't fully aware of it at the time and that may be just as well. I am a believer in ignorance being bliss. Sometimes. Still, I had the sense to go to the local guru. Ray Pitt was now executive producer at AKS. Speaking from his editorial experience, he gave me the best single piece of advice about film direction I ever got: always cover yourself with a cut-away. This confirmed the Hitchcock dictum: when I'm in trouble, I cut to a laughing Chinaman. Seriously, the advice is, look for a story which has good sub-plots offering parallel action.

I had read the few books on the subject of directing that were available, mostly from Russia and by or about Pudovkin and Eisenstein. As soon as the Great War ended, the Russians seized upon the silent cinema as the most effective method of propaganda so far invented. Its universal appeal was clearly the perfect vehicle for demonstrating a nation's politics and culture. The Russians were the first to realise this and some of their films of that period are masterpieces. The Brits have never understood it, even today, when trade may still follow the flag in some places but in most places trade follows the film.

The most valuable experience was to be gained at the London Film Society, which ran a series of showings on Sunday afternoons at the Scala Theatre in Charlotte Street. I caught up with most of the classic films and am only one of hundreds of people who are forever grateful to the devoted organisers, one of whom was the great Olwen Vaughan.

The Russians had the fullest understanding of the effects that can be obtained in the cutting-room and gave rise to the idea that the editing process is the dominant factor in filmmaking. If I may repeat the famous explanation of the process: suppose you take a close shot, in Paris, say, of a man looking down camera left and you then take a close shot, in Moscow, for instance, of a dog looking up camera right. You cut the two together and the audience will believe that the dog and the man are together in the same place, looking at each other. Montage it was called and it was in the top ten of the 50 OK words.

GW Pabst and Carl Dreyer were two more heroes of the pre-war days whose films – in my opinion – were not exactly the cat's pyjamas. Slow and stately and literary in concept, I thought. I've never forgotten one instance of this which I came across when I was preparing for a picture about vampires. I looked up some of the earlier vampire films and in *Vampyr*, which was based on a novel, they actually held on a close-up of a page of the book so that the audience could read it. No wonder the audiences were enthralled with the Westerns. DW Griffith was the man for me. René Clair was at the great man's funeral and he pronounced the finest epitaph a director could desire. He said, 'Nobody has invented anything since.'

A lot of producers have eagerly demonstrated how much they can improve a film after shooting has been completed, by throwing the director out and huddling over the Movieola with the cutter. They adopt the sobriquet 'creative producer' and the result is usually disaster. In Hollywood the long established and dearly cherished method of shooting was to plod through every scene as a master scene, with long-shot, mid-shot, three-shot, two-shot, close-ups, covering it all like a tent. As soon as the last set-up was in the can the director was often shunted off to shoot another picture, thus leaving the cutting room door invitingly open to the producer.

The way for the director to circumvent this is to do the cutting in the camera and shoot everything with a minimum of coverage so that the scenes will only go together one way. Ideally, one should not shoot master scenes at all. Using this procedure, it is amazing how, after Herculean struggles between the producer, the editor and the film itself, the scenes appear in the final film just as the director intended. As mentioned before, it cannot be too strongly emphasised that once shooting is completed, nothing and nobody can alter the film, unless re-takes and extra scenes can be filmed. Editors undoubtedly do bring out the virtues and suppress the shortcomings of the material they have. The edited version should at least look better than the rushes, but there are limits to what the editor can achieve. True, there are now many more facilities available to the editor for manipulating film but it is dangerous to depend on them and more expensive than doing an extra take to get it right.

Shooting to an editing plan is also economical, especially in these days of short schedules and even shorter budgets. A minor advantage is that it doesn't wear the actors to a frazzle before you get to the close-ups. If one confines oneself to shooting only the necessary material, there is more time to be spent in other important activities: for instance, thorough rehearsals. When shooting episodes for television the biggest problem of all lies in creating enough time for rehearsals. The production department attitude seems to be: the actors are dressed and know their lines, the director has done his homework, so call 'em all on the set and shoot it.

The *Home Guard Town Fighting Series* was photographed in four weeks in Birmingham, where the German bombing had left vast areas of wrecked streets, offering authentic battle locations. It was completed at Wembley and duly approved by HQ Home Guard Training.

I was delighted to be given another assignment straight away, this time with actors, studio sets and locations and a script by Jack House. The story, called *According To Our Records...*, was to emphasise the importance of keeping personnel records accurate and up to date. The production manager was Campbell Logan, who came from the BBC. He also acted as casting director and produced a long list of excellent actors who came along to do their bit for the war effort for the statutory fee of £5 a day for expenses – including Mary Clare, who was charming.

The productions were becoming more elaborate and the Army was beginning to see the value of them. In instruction, the films were an ideal way to ensure that the identical message was conveyed to all units, exactly as the originating directorate required. After the showing they prompted valuable discussion. In general, they also contributed to morale. The next job for me was a three-parter teaching instructors how to teach, sponsored by the Army Education Corps. It was particularly useful and was shown extensively and over a long period of time.

What a varied life it was at AKS! Next I made a set of three-minute flashes on security. 'Careless talk costs lives' sort of thing. One in particular would have benefited a lot of people today: the message was, 'Speech on telephones is NOT secret'. Jack Warner spoke the commentaries, which were written in rhyming doggerel. The action and settings were played in crude, theatrical style: Expressionist, I called it, but I'm not sure that was the correct word. It was all very exciting and quite a lark: nothing flatly documentary about that.

It was about this time that I bumped into Jack Cox, walking along Piccadilly. He asked how we were getting on at Wembley and I began to enthuse '...and we're learning quite a lot'.

Sardonic as ever, Jack asked, 'Oh yes – who's teaching you?' Good question. Well, nobody was, at the moment, but I was beginning to realise the influence of Stevenson, Reed and Hitchcock.

The next job was titled *What's the Next Job?* It may seem incredible, but as early as September 1944 the Ministry of Labour decided to make a film offering the troops a general explanation of the plans they had worked out for the resettlement and retraining of hundreds of thousands of men and women – after the war was over. There was no doubt about who was going to win it.

The script was by the redoubtable Jack House and we had an excellent cast: Moore

Marriott, Alfie Bass, Peter Cotes, Lesley Brook, Brenda Bruce. The art director was Lawrence Broadhouse, a true artist. I had met him at Gainsborough and Gaumont-British and took a great shine to him. The music was composed by William Alwyn, no less, with Alan Rawsthorne supervising. Our standards were now on a fully professional level.

Eric Ambler was now established as head of production so we were working together frequently and with increasing confidence. I asked his advice about the prospects of a return to civilian life. I didn't relish the idea of going back to Gainsborough as a second assistant director. Sensibly, Eric counselled patience. The war was by no means over; indeed the V1s were beginning to drop out of the sky. The random bombing of civilian populations had been a favourite technique of the Germans ever since Guernica in 1936; the conventional air-raids had faded out, but this new weapon caused some anxiety among forces overseas about the Home Front.

Elsie and Doris Waters came along to Wembley to make a series of featurettes. These gave general impressions of everyday life in the UK: children in school, a factory at work, girl guides, a fish and chip shop, and so on. Despite the V1s and later the even nastier V2s, life on the Home Front was going on as normally as possible. It was true, too. The days were long gone when everything stopped dead as soon as the sirens sounded an alert.

Eric now revealed to me his plan for peace time. He was involved with Filippo Del Guidice of Two Cities Films, the intention being that Eric should write a script of *Uncle Silas*, a novel by J Sheridan Le Fanu, to be filmed as soon as he was released from the Army. He would also produce the picture. He then asked me to read the book, and how would I feel about directing the film?

I was staggered by the offer. This was far beyond anything I had hoped for. Soon I was invited to lunch with Del in his flat at Grosvenor House. This was quite an occasion for me. As I said goodbye Del said, 'You have the talent. I know. I have the nose'. I had passed muster.

This was all very heady stuff but there was still work to be done at Wembley. The next script was the biggest I had tackled so far. Jack House was absolutely the right man to write it. It was called *Read All About It!* Its purpose was to dispel two widely-held beliefs:

a) You can't believe anything you read in the newspapers.

b) I saw it in the paper so it must be true.

Jack was a dyed-in-the-tweed journalist of long experience so he knew what he was talking about. He turned in an entertaining, well-balanced display of the pros and cons of the above propositions. He took us behind the scenes, into editorial conferences, into the print rooms, giving a genuine feel of the writing and publishing of newspapers and how the news is treated, from the tabloids to the broadsheets. Furthermore he had worked for years at Express Newspapers in Glasgow, so he was able to get full co-operation from the Fleet Street HQ. They were extremely generous in providing facilities: the film contains interesting footage of hot-metal printing, type-setting and printing machines.

The film was re-discovered in 1998 by the Imperial War Museum, in an Army establishment in India. Paul Sargent arranged for it to be shown at the National Film Theatre, together with *The New Lot*. It stood up quite well, I thought. Peter Newbrook, who was a cameraman and director at AKS, has also been doing a lot of detective work in this area.

Jack House was a good friend to me during the AKS years, being somewhat older and considerably wiser than me. Ask him what he would do when the war ended and the answer was: go straight back to his beloved Glasgow, the finest city on earth. For the time being, Jack had to make do with London and a good, cheap restaurant he had discovered in Soho, called Fava. We often went there for supper. Most times we were joined by a colleague of Jack's, Stephen Watts, also from Glasgow and before the war, film and theatre critic of the *Sunday Express*. Stephen was in the 60th Rifles and worked in Intelligence. Fava was decidedly Oriental in style and it amused the two Scotsmen to arrange a Burns Night dinner there, complete with haggis and whisky. That was a jolly evening and nice of them to ask me.

The Germans had just surrendered but the Japanese were still going on. However, by the time we finished shooting *Read All About It!* the Japanese understood the message of the atom bombs and the end was in sight. Jack being a broad-minded man of judgement and wit, it's no wonder he attracted such an enormous audience when he took up broadcasting after the war, beating all comers in *Round Britain Quiz*, as well as picking up where he left off as a leading figure in the Scottish press. Stephen returned to the *Sunday Express* as theatre critic, which was good fortune for me, because he often invited me to go with him to first nights. This gave me a crash course in the London theatre during one of its most intensely successful periods, with the famous Olivier/Richardson season at the New, *Okhlahoma!, Huis Clos* and so on.

I had one final production to make for AKS. The script was written by Thomas Browne and he titled it *Think It Over*. The intention was to teach lieutenant-colonels, when promoted to the rank of Brigadier, how to think: that is, strategically instead of tactically. It was an intellectual exercise but Thomas dressed it up skilfully and the end result was satisfactory. What effect it had on the lieutenant-colonels I don't know. Anyway, my mind was on other things.

DEMOB

Eric had already established an office at Denham Studios, where *Uncle Silas* was to be made. That in itself was a dream come true: to be making one's first feature picture at Denham, which was a top class studio. However, it turned out to be lacking in one essential quality. The film was to start shooting in November 1946 and we were in for the bitterest winter weather since the Norwegians invented skis. Unfortunately the brilliant government of the day had persuaded industry to change its heating systems over from coal to oil. The Rank Organisation dutifully complied. The existing equipment was taken out of Denham, ready to receive the new gear, so we were left with nothing. Of course, the oil-fired machinery failed to arrive. I believe it was eventually installed the following spring, in time for a warm summer.

I had read a lot of Sheridan Le Fanu's books, but not *Uncle Silas*. It is unusual amongst his works, because there is no supernatural element in it, which is predominant in all the others. It is a first rate suspense thriller. Published in 1864, it qualifies as a Victorian melodrama but with Eric's strictly logical style it would be a script to be thankful for. It would be set in its mid-Victorian period, with all that would be entailed in costumes and sets. In the midst of the post-war austerity I reckoned I could enjoy that. What is more, the lead was to be played by Jean Simmons, who was ideal casting. It was perfect. One could not reasonably ask for more.

Suddenly Eric told me we were not going to make it after all. The powers that were at Rank-Two Cities wanted a film that was an original Eric Ambler story, not something based on some one else's work. It was a sensible point of view and there was no arguing with it, but it was a dreadful blow for me.

So Eric wrote *The October Man*. This is the story of a man who is badly injured in a bus crash. A child he is looking after is killed. Partially recovered, he takes a room in a boarding house, to be near his job. One of the other boarders is murdered and, through no fault of his own, he becomes the chief suspect in the murder inquiry. To begin with, he naturally protests his innocence of the murder, but his mental state is fragile. He feels guilty about the death of the child, although it was not his fault at all, and he begins to believe that he may have committed the murder. He is tempted to confess to a crime he didn't do. He decides to commit suicide but the real murderer is at last revealed.

A psychological drama of some power. The setting was a gloomy boarding house on the edge of Clapham Common. The lighting cameraman, Erwin Hillier, gave it the right sort of heavy photography that the subject demanded. Erwin was one of the leading cameramen and had photographed *The Canterbury Tales* for Michael Powell. And I couldn't get on with him at all. Also, his operator, Bob Thomson, was one of the most cantankerous men I have ever come across. Doubtless they also found me difficult.

These were the days when the technicians were in control. One of their little habits was enough to try the patience of a saint. When the lighting cameraman was satisfied that all the lights were in the right places, with a forest of diffusers, gellies, goboes and what-all cluttering the floor, so that it was difficult to get into the set, a test was run. The actors were placed on their marks and a 30-foot silent test was run in the camera. The magazine was taken to the camera department dark room by the clapper/loader. He developed the film, selected a frame in the negative and made an enlarged ten by eight paper print of it. This was then carefully examined by the lighting man and any corrections he thought necessary were made. All this took far longer than it takes to tell and of course, during this time, nobody did anything but wait.

Joyce Carey was playing an interfering resident of the boarding house. Brilliantly sharp and quietly witty, she introduced me to the *Times* crossword. At least the delays enabled me to become a competent practitioner, although I have never won the atlas or the fountain pen, nor yet the malt whisky and stationery rack. So far.

Nowadays it's only a £20 book token. After 50-odd years I'm beginning to lose heart.

There was a continuous battle between the camera department and the sound recording team. They never seemed to realise that their insistence on the ultimate technical perfection was stultifying to the actors, putting them all in straitjackets. They would only have been satisfied if they could have bolted them all to the floor. The actors could only move – if at all – on a precise cue which must not vary by half a second. Then they must stop on a mark exactly.

The result was immaculate, but static. A drama of this type can be allowed to be heavy and slow-moving, provided the script is packed with incident and a few surprises, but it must not be static. We had an excellent cast, led by John Mills and Joan Greenwood. They all did wonders in a very constricted atmosphere. Together with Joyce I had Kay Walsh, Catherine Lacey, Edward Chapman, Adrienne Allen and Sydney (as he then was) James with one line.

Joan Greenwood was discovered by Sydney Box, who put her in a charmingly funny film about a woman who infuriates everyone around her because she never stops talking. She was delightful in it. *The October Man* gave her a more serious part and she responded beautifully. We worked together with confidence and understanding. Our paths never crossed again. I wish they had.

I must admit that I was appalled by the general attitude in the studio. It was the fashion that all productions ran over schedule and any that were completed on time and on budget were looked upon as second-rate. It may well be that I did not do enough to hide my opinions. I had just spent six years in the Army where a different outlook prevailed.

In civilian life, if the slightest thing went wrong, everybody downed tools and stopped work completely. While the hold-up was being dealt with, whatever it was, everybody else simply sat down and waited for it to be cleared up. Nobody cared. They simply said: 'Oh well, it's only a few more bags of Uncle Arthur's flour!' I wonder what J Arthur would have said if he'd heard it. But then, he was another of those great leaders of modern industry who never go near the seat of production, or ever try to find out how the process works.

The October Man was scheduled for 12 weeks, which was more than enough, but it took seventeen weeks to complete, working a six-day week. In these conditions the most frustrating job I had was to try to keep the momentum of the production going and to maintain the morale of the cast, which was as much of a strain on everybody else's nerves as it was on mine. There was a general lack of support from the production department, headed by PC Samuel, and by the time we were into the tenth week's work, I knew that I had lost Eric's confidence, not entirely by my own fault. One quickly learns that stamina counts for a lot in this game and there is no place for five-furlong horses. We got there in the end, 25 days over schedule and a daily average screen time of one minute, one second. The number of set-ups per day was four. Laughable, if it wasn't so serious – but nobody was taking it seriously.

The October Man was sneak previewed and moderately well received. The final cut ran 95 minutes. Eric decided to join with Cineguild: Anthony Havelock-Allan, David Lean, Ronald Neame, Stanley Haynes – probably the best group of filmmakers around. Two Cities decided not to take up their option on my services. So I waited for the premiere at the Odeon, Leicester Square, and the critics.

I was exhausted, but not particularly worried. I felt that I had got through a very trying time. I knew that I hadn't exactly got everything right. The film was too slow and should have been cut more sharply, but it was well made and I had achieved my first credit as director of a first feature of quality. This seemed to me to be satisfactory enough to be going on with. I had no ambition to conquer the world with my first picture. It was shown at the Dinard Film Festival in 1993, where there was a retrospective of seven of my films. Several people in the audience said they were surprised to be told that it was made 45 years ago: it looked so modern. So it can't have been too bad.

I was immovably determined on one thing: I had made a modest but sound start as a director and I would never do anything else. To me, it was a job for life. It is regrettable, looking back over nearly 50 years, to recall the very large number of people – dozens of them – who got to direct their first film and then never made another one.

The notices were very good indeed, some of them very complimentary to me; CA Lejeune made me her Man of the Month. So, a good boost to morale, but I now had to face up to the most difficult aspect of a director's life: finding the next picture. I tried to remember all the books I had read and the plays I had seen. I tried to keep up with the current offerings. I tried to write a thriller, but it soon turned into a dull detective story.

After only a couple of months, talks began with Paul Soskin, not the Soskin who built the new studios at Borehamwood – that was his uncle. Paul was going to make Esther McCracken's play *No Medals* into a movie for Two Cities. It had a successful run in the West End in 1944, playing to full houses for over 700 performances, the story being about the difficulties of a wife and mother, struggling to keep home and family together in war time.

Two Cities was becoming more and more absorbed into the Rank Organisation and so for the first time I met Earl St John during these early discussions. Originally with Paramount on the exhibition side, he was now head of production for Rank. He was an American, from Alabama and was to be part of the major effort that Rank was mounting to gain a showing for his films in the United States.

In January 1948 we settled down to serious preparation. My copy of the script is packed full of re-writes – never a good sign. It was written by Miss McCracken and Paul Soskin, with additional scenes by Val Valentine. Valentine was the only one with experience as a film scriptwriter. Soskin seemed to have the idea that the director should be excluded from discussions of script and simply accept what was handed over when the producer was satisfied with it. Still I was glad indeed to be back at Two Cities. A good cast was gathering: Ursula Jeans, Cecil Parker, Joan Hopkins, Derek Bond, Lana Morris, Thora Hird.

Then Paul announced the good news. He had managed to get my favourite cameraman: Erwin Hillier. Once more, this film consisted almost entirely of interior settings, a small scale domestic story. It had nothing to offer Erwin. The only thing it did offer was a beach scene on the sands at Margate. We arrived there on a brilliantly sunny day in June and Erwin refused to shoot because there were no clouds in the sky. However, most of the crew were less intractable: the operator was Eric Besche, a most agreeable colleague, and Vetch was again the art director.

Esther McCracken had a number of successes, such as *Quiet Weekend* and *Quiet Wedding* which were later filmed well and were not dated. *No Medals*, now endowed with the enticing title *The Weaker Sex*, appeared two years after the end of the War and people didn't want to be reminded of those problems; they were having enough trouble trying to cope with the peace. It was a neat and tidy job, but it did nothing to enhance the prestige of anyone concerned.

Next I was offered a film to which one special condition was attached: whatever happened, it must not go over schedule or over budget. The penalty for failure in either respect was instant consignment to outer darkness. Black holes hadn't been invented but, looking back, I think that would have been the idea. The schedule was seven weeks, which seemed adequate. I was never shown the budget or even told the overall figure, so how I was supposed to comply with these strictures I don't know.

This was *Paper Orchid*, with a screenplay by Val Guest, based on a novel by Arthur La Bern, who was also the author of *It Always Rains On Sunday* and *Good Time Girl* which were made into successful movies. The production was backed by Columbia and the executive producer was William Collier who, as Buster Collier, was a famous American film star. The producing company was called Ganesh, after the elephant-headed Hindu god of foresight, who failed to exercise his gift and gave no warning of what the end of it all was to be. The filming was to take place at Nettlefold Studios, a small and efficient outfit where we would be the only picture in production and therefore all effort would be concentrated on our picture.

The producer was John R Sloan, a most genial man of boundless energy, enthusiasm and experience who usually worked at the Warner studio at Teddington. He was tireless in his attention to detail and a great all-round support. The cameraman was Basil Emmott, whose experience went back to the silent days. He lived in France and was immensely proud of his beautiful drop-head Citroën; so rare that even Maigret couldn't aspire to own one. I knew I could rely on him completely.

The cast was also strong in talent and experience: Hugh Williams, Hy Hazell and Sid James (to give him his later title). The shoot went off very smoothly, and we dutifully finished shooting on time and – I suppose – on budget.

As soon as it was completed I got a letter from Switzerland, from one Othmar Gurtner. He had seen *The October Man* and liked it. He was planning to make a film and would like to talk to me about it. On the strength of this letter I was allowed to buy some Swiss francs from the Bank of England and on Christmas Day off we went to Zurich. Taking the *Wagons-Lits* from Calais, it appeared that when we arrived at Basle the dining car was changed. The Swiss preferred their own diner and I soon found out why. That breakfast is something I shall never forget. Pure white bread, black cherry jam, fresh eggs, ham, cheese, excellent coffee – none of that had been seen for six years. And the shops in Zurich were something to see.

Gurtner's idea was to film a famous Swiss novel called *Derborence*, by CF Ramuz. I can't remember any of the details now, but it was a heavy drama and very static and I really couldn't see much hope of it being made. Gurtner was a charming man and a generous host. Apart from his interest in films he had something to do with preventing avalanches: when a potential fall was sighted he would call out the Army artillery to fire a few shells at it to bring it down. Presumably he cleared the area first. Nothing came of it in the end but I was grateful for a breath of Swiss air.

Then, back at Nettlefold's, Robert Farnon came in to compose the music and *Paper Orchid* was ready for the statutory trade show in April 1949. After that, silence. I saw a squib in one of the trade papers saying that the picture was to be premiered in Brighton and shown at various seaside resorts during the summer. I don't know if this happened or not. There was some sort of showing at Swansea. There never was a press show. There never was a release of any kind, perhaps because the circuits refused to take it. The movie was just left on the shelf.

Perhaps Columbia had been making a quota quickie, but even so, they would have had to get a showing for it in order to qualify. It can't have been all that bad. The original book was good if a touch melodramatic: Fleet Street and a murder mystery. Val Guest's script was sharp and concise. He had worked in newspapers at one time and he had lost none of the authenticity of the book. The performances were all good, with actors like Andrew Cruickshank, Walter Hudd and Hughie Green in support. There it was. And still is, unless somebody cut it up for banjo picks.

Gradually I was beginning to worry. Spring came, but everything was dead, as far as I was concerned. I had directed three pictures, but I was travelling on a descending curve. Looking back, I remember it as an agonisingly long and depressing time. Now that I am checking the dates in my diaries I find that the ages spent waiting for the phone to ring were in fact quite short. I also remember, this time with accuracy and gratitude, the encouragement I had from some good friends: Norman and Pamela Hackforth, Stephen Watts, Nicholas Phipps, David Tomlinson and especially Kay Walsh, who was having a miserable time herself. They buoyed me up no end.

Kay was working at Elstree in July, in Hitchcock's *Stage Fright*. It was now Hitch's habit to lunch in the studio restaurant, where he presided over a long table seating a dozen or more people. Kay invited me to go along one day so I found myself sitting with most of the cast of the picture: Jane Wyman, Michael Wilding, Dame Sybil Thorndyke, Alastair Sim, Joyce Grenfell. Hitch greeted me most affably. On the other side of the table from me was another member of the cast, Marlene Dietrich, who wanted to know the date of my birthday. I told her, 19 December.

'Aaaah!' she said. 'Sagittarius...'

It seemed I had said the right thing. While I was frantically trying to think what to say next, a marvellous piece of luck came my way. I was surprised to be called to the telephone. This is of course the best thing that can happen to you when you are lunching at a studio, but it has to be genuine. It's no good arranging for a chum to ring. This was genuine. It was Jay Lewis on the phone. I hadn't seen him since the War; what could he want with me?

MORNING DEPARTURE

Would I call at his office in Wardour Street and collect a script? There Jay introduced me to his partner, Leslie Parkyn. The script was about a submarine disaster, based on a play called *Morning Departure*.

The story was about a submarine on peace-time exercises in the Channel which triggers an old magnetic mine and sinks to the seabed. The play was written by Kenneth Woollard and the script was by William Fairchild. This was one of those rare occasions when I read a script and I knew with absolute certainty that the film would be a big hit. Shooting was to begin in August on location at Portland. We had the full co-operation of the Royal Navy. We had a submarine, HMS Tiptoe and the mother-ship HMS Maidstone at our disposal. There was a lot of work to be done and Maidstone was scheduled to leave in two weeks. The weather was good and we completed our task on time. The cameraman was Desmond Dickinson, another veteran of the silent days; a delightful man and ideal casting for this subject. I was confident that the rushes were good and I was looking forward to the studio work at Denham. Little did I know...

The day before main photography at Denham was to begin, Jay invited me to take a walk with him around the back lot. As soon as we were away from the main buildings, he stunned me with a long lecture about the Portland location. Now he had time to look at the film I had shot he was appalled by how bad it was. With skilful editing it would just about do, we'd get away with it, but now that the serious shooting was about to start, it was obvious that he would have to be on the set with me all the time to supervise everything. Not only was he worried, but the financial backers were scared too and were looking to him to ensure that nothing further went wrong.

Looking a long while back, I wonder just how much of this was true and how much invention, because all the work I had done was included in the final cut of the film. But at the time it was a devastating attack and it took the wind completely out of my sails, all the more because it was such a surprise. Up till then I had not had one word of criticism about the rushes from anybody. As far as I knew everybody thought they were satisfactory, as I did. However, if Jay insisted on sitting on the set all day, there was nothing I could do about it.

In the event Jay's ploy was to second-guess me after every rehearsal. My method was, and still is, to present – with the actors – a complete mechanical layout of each scene as it came along, so as to enable the crew to get to work. Everyone then knows what the requirements are for the whole scene and what the covering angles are going to be. Once the crew have finished their arrangements I take the actors through two or three rehearsals, during which all the minor details are ironed out and the final polish is applied and the actors are led naturally into the first take. This is the tried and tested procedure used by almost every director in the world. But as soon as the crew start to set up, anybody can barge in with comments and suggestions, mostly concerning the minor points which will anyway be dealt with at a later stage.

Jay's interventions led to long discussions and arguments, much to the discomfort of the actors; they find it difficult to listen to two voices. Of course some of his observations were perfectly valid, but would be taken care of at the proper time, when the actors were preparing themselves for the take. This interference was simply interference for its own sake, but the biggest danger I saw was that he was constantly trying to hype up the drama into a melodrama; this film was a serious, utterly realistic, drama. It required the most delicate treatment; one lapse into cliché acting would plunge it into a cheap exploitation of a true-to-life tragedy. Nobody then had the faintest idea how important this discipline would turn out to be.

I had already had straight-from-the-shoulder talks with two of the actors about their performances, which were routine and superficial. Nigel Patrick was presenting his first lieutenant as a handsome, dashing officer and the character was all of that, but he was only skimming the surface of him. James Hayter had an entirely conventional character as the lower-deck comedy relief and was playing it as written. Once he saw that there was more in it than met the eye he grabbed the chance with both hands. These admonitions were accepted whole-heartedly by both actors. In the end they both turned in superbly sincere characterisations.

On other occasions I'm not sure that I have always put comments to people in what is known as an acceptable way. I may have upset a lot of colleagues and not done myself any favours. The trouble is that I have a firm and ineradicable conviction that the project on which we are all working is far more important than any of us individually. Whatever manner of speaking one chooses, all instructions must be concise and simple; queries and objections must be dealt with directly. If the director doesn't know his own mind the cast and crew will be at sea and the film in jeopardy. That deathless line, 'Let's not fight this thing – it's bigger than both of us' will do well enough for me.

Early on in the shooting of *Morning Departure* I realised that Jay was trying to get rid of me and take over as director. If I gave him the slightest opportunity he would seize it with relish. I knew I had to make a superhuman effort, that I must not be induced to resign or be sacked. I was directing the picture and at the end of it I would be entitled to the credit.

Then fate took a hand, or the financial backing did. I had not seen much of Leslie Parkyn, Jay's partner. He was a quiet, reserved man, scrupulous to a fault. He had a shrewd, sharp eye and sound judgement. The finance came from the recently invented British Film Finance Corporation which was headed by David Kingsley. He was a banker and I had met him once during the War with a mutual friend, Jack Clarke, who was my first assistant at AKS.

So far the BFFC had contributed small amounts to the budgets of a few films, but this time they had been moved to take the whole risk. All £125,000 of it. It doesn't sound much now, but it was serious at the time. Therefore they were carefully monitoring everything that happened. At any rate a decision was made, I shall never know by whom, that Jay should go off to Dover with a second unit to film the salvage operation above sea level.

Jay and I had a conference about how his scenes should fit in with mine and off he went. The last two or three weeks of shooting, which in many ways were the trickiest, went off without a hitch. We went through the final completion stages of post-synch, music and dubbing early in the new year, 1950. Thank heaven, nobody wanted any music at all in the film. Only the opening and closing titles have music, and this was borrowed from *The October Man*.

The premiere was fixed for 27 February 1950. Suddenly, a couple of weeks before this, an appalling real-life disaster took place. A submarine, HMS Truculent, a sister ship of Tiptoe was motoring quietly up the Thames. It was dark and the light was bad. Coming the other way, down the river, was a large freighter. There was a collision. There were four men on the deck of the submarine. They were all thrown overboard as the boat capsized. The hatch of the conning tower was still open. All the rest of the crew were below and the boat flooded. All 64 hands perished.

The film had been shown to the Royal Navy as soon as it was completed. At first sight it seemed to us that to go ahead and show *Morning Departure* would be in the worst possible taste. On the contrary, the Navy saw no need to view the film again and decided that it should be shown, just as it was, with no alteration. Thank goodness the integrity of the drama had been preserved.

The grim truth has to be faced that the tragic loss of Truculent contributed to the enormous public interest in the film. The press was unanimous in endorsing the decision to show it. One can only hope that no one was distressed by it. When I gave the *Guardian* Interview at the National Film Theatre I had talked about this. Afterwards a stranger came up to me. He explained that he had a close relative who had died in HMS Truculent. He assured me that nobody involved in the disaster had been distressed by the film. On the contrary they had taken some comfort from a truthful account of the risks that submariners face. Here again, a reflection on a past effort pops up after 50 years.

The critics' reviews were staggering in their praise. *The Times* managed to dig up the customary disdainful note, about the opening sequences which showed the domestic backgrounds of the main characters. I agree: these scenes were weak and nowadays I think they would be dispensed with, but they were conventional because the lives they portrayed were conventional. Such rave notices are hardly ever seen these days. People wrote to me to say how much they liked the picture. I was thrilled to get a long letter from Joyce Carey, and one from John Boulting, but the one that gave me the most satisfaction came from Leslie Parkyn.

The premiere was at the Gaumont Haymarket. In the crush we slowly climbed the stairs to the circle. Ahead of me was my agent, Jack Dunfee, who turned to look back and spotted me. For the benefit of the crush he shouted 'Give me a ring in the morning, Roy – it's HOLLYWOOD!'

HOLLYWOOD

OR 'THERE AND BACK – TO SEE HOW FAR IT IS'

The following morning Dunfee outlined the interest in my services shown by 20th Century-Fox as reported from MCA Hollywood. Nothing was definitely decided, but they were considering the possibility of making an offer. This was something quite unlooked for. I had never thought of working in Hollywood. At that time Fox was the best studio with Zanuck scoring success after success. I agreed that if asked I would be willing to go, but it was all slightly too good to be true. Probably nothing would come of it.

Only two weeks after the opening of *Morning Departure* Eric Ambler gave me the script of *Highly Dangerous*, which I think he said he had based on one of his earlier novels. Sydney Box was going to produce it for Rank as a vehicle for Margaret Lockwood and an American male star. It was pleasant to be seeing Eric again after a period of estrangement. He thought I might get an offer to go to America, but he also thought I should not go, at least for the time being; I was young and there would be plenty of time to go later on.

I was summoned to meet Earl St John, head of production, who was ensconced in the Rank Organisation's head office in South Street. The building was originally a magnificent town house in Mayfair and Earl's office had previously been somebody's bedroom. It was huge. There was a high semi-circular daïs at one side, which I suppose was intended to support a splendid bed. Now Earl sat up there, behind a large walnut desk. With a grin, he invited me to climb up and join him.

We discussed *Highly Dangerous* but the only thing I remember about our talk was when the subject came up of the possible offer from 20th Century-Fox. Earl expressed his admiration for my work on *Morning Departure* and how keen he was that I should direct *Highly Dangerous*. He then gently explained that *Morning Departure* was marvellous but it simply wasn't the kind of movie that would interest Hollywood. Neither would they be interested in the director of such a film.

At that moment I absolutely knew as a certainty that a firm offer would be made. I don't know why. It wasn't because I thought Earl's views were worthless; he had voiced a sound opinion. I just knew it would happen. Unfortunately I didn't act on this hunch.

The great success of *Morning Departure* had produced a turmoil in my life and

I was in no state to make proper decisions. It would have been quite enough for me to settle quietly down to consider the consequences of a Hollywood offer and analyse just what it would mean to uproot myself and my wife, who was expecting a baby in August, quite apart from the strain of making one's first picture in Hollywood, where the standards were high. To take on a major feature picture starring Margaret Lockwood was also a serious undertaking. I didn't stop to think that I might find myself involved in both projects, all within the space of six months.

But suppose the chance didn't come again? Was it not better to plunge in at the deep end? I was well aware that I had directed only four pictures and those with varying degrees of success, but my self-confidence was intact and indeed somewhat bolstered by having weathered the pressures of making *Morning Departure*. Neither had I any wilful intention to disregard good advice, but I must confess to the thought that some part of Earl's and Eric's attitudes might be because they wanted me for *Highly Dangerous*.

Anyhow, 20th Century-Fox were still talking but hadn't yet put forward a definite proposition. I was beginning to doubt their intentions. *Highly Dangerous* was due to start straight away, so I decided to do it.

Location spotting started and I took Vetchinsky on a recce trip to Trieste. We flew to Nice and then enjoyed the trip by train along the coast to Genoa and thence to Milan. From there, onward to Venice where we just had time for dinner. It was pouring with rain, I remember. At last, after a three day journey, we arrived at Trieste.

The atmosphere here was tricky. The place was originally a free city under Austrian influence, but it was ceded to Italy at the end of the First World War. At the end of the Second World War the Yugoslav Army had occupied it and were still firmly established in one half of it, while the Italian civilians kept their distance in the other half, heavily supervised by the British. We roamed about freely but were warned not to stray over the dividing line. The Jugs, as they were called, often had difficulty in distinguishing friend from foe. So what else has changed?

After a week of rooting about I was summoned to Paris for the premiere of *Morning Departure*. There was no hopping on and off aeroplanes in those far-off days of not so long ago, so I took the overnight train back to Paris. John Mills came over from England and joined in a hectic three days of interviews on television, radio, etc. Not that it wasn't very exciting indeed. Johnny was on his best form and he can be hilariously funny, believe me.

One of the best moments was provided by the Rank office, in the person of Serge Ovzievsky, their PR man. He organised a dinner at Monseigneur – an excellent restaurant where the theme was Old Russia. There was a splendid string orchestra of 20 musicians all dressed as cossacks. When the food was served it turned out to be kebabs such as you've never seen: four more cossacks swept over to our table, bearing the meat on flaming cavalry sabres. The orchestra struck up a rousing song, marched across the dance floor and surrounded our table. Some showmanship!

It was all worth the trip, even including the dreary train journey back to Trieste. I didn't feel tired at the time, but looking back I realise I must have been exhausted.

A small camera unit had arrived from England and we spent ten days shooting background plates for back projection. In the middle of this, a firm offer came after all from 20th Century-Fox. Presented with a Hollywood contract, coming from the best studio at that time, with Zanuck being top dog, it was very hard to resist. I was far away from home and family and friends with whom I might have discussed this, though I doubt, in my present state, I would have been able to profit by any advice that might have been offered. At that time there were few precedents: as I recall, Compton Bennett – after the success of *The Seventh Veil* – was the only post-war example of a British director going to Hollywood.

Lew Wasserman, the head man at MCA, was now in London and I fell under the spell of his high pressure description of the delights that awaited me in the US. A simple, straightforward script would be my first assignment, to allow me to settle in and learn the ropes; bigger things would follow. After all, there were one or two directors under contract at Twentieth who were nearing retirement...

There, you see, is the old Hollywood studio system: each one maintained a stable of directors who could be trotted out any time, as they also did with producers, writers and actors and actresses. Of course I should have insisted that they offer me a specific deal for a specific film – which might well have aborted the whole project. So what if it did? I was in demand in England anyway. Of course this, of course that – and the other. All hindsight. In fact, at that time, I had no idea how strong my position was. Believe it or not, it's true. I have on several occasions been chidden for putting myself down. For one thing, I had absolutely no talent for personal publicity, which was positively discouraged anyway. Raking over the past as I am now, I am beginning to accept this estimate. Certainly I can now see that it has been a detrimental factor in my decisions on at least two more occasions. The conditions in the summer of 1950 were entirely different from now, especially for one as inexperienced as I was in negotiations of this kind. In fact no previous experience at all. I accepted the offer. So now I had landed myself with both the problems.

I was now introduced into the orbit of the 20th Century-Fox office in London, in Piccadilly, just by Hyde Park Corner. It was run by Freddy Fox, with Ben Lyon as casting director and – much to my surprise – Robert E Dearing, dear old Bob Dearing, last heard of as the curmudgeon who ran the cutting rooms at Gainsborough, when they were still at Islington. He was now supervising editor for 20th's productions in England.

I at once remembered a trivial incident during the war. It was at the time I had just been commissioned. I was on leave in London and decided to look up old friends at the Bush. It was all very jolly. Billy Partleton was there and many others. Frank Launder and Sydney Gilliatt were their affable selves. We went to the pub on the corner, where we found some more people from the studios, including Bob Dearing. I greeted him – and he turned his back on me. It was quite deliberate and I have no idea why he did it. During all my time at Islington I had never had anything directly to do with him.

Seeing him again after seven years or more, in different circumstances, was quite weird. I did wonder what sort of help or hindrance he might be, but he wouldn't have anything to do with me, since the office had only to arrange my transportation to Los Angeles. That job fell to Ben Lyon, who felt it his duty to the company – I suppose – to arrange it in the most economical way. It wasn't exactly steerage, but it wasn't luxurious either.

The last stages of preparation of *Highly Dangerous* centred on long discussions about big-name American male stars, all of whom turned out to be unsurprisingly unavailable and eventually Dane Clark arrived, to be Maggie's co-star.

Now, Eric had written this script as a vehicle for Margaret Lockwood. It was a Cold War spy thriller, and it contained several set-piece scenes for her. She is an entomologist who is persuaded into a trip beyond the Iron Curtain to discover what may be afoot in the way of germ warfare spread by insects. Of course she is rumbled by the local chief of police the moment she arrives, but sails serenely on. When her contact is murdered she is all the more determined to press on. There was a lot of comedy in it, largely at the expense of the two main characters because, ironically, her brilliant plans to outwit the enemy continually go wrong, despite the efforts of the leading man to restrain her. Each time he has to bail her out, at some risk to them both.

This was my first experience, as a director, of a visiting American leading man. Having seen a lot of films at that time it seemed to me that some of them had a common set of principles: the hero must never show weakness, never betray a sense of humour and his attitude to women is 'aren't you lucky to have me'. These attitudes must never be jeopardised by the story of the film or its background or the character he is playing. All the other characters and their impact on his character may be disregarded.

However, this first impression turned out to be a misleading one: during my term in Hollywood my leading men were Tyrone Power, Richard Widmark, Gary Merrill and Robert Ryan and very lucky I was. Some of the ones who come to England suffer from some kind of jet lag I suppose, although Tyrone was here and he was just great. So I revised my opinion, albeit with minor reservations. Also, this was 1950 and since then all acting styles have undergone radical changes for the better.

Dane Clark had been working under John Garfield in the New York theatre for some time. On arrival here, he decided to be the next John Garfield. Not the first Dane Clark. He was amiable enough, but he was dreadfully worried that his character had to defer to the girl. She was the leading character in the story and everything in the plot happened at her instigation. Only at the very end did the hero save the day with outstanding bravery.

There is little else to tell about *Highly Dangerous*. I haven't seen it since I made it. I don't believe I ever had a real grip on it. I didn't do enough to subdue an over-enthusiastic performance from Marius Goring. I presented Maggie well but I could have given her more encouragement in the comedy, although comedy was never her forte. There's no doubt about it, I don't do well unless I can concentrate on the matter in hand, that and nothing else. Since then I have developed a special brand of tunnel vision when working. After eleven weeks shooting, on the last day, my wife gave birth to our son. Six weeks later the three of us were on board RMS Mauretania, bound New York.

A LIMEY AT THE COURT OF KING ZANUCK

One of the bonuses in going to the United States was that I could expect to see some old friends, Americans I had met in London during the War. The first of these was David Golding, who fetched up in England after being editor during the War of the American forces newspaper in Italy. He stayed on in London, becoming Korda's PR for some years. Now he was in New York and working for 20th Century-Fox. Standing on Pier 90, there he was, ready to whisk us into town in a huge limousine.

After the three-and-a-half day's train trip, we arrived in Los Angeles. Two more old friends were waiting to welcome us, Samuel Goldwyn Jnr and Alan Campbell. With them were two people we hadn't met before: Sam's wife Jennifer and Alan's wife Dottie – Dorothy Parker. A tiny lady, softly spoken – she never raised her voice – but for all her modest demeanour you'd never miss her in a crowd. She did not immediately let loose a string of epigrams, but she had a presence which was most impressive. She was charming and obviously a person to be respected. My new agent George Chasin, one of MCA's best, insisted on taking care of the enormous quantity of baggage we'd brought and then found himself chasing up the other half of it that had been left behind when we changed trains at Chicago.

I was staggered by my first view of the 20th Century-Fox studios. It has now been turned into Century City but in 1950 it was a magnificent film studio. It was vast, covering the area between Wilshire and Pico Boulevards, just outside the city of Beverly Hills. George Chasin showed me round it. On the back lot there was still the outline of Trafalgar Square, which had been built for *Cavalcade*. Along one side of this was a long row of garages which housed all manner of vehicles, dozens of them, from covered wagons and Model T Fords to a 1920 LGOC double-decker bus. As we walked, George apologised for the office I had been given, complete with secretary, but not in the main admin. block. I hadn't thought about it. I'd never had an office of my own before. Apparently this was a serious matter of prestige and George was determined to do something about it. As it turned out, I stayed in that office all the time I was at the studio. I never thought it was shabby: next door was the riotous, wonderful Sam Fuller; next door to him was Herman Mankowitz, who wrote the script of *Citizen Kane*. Good neighbours.

There was no doubting the warmth of the welcome we received from the natives. Stephen Watts was writing a regular Saturday column in the *New York Times* on the London theatre and cinema in general. This week's piece was all about me and how England's loss was Hollywood's gain. Most flattering and good of him to do it: it was a splendid build-up to my entrance, but the idea of England losing anything by my departure didn't register with me at all. Some of the London papers had coupled it with remarks about the dire state of British film production, which was becalmed in another of its periodic doldrums. I never for a moment saw myself as retrieving the situation single-handed and I certainly didn't think *Highly Dangerous* would do much for the situation either.

I was quite happy in Austerity Britain: we were all muddling through, despite the difficulties. True, bread had recently been rationed for the first time, four years after the war had ended; also the meat allowance was reduced to one shilling a week, something less than a pound in present day money. In Los Angeles this sort of thing was unbelievable. The locals commiserated with these half-starved refugees and congratulated us on our good fortune in escaping. American hospitality is legendary and it lived up to the legend.

Alan and Dottie gave a most enormous party at which everyone, but everyone, appeared: Fritz Lang, Otto Preminger, Laurence Olivier, so many names I can't possibly drop them all. Alan was the sort of man who knew everybody, although many of the guests were there to see Dottie, who didn't socialise much and indeed finished up as a recluse. They had not long been married for the second time, to each other, I mean. They married for the first time in the thirties. Alan was an actor who was reputed to be a look-alike for Richard Barthelmess but no great shakes on the stage. They came to Hollywood when Samuel Goldwyn asked Dottie to work as a screenwriter. Some time later they divorced and Alan turned up in England in the US Army during the war. I met him with Eric Ambler and also Samuel Goldwyn Jnr who was in the US Army. More than a dozen years later I was completely bowled over when Lillian Hellmann spilled the beans: not only did Alan know everybody, he was also all things to all men, women and camels. I never had an inkling. He was a plausible rogue.

I had some introductions to members of the British Raj. Nigel Bruce, who was always known as Willie, and Mrs Bruce, who was always known as Bunny made us welcome. She tried to dissuade Willie from telling his favourite story, which was the one about a woman phoning the Food Hall at Harrods. She is trying to trace a man called Jim, who worked there. The manager doesn't know any Jim: what does he do? – 'is he a pheasant-plucker?' and the woman says dolefully, 'No, he's a mean son-of-a-bitch.'

One of the curious aspects of Hollywood at that time was that the people working at any one studio formed a sort of club and didn't socialise with the people at any other studio. One ran with the studio one was at, so I ran with the Fox group and very jolly they all were. A couple of weeks went by; still no sight or sound of Darryl F Zanuck.

Unexpectedly I got a phone call from Jay Lewis. He was in town and wanted to see me. A few people were coming to the house for drinks that evening so I asked him to come along too. He had another man with him, tall, English. I had never met him and I have no recollection of his name or anything about him. Jay said he wanted a quiet word with me so we went out of the sitting room on to a balcony. The house was on the hill overlooking the Strip and a splendid view of Los Angeles. It was dark now and the enormous spread of the city was a blaze of lights.

Jay wasted no time on the view. He thought I should know that he had had a long meeting with Darryl Zanuck at which he had explained that he was the man responsible for *Morning Departure*. Roy Baker was credited as director but in fact had been supervised every step of the way by him, Jay Lewis, who had virtually taken over. In other words, Zanuck had got the wrong man.

This was a hell of a shock, especially as I had not yet seen Zanuck myself. Looking back, I cannot understand what Jay expected to gain by viciously misrepresenting the truth. He was certain to make a lot of money from the picture, which was already a box-office smash. He had stepped straight into a good reputation as a producer with his first feature film. This was apparently not enough. He must have been insane with envy, to deliberately try to destroy my position at 20th Century-Fox by telling Zanuck a pack of lies with no possible advantage to himself. Surely he didn't expect Zanuck to tear up my contract and offer him a picture to direct? I also wonder what satisfaction he got by telling me to my face what he had done.

A couple of weeks later my contract officially started. Not surprisingly, there was an air of uncertainty, coupled with oblique questions. The seeds of doubt had been sown. Still no meeting with Zanuck. George Chasin was puzzled but did his best to reassure me. I told him what Jay had done, that Jay deserved all credit as producer but he certainly hadn't directed the picture and it was my stubborn tenacity, demanding first class performances and my determination to keep the film true to its proper style – tragedy, and not contrived melodrama – that saw us through.

One day, as I was walking back to my office from lunch, I met André Hakim, Zanuck's son-in-law and a producer on the lot. He asked me about Jay Lewis, so I told him him the facts. I was the director of *Morning Departure* and no one else, despite Jay's interference. Whether I was able to dispel any doubts André may have had, I know not.

This was another of those periods of waiting which seemed so long at the time, but in fact it was only a couple of weeks before I was asked to meet Sol C Siegel. He was probably the most senior producer working at 20th Century-Fox and certainly the most respected. He was known in Hollywood as 'the Elder Statesman', although he was still in his early fifties. His manner was grave and dignified, but alongside it was a great sense of humour. He certainly was one of nature's real gentlemen. He showed me many kindnesses. I think he understood the behind-the-scenes problems I was coping with. He was a man of great wisdom and long experience. He took a considerable interest in me and I felt that he saw some possibility that my talent might develop usefully.

He handed me the script of a remake of *Berkeley Square*. This was to star Tyrone Power and a girl yet to be found. This all sounded fine, except that the picture was to be made in England, at Denham. Tyrone Power was spending two or three years in exile from the US for tax reasons and had to make one more film before he returned home, and this was going to be the one.

Some time before this, somebody's agent had discovered a tax law which had been enacted by Congress back in the 1920s. The purpose of it was to boost recruitment of engineers needed to work in the oil fields in the Middle East. The oil companies would provide maintenance for them and their families and, if they stayed there for five years, their salaries would be paid in America with no tax deducted. That is one of the reasons why so many stars and producers came over to Europe in the fifties and sixties. The other reason was blocked currency.

Was this picture being used incidentally as a convenient ruse to return me to England? I had come to Hollywood to make films there, not back in the UK, but I was now in a fix. There was no question of turning the picture down and putting myself on lay-off. After a lot of thought, in the end I reckoned that the only thing I could do was to make the best success I could of *Berkeley Square*. With my usual cock-eyed optimism I concentrated on the more attractive aspects of the proposition: costume, romance, 1784, Technicolor – all fresh experience for me.

Sol took me to lunch at his club. This was the famous Hillcrest Country Club and it was magnificent. There was a splendid golf course and tennis courts and everything the members could desire. The restaurant was luxurious and we sat at the bachelors' table, a very large round table for men only. The others at the table were: Groucho Marx, George Burns, Danny Kaye, Jack Benny – to name but a few. It was the most hilarious lunch I've ever had. They all enjoyed themselves no end, pulling the leg of this young limey. The food was good, too. Looking back, I'm beginning to wonder if Sol had set this up.

At last there came a meeting with Zanuck. Sol was also there and he and DFZ did most of the talking. There wasn't much to say anyway. It was finally decided that I should return to England to make the picture. Apart from that, I have almost no recollection of the meeting. Seven weeks after landing in New York we were back in London.

A footnote: This book started as a collection of notes made at the time I was searching for my family history. It is fitting therefore to record here the birthday earlier in this year 1950 of my Grandmother Ward. She was the last of her generation in my family. She was 87 in March and, three months later, she died. Whenever she had been out of the house, if anyone ventured to ask, 'Hallo Ma. Where've you been?' she always gave the same reply, 'There and back to see how far it is'. It seems to be an appropriate motto for this strange interlude.

The return crossing was made aboard Ile de France. The only difference between this voyage and the previous one was that in Mauretania they offered to show us the engine room. In the French ship they showed us the kitchens.

At the end of November, the Clean Air Act being six years in the future, we arrived back in the Smoke. The foggy atmosphere – 'a London particular' – pleased the Americans no end. Lots of jolly jokes, all justified. All was just as it should be, according to all the old Hollywood movies about London. In accordance with the income tax rules I no longer had anywhere to live in England, now being domiciled in USA. So now I was on location in my own home town, living in hotels and rent-

Left: John Mills
and Joan
Greenwood
(*The October
Man*, Two
Cities)

Below: Ursula
Jeans and crew
(*The Weaker
Sex*, Two
Cities)

Right: William Fairchild and Richard Attenborough (*Morning Departure,* Rank)

Below: Tyrone Power (*The House on the Square,* 20th Century-Fox)

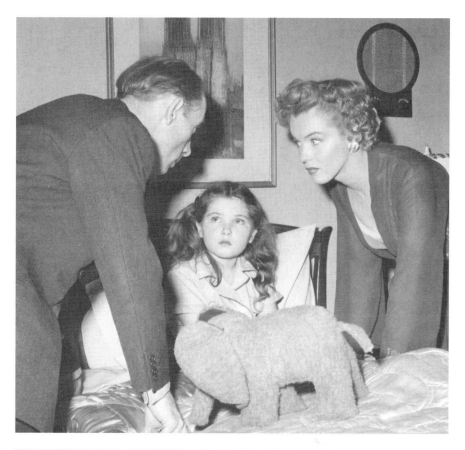

Above: Marilyn Monroe (*Don't Bother to Knock,* 20th Century-Fox)

Left: Richard Widmark and Anne Bancroft (*Don't Bother to Knock,* 20th Century-Fox)

Right: Two-camera set-up for 3D filming (*Inferno*)

Above: William Lundigan (*Inferno*, 20th Century-Fox)

Right: Robert Ryan (*Inferno*, 20th Century-Fox)

Above:
Anthony Steele,
Julian Wintle
and Diane
Cilento
(*Passage Home*,
Rank)

Left: How to fix
a catapult, with
Jacqueline Ryan
(*Jacqueline*,
Rank)

Above: Donald Sinden, Geoffrey Unsworth and Jack Atchelor (*Tiger in the Smoke*, Rank)

Right: Sharing a birthday toast with Hardy Kruger (*The One That Got Away*, Rank)

Right: Dirk Bogarde (*The Singer Not the Song,* Rank)

Below: Sylvia Syms and Johnny Sekka (*Flame in the Streets,* Rank)

Bottom: Michael Craze, Nyree Dawn Porter and Michael Crawford (*Two Left Feet,* RBP/British Lion)

ed flats. A ridiculous situation and, surprisingly, not a very comfortable one, which lasted for eight months.

The premiere of *Highly Dangerous* was not the happiest of moments. The reviews were not very good. It was depressing, but I was preoccupied with preparation for *Berkeley Square* at Denham, which was now well under way. The script was by Ranald McDougall and was based on the original 1933 film starring Leslie Howard and Heather Angel which had a screenplay by Sonia Levien and John L Balderston, which was based on the play by John L Balderston and JC Squire, which was based on a short story by Henry James called 'A Sense of the Past'. I hope I make myself clear.

McDougall provided a present-day sequence at the beginning of the film which was set in a bang-up-to-date nuclear research laboratory, where our hero is a scientist. He is American with English ancestors and goes to the house in Berkeley Square in which they lived in the eighteenth century. Standing on the doorstep in torrential rain he reaches for the doorknocker. Suddenly with a blinding flash of lightning and deafening thunder he finds himself back in the year 1784. There were a number of pseudo-historical scenes, taken from the original play, in which the hero meets Dr Johnson, the Duchess of Devonshire etc. The hero, being a scientist, tries to explain electric light, chloroform, vaccination and so on to the eighteenth-century people, hoping to bring forward the benefits of scientific discovery by a couple of hundred years. A somewhat fanciful notion. I admit I found it difficult to portray all this with conviction.

Tyrone Power was a nice man. Impeccable manners and a good actor of great experience. He had been a movie star for ten years or more and he enjoyed that, but his dearest ambition, which he never quite realised, was to succeed in the theatre, as his grandfather had. Totally professional and a dream to work with. In all the difficulties which soon appeared he was a tower of strength and overwhelmingly generous in his support of me.

The search was now on for the leading lady. Everybody has his story of how he turned down an actress who later turned out to be a star. Jack Dunfee asked me to see a new girl named Audrey Hepburn. I don't remember the interview but I do remember that I turned her down. Why on earth did I not at least test her? As will be seen, I'd have had to fight for her, but by golly it would have been worth it. A test might well have shown that she was ideal for the part. As was revealed later, she had exactly the right ethereal quality for it.

All sorts of names were being canvassed but Zanuck was pressing more and more for Constance Smith. Prior to *Berkeley Square* she had a tiny part as a housemaid in a 20th Century-Fox picture called *The Mudlark*. It was about Queen Victoria, played by Irene Dunne, directed by Jean Negulesco, and filmed in England. She had almost nothing to say but she was photographed beautifully and Zanuck was determined that she should now play the leading part opposite Tyrone Power. Some time previously a Hungarian film called *Extase,* starring Hedy Lamarr, was shown in Ireland and to promote it a competition was mounted. The idea was to find the girl who most resembled Hedy Lamarr. One of the judges was John Boulting. The prize was a trip to London and a screen test. Quite rightly, Constance Smith won it. She did look like Hedy Lamarr. She was beautiful, with perfect Irish looks: blue-black hair, brilliant blue eyes, a flawless complexion and a good figure to go with it all. But she had no experience of acting at all.

On the strength of her appearance in *The Mudlark* she was given a stock contract by Zanuck and taken to Hollywood. He now posted her over to us. Both Tyrone and I, and to a certain extent Sol, had expressed the obvious doubts about putting a girl whose experience was almost nil into a star part. No matter how impressive any of the other actors were, including Tyrone himself, the acceptance of this story by an audience depended on the actress who played that part. Despite the reality of her family around her, her mother, sister and brother, she had to convey an almost ghost-like, ethereal presence. It was not an easy one for someone of experience, let alone a newcomer.

We were doing costume tests and we arranged an elaborate test for Connie, complete with Tyrone and several of the other actors. It turned out poorly. Tyrone was worried and so was I. The test was sent to Zanuck, who told us to go ahead and shoot the picture with Connie.

Everything went well, to begin with. My only problem was Georges Perinal, the lighting cameraman, who was surly and unhelpful. He had photographed almost all Korda's great films and fully merited a high reputation. Now he was bored and took no pains to disguise the fact. *Ennui* is the French word and he was its exemplar, *par excellence*. We were shooting in Technicolor, with the old three-strip process. The camera was as big as an old-fashioned public telephone box. It was all agonisingly slow. When we got to Connie's scenes our progress slowed almost to a halt.

None of this was her fault. It was unfair and a grave mistake to put such demands on her and it did her no favours at all. Believe me, I know about this: I had another experience of this kind a few years later. With all the patience and encouragement in the world, after six weeks of shooting, we were getting nowhere. No doubt she felt that she was surrounded by implacable enemies. At one point she told me that the next time she saw Zanuck she'd have me fired off the picture. The way I felt about it, I wouldn't have cared. I was working hard to make her look as good as I could. It was not in anybody's interest to sabotage her performance: all our names would be on the credits for better or worse. If it was a success she would get her share of the applause.

Eventually everybody had to accept defeat. Ann Blyth arrived from Hollywood to take the part and we started shooting again, re-taking Connie's scenes.

At least one of the crew retained his sense of humour throughout. This was Bluey Hill, the first assistant. A redoubtable Australian with a blazing personality, he was a popular figure and there are many anecdotes about him. We had a small scene with a two-line bit in it for a buxom girl. When she arrived on the set I saw she was extremely nervous, almost shaking with fright; also, there seemed to be something different about her appearance as I had seen her at the casting session. I asked Bluey about this. 'Yeah, she does look different. She got herself in such a state this morning she rushed out of the house and left her tits at home'. The other tale I like is about a later picture, starring Yul Brynner. Bluey called quiet on the set, ready for a take and the unit settled down, but there was still the sound of some one whistling behind the set. Bluey shouted again. It still went on. Bluey threatened the culprit: when he caught him, he'd be outside the studio gate in no time. Still it continued. Bluey was just assembling a further blast when Yul Brynner walked on to the set, whistling merrily. Bluey paused for barely a second. Then he turned to the crew with a beaming smile and said, 'What a pretty tune!'

At last we finished shooting and assembled a final cut. This I took to Hollywood to show to Zanuck. The editor, Alan Osbiston, who had edited *Morning Departure*, came with me. We flew in the greatest luxury, in an aircraft which offered drinks at the bar before going upstairs to a five-course dinner. One then retired for the night, putting on pyjamas and crawling into an ample sized bunk bed. One was awakened in the morning with a complete breakfast in bed. What! No morning paper? The stewardess smiled politely and said, 'Please sir, don't suggest it. We have enough to do!'

The film was pretty and well mounted but beside being a period piece it was in another sense dated. It was grudgingly accepted by Zanuck and given two titles: *I'll Never Forget You* for America and *The House On The Square* for UK. It was agreed that I should be given another assignment soon, this time in Hollywood.

Now I had to fly back to England to finish the editing and dub in the music and effects. The return journey was not uneventful. The problem was trivial but may be worth telling in case it happens to someone else. American bureaucracy can be just as fraught with hidden traps as in any other country. All aliens with work permits must clear their income tax position whenever they leave the USA. This means a long journey downtown into the smog to City Hall and the offices of the Internal Revenue. There you get a chit which must be shown at passport control at the airport. I was confident that my withholding tax would amply cover my annual dues. Not so.

I had first entered the United States accompanied by my family. I then returned to England, also with my family. Now I had come back into the US alone. Therefore, according to the official into whose hands I fell, my tax for the whole year must be revised, assessing me as a bachelor, even though I had stayed only a couple of weeks and would return in five or six weeks. A large sum of money must be paid before I could be allowed out of the country.

I tried to contact George Chasin and failed. Nobody at the studio could help. It seemed everybody was away for the weekend or gone fishing. Eventually it was Tyrone who came to the rescue. He sent his business manager to sort me out. It was all settled in about half an hour, but before he went into action he asked me to sign a management contract with him. He was an excellent business manager, especially for people with complicated contracts, investments and large incomes, but not necessary for someone like me. For the rest of my time in Hollywood I paid him five per cent of my salary. The withholding tax at that time was 28 per cent. Other mandatory payments were one per cent Motion Picture Relief Fund, one per cent Directors Guild, ten per cent MCA. Altogether 45 per cent of one's income. So however grand a Hollywood contract appears to be you may reckon on about 50 per cent of it for yourself. The best advice for anyone negotiating a Hollywood contract is, whatever they offer, tell them to double it or leave it alone.

Also on the subject of contracts, I had, at the time of *The October Man*, signed a standard management contract with Jack Dunfee's firm, O'Brien, Linnit and Dunfee. This was one of the old-style documents which bound the artist to the agent for life. There was no way of breaking it, ever. Even if one changed one's work from film directing to professional boxing, it still held good. Of course I signed it, but I soon began to realise the implications of it and it engendered in me a considerable resentment. Soon after I arrived in Hollywood George Chasin asked me to sign a new contract with MCA America, which I was only too pleased to do; it abrogated the London contract. As will be seen, some years later this brought about a splendid bust-up with Jack Dunfee.

Back at Denham we settled down with Muir Mathieson, who would supervise and conduct the music, which was to be composed by William Alwyn and played by the London Symphony Orchestra. I had met this team before on *The October Man* and once or twice during the Army period. Muir was well established before the War as the most eminent producer of music for films, working mostly for Korda. He was noted for persuading eminent classical composers to write for films. He had made this territory his own and rightly so, because he was good at it. He was determined and forthright. When he came to view the cutting-copy with you there was slight air of 'let's see what our music can do to save this picture from total disaster.' This was merely his belief that the music was one of the most important elements in the enterprise, if not the most important. As the dubbing editors view it, the finished film is an illustrated soundtrack. Above all it should not be left in the hands of cloth-eared directors who couldn't distinguish 'God Save The King' from 'Rule Britannia'. I'm sure he had had some nasty experiences. We worked together very well on several pictures. He was a contributor.

William Alwyn was one of the people I am proud to have worked with. Quiet, sensitive and wonderfully responsive to the style of the film and the varying moods of the scenes within it. And in complete command of the means of expressing them. Mad on cricket. A charming man and a gent. Once during the recording session both he and Muir wanted to go into the sound booth to listen to a section of the score. This meant there was nobody to conduct the orchestra. Muir offered his baton to me and said, 'Here – you take them through it'. What a thrill! To command those magnificent players, greater even than driving a steam train or taking my car round Brooklands. I had the chance to allow it to be known to generations yet to come, 'I once conducted the London Symphony Orchestra.' Well, once. A chance like this comes but once – and I refused it.

The return journey to New York was made in the Queen Mary and we were met once again by David Golding, who once again laid the town at our feet. The two days before the Super Chief left for Los Angeles were a riot of lunch at Lindy's, lunch at Sardi's, dinner at The Stork and lunch at 21, which covered the territory reasonably well, I thought. We fitted in the premiere of *Bathsheba*, a Fox biblical offering which has not stayed in my memory, probably because David – Golding that is, not King David – introduced us to Gary Merrill, who introduced us to his wife, Bette Davis. We were all headed for Los Angeles, Gary by air, but everybody else was booked on the Super Chief.

This train was the only one which took you right through to Los Angeles. The others all tipped you out at Chicago, as on the previous occasion, when half the luggage was left behind. You then had to make your way across town to another railway station and another train out west. This was a relic of the portage system between two rivers, the Chicago river and the headwaters of the Kankakee, which brought Chicago into existence. This monopoly was still being jealously guarded by the interested parties. However there was now one concession: the Super Chief had a through carriage which they shunted across Chicago, so everybody could remain on board. It was splendidly appointed and very comfortable but for two families to be thrown together in a train for four days will produce either a life-long friendship or mortal enmity. We all came out smiling and Miss Davis proved to be one of the best friends I ever had.

The first proof of this was manifested after only a few days. While I was back in England I continued to pay the rent for the house I had leased in Los Angeles and wrote to the owner renewing the lease for a further six months. When I was about to leave England I got a letter announcing that I couldn't come back to the house because it was already occupied by another party. As soon as I left, the owner had re-let the place, still taking my rent, reckoning that I would never come back. I had no option but to go to a small hotel at first, while looking for another house.

When Bette heard about this she was disgusted, but said no more at the time. The Merrills had rented a house on the beach at Malibu and she invited us to lunch the day after we arrived in Los Angeles. She had already found a suitable house for me, three doors away from her own. It was a snip and saved me infinite trouble and expense. Bette was appalled that anyone could treat a stranger in this way, especially if he was English: Bette was a dedicated Anglophile.

Bette Davis was the example of the total professional. Never mind how she drove other people; she never drove anybody harder than she drove herself. She didn't suffer fools gladly. She was tough. But she was the supreme film actress of her generation. A great star, she had limitless courage and would tackle anything, taking enormous risks, sometimes disastrously. As will appear later, she was very nice to me and I don't believe I am unique in this respect.

DON'T BOTHER TO KNOCK

– JUST SAY ZANUCK SENT YOU

I started writing this book in the 1960s, when I began to investigate my family history, largely to satisfy my curiosity and to amuse any descendants I might have. During the seventies my younger colleagues in the studios began asking me questions about pre-war film production and I also began to collect notes about that. This required some research because my complete set of the 38 scripts I had worked on during that period was lost during the war. Anyway, spasmodically, I have been adding sections to this book ever since. The reason for this preamble is that until quite recently, I had one firm intention, which was that however far this book grew, I was definitely not going to join the Marilyn Monroe Industry. We worked together for only a couple of months under extreme difficulty, but I adored her and I have no wish to find myself in any way associated with the people who have created such an edifice of fantasy around her.

More and more of the so-called biographers have drifted farther and farther away from the original sources of information and relied more and more on their imaginations to cook up a book. It should be remembered that most of the original sources are tainted anyway, because Marilyn's most unfortunate characteristic, which did her more harm than anything else, was her uncanny ability to attract to herself the sort of people who only wanted to exploit her. They may have been useful to her in bolstering her ego, but as far as I can see, with one or two shining exceptions, few of them ever contributed anything of value to her. Indeed her mind was cluttered with high-falutin' gobbledegook which, considering that she had started with enough handicaps anyway, only made her life more difficult.

So here I am, adding to the Marilyn Monroe Industry after all. At least I was an eyewitness, for a short time, during one of the most important periods in her career.

Don't Bother to Knock was based on a novel by Charlotte Armstrong called *Mischief* and could be described as the one about the baby-sitter who just happens to be a psychopath. Almost any story can be reduced to crude terms according to the degree of cynicism brought to it. A slightly longer version goes like this:

Jed is an airline pilot who has a girlfriend called Lyn. She works as a dance band singer in a second-rate New York hotel. Their affair has reached the stage where she wants marriage and he is being evasive. She accuses him of being thoroughly selfish and ruthless. The argument develops into a row and Jed stumps off to his room upstairs in the hotel.

Mr and Mrs Jones are in town for a company dinner. They want a baby-sitter to look after their nine-year-old daughter and Eddie the elevator operator has obligingly offered to provide one. The sitter is his niece, Nell. She is in her early twenties, very plain and ordinary-looking and dressed in an ill-fitting cotton frock.

The parents go downstairs to the dinner and the child goes to sleep in a small bedroom. Once she is alone, Nell starts to play with Mrs Jones' make-up and the dresses in the wardrobe.

Jed in his room glances idly out of the window. He can see into the Jones' suite. He catches a glimpse of Nell, now made up and in a borrowed negligee.

Jed comes to visit and some of the things Nell says make Jed uneasy. He notices that her wrists are badly scarred. It comes out that Jed is an airline pilot, who flew bombers during the war and has had a crash in the sea. Nell firmly identifies him as her lost lover Philip.

The child wakes and interrupts them. Jed leaves Nell to put the girl back to bed. Nell is increasingly disturbed and is tempted to push the child out of the window. Finally she tries to slash her wrists again.

The main point of the story emerges as – for the first time in his life – Jed's sympathy has been aroused by the plight of another human being and he does what he can to help Nell, or at any rate to see she gets the expert help she needs. And so his attitude to Lyn is altered too.

The story is certainly not one of world-shattering importance. The script was written by one of Hollywood's most distinguished writers, Daniel Taradash. The minor characters are rather two-dimensional but the supporting cast was excellent and made a huge contribution. Taradash's construction was beautifully crafted and his dialogue short, sharp and effective. I was surprised to find that Taradash is quoted as being disappointed in the film, aiming most of the blame in my direction. *Les absents ont toujours tort.*

When the news came from Zanuck that the part of Nell was to be played by Marilyn Monroe, the executive producer Julian Blaustein was apologetic; the producer, William Bloom was horrified. I knew far less about Miss Monroe than the others but from my memory of *The Asphalt Jungle* and *All About Eve* this seemed to me to be a grotesque piece of casting. But Zanuck had spoken.

Both Julian and William had worked previously at Columbia, William in the story department; both were delighted to be free of the fell influence of Harry Cohn. Julian had made a big hit with *Broken Arrow*, which was generally agreed to have broken new ground for the Western. Zanuck had recently put him in charge of half the product at Fox. At that time the studio was turning out 25 films a year and it was decided that in future Zanuck would be responsible for half the product, the top half, and Julian would take care of the other half. Julian and Bill were highly literate, movie professionals. We got on well and they were a considerable support to me all through the rest of my time at Fox.

Thinking about this episode so many years after the event – it was December 1951 – has brought up one or two questions which I might have asked at the time. Whose idea was it to make this subject? – and with Marilyn? Was it put up by Marilyn herself? Who had the idea to have me as director? Or were all the other directors in hiding? One can sum up the answers to these questions as follows: Joseph Schenk, who was the boss of 20th Century-Fox and had formed the company in the first place, decided that the picture should be set up as a present for his friend Marilyn. Zanuck, who thought it a waste of time, decided to make it as cheaply as possible.

The general opinion was that Miss Monroe had been around a long time and was a no-hoper. She'd never be anything more than a blonde broad with big boobs. From her own statements, made much later, it appears that Mr Schenk had good reason to indulge her. If I seem to be putting these suggestions with more delicacy than is customary these days, it is because I refuse to write explicitly about matters of which I have no personal knowledge.

Zanuck never liked her. He thought she was a nuisance, especially over a recent fuss about a notorious nude calendar photograph. She had been under contract to Fox once before, subsequently under contract to MGM and now under contract to Fox again. She had worked at RKO and Columbia as well; altogether she'd appeared in small parts in 14 films before this one, so she wasn't without experience of the studios and how they worked.

As the character in the story is described above, it was simply unbelievable that a girl with the appearance of Marilyn Monroe would ever find herself in such a position. I was unaware at that time that Marilyn's own background had been similar to Nell's – if anything, worse. That was the sole connection between the actress and the character. Otherwise her appearance and personality were totally at variance with Nell. It was a part for Jane Wyman, for instance.

As soon as he got a chance to read it, Richard Widmark wanted to play Jed. This was good news. He is a good actor apart from being a star. I had met him with Tyrone Power and I was certain he was right for it. Dick had his own reasons for wanting to do it. He had made a great reputation as a heavy, famous for his maniacal laugh ever since he had – laughingly – pushed an old woman in a wheelchair down a flight of stairs. He thought quite rightly that Jed would help to foster a new image for him. Whatever personal interest he may have had, he wouldn't have wanted to be in a rotten movie just for the sake of playing a sympathetic character.

However, the studio extracted a quid pro quo from Dick. They wanted him to play in a magazine picture compiled from three or four short stories called *O Henry's Full House* and the part was once again a heavy with a maniacal laugh, which he didn't want to do at all. But if he wanted to play in *Don't Bother to Knock*, surely he'd agree to do his number in *Full House*...? Marilyn was also drafted into it.

For the part of Lyn the casting department suggested a new girl called Ann Marno. She had been tested for a projected film of a novel called *The Girl on the Via Flaminia* which was never made, but the test was so good that the studio put her under stock contract. I saw the test and I agreed. She may have been inexperienced but she turned out to be first-class. Nearly all her scenes were with Dick Widmark, who was a great help; another bonus for her was that she had no scenes with Marilyn, except at the end of the film and that was a reaction, which she did superbly, making a great contribution to Marilyn's performance.

There were no exterior locations in the script so the whole film was shot in the studios. The sets were all interiors of the hotel and could be built as two complexes: one, the ground floor entrance with a small bar and restaurant; two, the sixth floor with the Jones' suite, Jed's bedroom and corridors. Both were built on one large stage at the old Fox studios on Western Avenue in Hollywood and they were dressed and ready to go one week before shooting commenced, so we were able to rehearse in them with most of the cast.

Several more people came into my life at this point. One of the best cameramen I ever worked with – and I've had several – appeared: Lucien Ballard. Quirky, quite the eccentric and proud as a peacock, he claimed to be a Cherokee Indian from Okhlahoma. He was tall, slim, good-looking, fit as a flea and always elegantly dressed. At one time married to Merle Oberon. He was a great help to me and we got on so well he photographed the other two pictures I made in Hollywood. He was a great joker and he was the only one who could jolly Marilyn along – occasionally.

My first assistant was Eli Dunn, who had come to Hollywood many years before this. He was William Fox's secretary and he knew all about the old Western Avenue studio. I remarked on the great size of the theatre where we saw rushes. Apparently it was built in the late twenties especially for a new widescreen process, which was to be known as Grandeur Vision. Around the same time the talkies came in with a headlong rush so the new process was dropped on the ground that 'we've given 'em sound, so widescreen can be saved for another day'. Eli told me that there was another unit working in the next studio and the director was John Ford. At once I was eager to meet the great man but Eli strongly advised against it and put me off completely. I won't repeat the words he used but Mr Ford was clearly not popular. Eli claimed that technicians would pay money NOT to be on a film with him. That was a surprise. Eli was too polite to say so, but I found out later that Ford was a besotted Irish-American who loathed the British.

I think the first time I met Marilyn was when we were discussing costuming with the designer, William Travilla, who became devoted to her and dressed her in almost all her films. At any rate I do remember that she had two fat books under her arm, by Stanislavsky. We made her look as plain as possible at the beginning of the story, with little make-up and wearing an ill-fitting cotton dress – all of which made her look if anything more attractive. Then when she appeared in the later scenes in full make-up and a dark, coffee-coloured negligée she looked like the dazzling star she was destined to be.

Also attached to the picture with some kind of watching brief was one J Watson Webb Jnr. A scion of the East Coast aristocracy, he had started at Fox as a messenger in the mailroom and by this time was one of the leading editors in the cutting rooms. I think he was supposed to intervene if I made any dreadful mistakes in the set-ups so that they wouldn't cut together, or some such. It took him about ten minutes to decide that this was highly unlikely so he sat back and watched the struggles on the set with profound disapproval. He was genial – his favourite word – and a perfect gent. As soon as he realised I had only one car he appointed himself as my chauffeur, picking me up in the morning and delivering me back home in the evening, so that my family had transport available during the day.

The other attachée was Natasha Lytess, who in fact attached herself. She had firmly established herself as Marilyn's drama coach while Marilyn was working at Columbia and Zanuck had been persuaded to put her under contract to 20th, with some limited responsibility for the other contract players. It was put about that she was Russian, but I believe she came from Germany, having worked with Max Reinhardt and the Berliner Ensemble. She had a deep voice and from time to time she would grasp her lower abdomen in both hands and growl, 'It comes from here!' Her most precious possession was her mesmeric influence over Marilyn, which she was determined to defend at all cost.

It so happens that, ever since I started directing, I developed strong views about dialogue directors, drama coaches, and so on. It was a job that was invented at the beginning of talking pictures, when so many silent stars didn't know how to speak lines, generally because they had never acted on the stage. Certainly it is no concern of mine if an actor goes to classes between pictures, or wishes to talk over a script with his teacher, or confidant, agent or whoever, before the picture starts shooting. He should also consult the director. Once shooting starts he should talk to nobody other than the director. No actor can listen to two voices. Too often I have had young actresses under the influence of some third party, generally a production assistant with ambitions to be a great director. Well, he isn't a great director yet and above all, he isn't directing this picture. I am.

Schools of acting are a fine thing, a very necessary thing; there are several good ones in this country and they do good work. However, as soon as the student graduates he should realise that his learning period is over. He now has to start at the bottom and spend the rest of his life accumulating experience. There is nothing else he can do. The same idea applies to directors and certainly to writers. They too can learn only by experience.

Rehearsals started on 7 December 1951 and it seems that Marilyn made a request to Zanuck to have Natasha Lytess with her on the set during the shooting. Zanuck's reply, dated 10 December, is quoted in full in the book *Memo from Darryl F Zanuck*:

Dear Marilyn,

Your request to have a special dialogue director work with you on the set is a completely impractical and impossible request. The reason we engage a director and entrust him to direct a picture is because we feel he has demonstrated his ability to function in that capacity. Whether the final performance comes out right or wrong there cannot be more than one responsible individual and that individual is the director. You must rely on his individual interpretation of the role. You cannot be coached on the sidelines or the result will be a disaster for you.

In Asphalt Jungle *you had a comparatively simple part, in which you were very effective, but it did not particularly call for any acting as compared to the role you are going to play at the present time. It is more than ever important that you therefore place yourself completely in the hands of the director – or ask to be relieved from the role.*

Either Mr Baker is capable of directing you as well as the rest of the picture or he is not capable of directing anything, but since he is the director we must place our responsibility in him.

I am sure you realise how ludicrous it would be if every actor or actress felt that they needed special coaching from the sidelines. The result would be bedlam, and whatever creative ideas the director might possess would be lost or totally diffused.

I think you are capable of playing this role without the help of anyone but the director and yourself. You have built up a Svengali and if you are going to progress with your career and become as important talent-wise as you have publicity-wise then you must destroy this Svengali before it destroys you. When I cast you for the role I cast you as an individual.

Best always,
Darryl Zanuck

Wise words. I knew nothing of this until the book was published in the USA in 1993 and I am indebted to Roy Fowler who told me about it. There is some compensation in living to an advanced age after all.

Despite being turned down by the boss, Miss Lytess seated herself comfortably at the side of the set. The rehearsals went well but as soon as we started shooting a lot of problems appeared. Marilyn was quite incapable of punctuality. It took her an extraordinary effort of will to get on to the set at all and always late. I believed it was simply stage fright and I was sympathetic. What a charitable chap I was! Another factor that I didn't find out until many years later was that Marilyn was up every night until three and four in the morning, chewing over every word and move in the next day's work with Lytess. The tardiness didn't bother me all that much, but in the Hollywood of those days it was a dreadful sin and the whole production department was hostile, which didn't help to develop the atmosphere of calm professionalism which we prefer.

It didn't please the other actors, either. They had been ready to go, word perfect, since 9.00 am and it's now 11.30 and no Marilyn. They also had great difficulty in playing scenes with her. Despite all the detailed work that went into the rehearsals, they could never be absolutely sure when she'd give a cue, or accept one, or make a move; and when she did do roughly what they were expecting her to do, it might not be anything like the rehearsal or a previous take. Between takes there was a good deal of whispered advice from the lady sitting at the side of the set. In cases like this the other actors begin to worry about their own performances and begin to get angry. Among them there were highly respected professionals like Elisha Cook Jnr and Jim Backus. I had a great deal of work to do reassuring them.

Widmark was decidedly put out and said so.

It soon became clear to me that this movie would have to be put together piece-meal. I must stage the scenes so that I could isolate Marilyn's coverage as much as possible. There could be no such thing as a master scene and there is no case in the film of her performance in any one scene being delivered in one take. They all consist of single lines and reactions from several takes. This probably worried her, but there was no alternative. Also, I began to suspect that if she felt that something had gone wrong with the take, she had got hold of the trick of making a deliberate mistake in order to abort it. She may have been receiving signals from the side of the set. Sometimes I would print the take anyway because it had an earlier line in it which was good. This may have worried her all the more.

The basic problem was that Marilyn was burning to ACT. The difficulty comes in trying to explain that the one thing you don't do in front of a camera is act. You don't act the character – you simply have to be it. Dialogue directors and coaches encourage their clients to act and the result is always fatal to the performance. Perhaps I was ahead of my time. Even in the theatre, where acting was at one time the principal part of the effort and acting was what the public came to see, a new realism and sincerity burgeoned in the sixties.

This is not to say that the minimalism we have seen from Peter Sellers, or Dustin Hoffman, or even the great Sir Alec Guinness is to be pursued to the extinction of all expression, but they are all on the right track. In many cases this sort of actor has chosen to play a character who lacked expression anyway. The risk lies in such a performance becoming downright dull and boring. This is where the indefinable magic of a star comes into play, carrying the audience with him. This is what makes the star indispensable. Many directors dislike the star system and would like to do without it; for one thing, the billing usually gives away the plot. It is true that the writer, producer and director and all the other people involved in any production are responsible for 95 per cent of the creative effect of a film. The other five per cent is supplied by the actors, the cast as well as the stars. Unpalatable it may be to some people, but nevertheless it is true that it is this five per cent that puts the picture over to the audience.

Sadly, some of these beautiful people can be ungrateful and pay scant regard to the support they have received. In interviews with the stars, how often do you read any mention of the director, or the producer, or the writer, or anybody other than ME? Where do the story and the dialogue come from? How do the scenes come to be photographed and recorded? Does the music come from thin air? Costumes and make-up? Does the camera point itself in the right direction? Is the editing done by Edward Scissorhands? Who conjures up the backgrounds, the settings and locations? Who supervises all this and is finally responsible for the hundreds of decisions that must be made? It may be an unpalatable lump of gristle to swallow, but the answer is, the director.

Marilyn accepted what I told her about the content of each scene and its context.

She never argued with me. She followed the staging of the scenes happily enough, but she always referred back to Miss Lytess. This may have been some comfort to Marilyn, but it did nothing to improve her performance. The straw that finally broke this camel's back was when Marilyn delivered one line with a pronounced German accent.

Charlie Hall, a tough production manager of long experience, was by now worried about the schedule, which to him was sacrosanct. I didn't share his anxiety because I was confident of the end result. I was already convinced that Marilyn would be a great star. The only thing that bothered me was the continued influence of Miss Lytess. Charlie pointed out that I could bar the lady from the set. I wasn't aware of this power and I agreed straight away. Charlie said he would tell them, but I insisted I tell Marilyn myself.

So, on Christmas Eve I went to Marilyn's dressing-room. I told her the picture was going well, she was doing fine, but there was no need for her to have a coach; it was more of a hindrance than a help, and much more to the same effect and at considerable length. She was surprised and disappointed, but quietly accepted what I said. We agreed to start again on the new basis after the two days' holiday.

Some time later, Marilyn was quoted as saying, 'I was so confused back then, I'd let any guy, or girl, do what they wanted if I thought they were my friend. I let Natasha, but that was wrong. She wasn't like a guy. You know, just have a good time and that's that. She got really jealous about the men I saw, everything. She thought she was my husband. She was a great teacher, but that part of it ruined things for us. I got scared of her, had to get away.'

There seems to have been a continual craving for reassurance which I tried my damnedest to supply and occasionally with a modicum of success, possibly because I was a new person in her life and I wasn't prejudiced against her like so many people in Hollywood were. Neither was I involved with her emotionally, except in the professional sense. Still, there was always an underlying determination that every single detail of her appearance on the screen should be exclusive to Marilyn.

Certainly she had one over-riding ambition beside which nothing else mattered. That was, to be a great big international star. Time and again she would ask me, did I really believe she would be a star? I was able to answer quite sincerely, yes. I had no doubt whatsoever. I had some private reservation about whether the studio system would make the necessary accomodations, but I was absolutely sure that if they could, it would be worth the trouble. Sadly, they never did.

This was still the old Hollywood where any misbehaviour on the part of actors or actresses was dealt with severely. Several of the directors of her later successes were still pushing her around as if she was some no-account blonde. Even though the Hollywood attitudes changed later, it was too late to be any help to Marilyn. It is a pity. All that was needed was a little bit of patience. Not indulgence, but patience. She was, after all, in their own coarse terms, valuable. An extra week or so on the schedule meant nothing. I shall be told that this is me, being naïf – look what happened when the actors (and their agents) eventually took control: the result was chaos. Ah well. It may be worth remembering that the often quoted remark about 'putting the lunatics in charge of the asylum' is not a recent invention. It was originally made a long time ago, in the early twenties, when Douglas Fairbanks, Mary Pickford and Charles Chaplin took control of United Artists.

Dick Richards, who was film correspondent and critic of the (London) *Daily Mirror*, was in Hollywood while I was shooting *Don't Bother to Knock*. We knew each other well and he came to visit me on the set. I felt by introducing him to Marilyn I was putting him on to a piece of hot news. He could be the first to announce the arrival of a great new international star. He didn't believe me. When he got back to London he wrote not a word about it, but later he dined out on the story for a long time.

My intention in this book is merely to offer a few comments on each of the films I have directed, as each one might prompt some reflection or other on the general run of a film director's work. But I have described this tale at some length because *Don't Bother to Knock* has attracted so much comment ever since it started Marilyn Monroe on her magnificent career. Most of this comment has come from people who never met Marilyn; some of it is so boss-eyed that one wonders if they have ever seen this film. Some of it has been personally insulting to me, from people who have never met me.

As I said before: 'The absent are always in the wrong'. Some of these writers assume that I must be dead, or since I have not made a picture in Hollywood since I left in 1953, I may as well be dead. So they feel free to say what they like, anything goes. I have read only three or four of the flood of books that have been published about Marilyn, but there are two I know of which require mention here.

The Marilyn Scandal by Sandra Shevey quotes extensively from a long interview I gave to the author in London in the 1980s. Apart from one or two unimportant inaccuracies it is correct and it is substantially the same as I have written above. However the main burden of the book is that Marilyn was murdered because she was about to reveal a long affair with Robert Kennedy, Attorney-General and brother of JFK. The source of all these allegations is one Robert Slatzer.

The other book, *Marilyn Monroe The Biography* by Donald Spoto, is most scrupulously and exhaustively researched and carries great conviction. Spoto utterly refutes Mr Slatzer's allegations and says that his claims of intimate friendship with Marilyn are entirely bogus. Slatzer even claimed that he and Marilyn were at one time married. Spoto accepts that Marilyn and JFK spent the night together on one occasion only and he offers convincing proof that there could not have been an affair with Robert Kennedy. Nor was Marilyn murdered, by the mob, the CIA or the FBI. His account of the last weeks of her life is tragically moving, when she was dominated by psychiatrists and pills. Undoubtedly the reader must accept Spoto's book as authoritative. Despite his hagiographic attitude to Marilyn, it is well-written, fully documented and readable, if repetitious.

However, the author has little good to say about my picture, although he does admit that it showed that Marilyn could succeed in a leading part in a serious film, despite many drawbacks. His description of me is ill-informed and quite funny. It is amusing that he has scarcely a good word to say about any director of any Marilyn Monroe film. Incidentally, Mr Spoto is, or was, a monk who has published seventeen books, mostly about film people. His latest book is a life of Jesus Christ.

The final cut of the film was received by Zanuck with little interest, except to give it its stupid title. However, he made one good decision: the girl who played the part of Lyn, Ann Marno, should henceforth be known as Anne Bancroft. She was good news. And she never looked back. So the picture made two stars; it did Richard Widmark no harm either. As soon as it was released Marilyn was established with the public and films would be mounted for her. Even Zanuck had to take her seriously. She was now launched on what might turn out to be a great career – and so it did. Natasha Lytess jumped smartly back into her Svengali act with Marilyn. I went off to have a much-needed rest, but two weeks later I was back on the lot, to do another picture with Julian Blaustein.

NIGHT WITHOUT SLEEP

– AND A SLEEPLESS NIGHT

This was to be *Night Without Sleep*, a novel by Elick Moll, who wrote the screenplay with Frank Partos. The producer was Robert Bassler and the leads were played by Gary Merrill, Linda Darnell and Hildegarde Knef, whose name was later spelled Neff. It was shot in five weeks and I suspect it was made only to tidy up some outstanding contractual commitments, so that they could be written off. It was a slight story, about an alcoholic who wakes up with an almighty hangover. He has no memory at all of the previous 24 hours. He retraces his steps and begins to think he may have murdered somebody, perhaps his wife, or his mistress, or perhaps a new, true love that he met last night. One by one they are cancelled out so when he finally returns home he finds a body in the bathroom. After all, he has murdered his wife.

It was well constructed but too thin and overweighted with psychiatric jargon. In fact, the story was told entirely in dialogue, with six and seven page scenes, in one case with only two characters sitting at a restaurant table; no action at all. I had one surprise during the shoot. This was a scene in a nightclub, when the leader of the band strolls over to greet our hero; they are friends. My assistant, Gerd Oswald, told me that my picture would never be shown in the Southern States because of this brief exchange. The band leader was black and he was Benny Carter, one of the best saxophone players of all time. I couldn't believe it; anyway we shot the scene and it was in the film. Whether it was cut in the Deep South I know not. Maybe Gerd was exaggerating.

We all did our best with it. Gary was great to work with and a good actor, Linda was charming but had little to do. The one I really fell for was Hildegarde. Before we started shooting I suggested we have lunch together in the studio commissary, to talk over the script. We studied the menu first. 'What are you going to have?' she asked. 'Steak'. 'Good', said Hildegarde, as she looked around the canteen. 'All these people, living on cottage cheese and salad. Rabbits' food'. She had a very small part but she was very effective and played it beautifully. She was definitely the bonus in that particular package.

One week after shooting we viewed the rough cut with Julian Blaustein. As Julian and I walked across the lot he casually mentioned a picture he would like me to do next. It was a book called *White Witch Doctor*.

It was disguised as a novel by one Louise A Stinetorf, but in fact it was an autobiography of her own experiences. Born and raised on a small farm in Indiana, she was a spinster of nearly 40 when she applied to go to Africa as a missionary. The mission refused to accept her, saying she was too old to start such work but she was determined to go, so she took a three-year course and qualified as a registered nurse. At last she was accepted – as a medical missionary. She was 43 when she arrived in Léopoldville and she stayed in the Congo for 25 years, all of it in the remotest territories known as 'up country'. She returned home in the late forties, so the period is roughly 1920 to 1945. She started with nothing and she left behind a compound of over 30 buildings, including a hospital, a dispensary and two operating theatres, with a native staff of over 60 men and women in training as nurses and midwives. Also dozens of village schools, spread over hundreds of miles.

The book has many very moving episodes and some hilariously funny ones. A perfect part for Margaret Rutherford, you might say, or an American equivalent. There should be one. After all, Marie Dressler was no chicken when she was a star. The studio said, Susan Hayward. Well, I suppose she could play it. Not quite the character in the book, though. And this white hunter, this uncouth brute who turns out to be a hero...? Not in the book at all. Mm.

The scheme was to go to the Belgian Congo, later Zaire, now the Congo again, to shoot backgrounds, long-shots with doubles, etc. I would leave in two weeks time and a second unit would join me in another couple of weeks. The producer was Otto Lang and he had already looked over the possible locations in the Congo. He would show me round before the unit arrived. There were magnificent sites, waterfalls, rapids, riverboats, jungle and in particular a splendid village where the main action was centred. This village was very big and had been built as a series of high, thick fences, arranged in concentric circles, like a huge maze. It all sounded marvellous.

Otto Lang was pleasant enough. He had been an Olympic gold medal skier before the War. Zanuck occasionally went to the winter sports resort at Sun Valley, Idaho, where he met Otto Lang.

Julian insisted on making me a solemn promise. I saw no reason for any promises but he insisted. If I went on this trip, he would guarantee that I should complete the picture on my return home. It seemed to me to be unnecessary to make such a statement and I took no notice of it at the time. Of course the penny dropped later when I suspected that I had been elected for lack of volunteers. Henry King, Henry Koster, Jean Negulesco, Sam Fuller, Henry Hathaway and Uncle Tom Cobleigh were all under contract, but were all terribly busy, I guess. I imagine that, in the past, there were cases where some sucker was sent off to shoot the tough, foreign locations, with the understanding that he would direct the picture. When he returned he would be quietly dropped.

I will admit that I was excited about going to Africa. Two weeks later I was in a train on the way to New York. Thence by air to London and Brussels. The Belgian representative of Fox met me at the airport and installed me in the Metropole Hotel. I handed over my passport at the reception desk. I thanked the 20th Century-Fox Man in Brussels for meeting me and assured him I would find my own way to the airport for the flight to the Congo next day. Stupidly I didn't take his office phone number nor his home number.

It had been a long journey already and I was booked on the next flight to Léopoldville which was taking off at 5.00 pm the following day. It was essential that I be on it, because this flight ran only once every two weeks. However there was plenty of time and I was ready for a good sleep. Knowing nobody in Brussels I dined early in the hotel and went to bed.

Suddenly, in the middle of the night, I was awakened from a deep sleep by a furious knocking on the bedroom door. I staggered out of bed and opened up. Three men barged into the room, one of them a policeman in uniform. Another was the night porter of the hotel. They had come to arrest me. They told me to dress at once; they were taking me to the police station.

I was bewildered. I protested. I demanded to know what this was all about. They said, there was some problem about my passport. It was a simple formality, a question of paying a fine of $60. I scrambled into some clothes and was hustled downstairs. I changed $60 into Belgian francs with the night porter and set off into the night with the other two.

It seemed we were walking for miles. I offered to pay for a taxi. They refused. It was now about 3.30 am. At last we arrived at the police station. I was booked in and told to sit on a bench. The inspector would see me later. He was asleep. Probably he would be awake at about six.

There was nothing I could do, no one I could telephone. My only concern was that I must not miss the plane this evening. If I did I should have to wait in Brussels for two weeks. Above all I was absolutely determined that I was not going to pay a fine of $60 for nothing.

Eventually the inspector appeared. He had examined my passport, which he declared was false. He had decided that I was one Robert Baker, born at Brighton on the same day and date as I was born. It is well-known, he said, that the name Roy is a diminutive of Robert and Brighton is a suburb of London. This Robert Baker was wanted by the police. He was a building worker who was working in Brussels in 1946. He was convicted of having immoral relations with a woman but he disappeared and never served his sentence.

It took ages to convince this obstinate, pig-headed clown that there was no possible connection between me and Robert Baker of Brighton. I was undoubtedly Roy Horace Baker, born in London, presently of Los Angeles, a film director *en route* for Léopoldville on the plane leaving this very afternoon. Now he changed tack, saying that he could accept a $60 fine and nothing more would be said. So that was why I had been told to bring the money. I refused, because if I paid I would be admitting an offence I certainly hadn't committed. It was now obvious that this farrago was a con and I was all the more determined not to part with $60, which was about £20 in those days; a paltry sum and the firm would have paid anyway – but it was the principle of the thing.

Finally he agreed that he would let me go, but first he must get clearance from Antwerp. The office in Antwerp wouldn't be open until 9.00 am. After another long wait he gave me my passport and I stumbled out into the fresh air. I had no idea where I was. I eventually found a taxi and got back to the hotel. The manager there suggested that the police had learned this trick from the Germans during the War and often used it to make a bit of money on the side.

I will admit I was very shaken by this experience. I realised how difficult it is to prove a negative: No, I am not him – I am me. Since then, I have had two more problems of identity and I still haven't got to like it.

The flight to Léo was smooth and uneventful. I only remember the one stop at Kano in the early morning, washing and shaving in the gents' lav. There was a rectangular hole in the wall where one day somebody would put a window. I looked outside. There was a vast expanse of sand, a group of palm trees and a man in a long white night shirt walking past, moving right to left, leading a camel. This must be Africa.

All very exciting, but leading only to a crashing disappointment. The research, reconnaissance and preparation for the film had been hopelessly inadequate. The whole enterprise became a desperate struggle to salvage something from the wreck. It was a farcical example of some crazy film people making fools of themselves and I can laugh about it now, but then, it was the toughest job I'd ever had. There is little to be said and I will simply quote some remarks from a long report I made to Blaustein:

'...the evidence is overwhelming, from people who know other territories in Africa, that the Congo has far less to offer as to scenery and natives...

...it consists entirely of a vast plateau covered by dense, trackless forest in which it is of course too dark to shoot, especially with three-strip Technicolor ... what little open country there is seems to be enveloped in a haze you could cut with a knife ...there are mountains only in the far east, in Ruanda Urundi which is too dangerous and at present inaccessible; waterfalls are rare and mostly in the form of rapids...

...the Belgians took over in 1908 and started development only in 1940 ... roads are few and bad, telephones non-existent...

...the famous village built in concentric circles – Mushenge, the principal village of the Bakubwa tribe – turned out to be nothing like the description in the script, which seems to have been taken from the book *The Leopard Hunts Alone*. The original Mushenge was on a different site and had not been laid out that way for many years ... extensive rebuilding was necessary...

...the Bakubwa are a dying race. M Schilling, the Belgian administrator who has lived with them since 1939, estimates they will all be dead or dispersed in ten years ... the young men have already gone and the old men who are left do not make good movie warriors...

...travelling up the Ruki river we had two wood-burning paddle steamers ... the captain in charge was probably an ex-bargee from Bruges who spoke only Flemish ... the crew, all local talent, was an undisciplined mob...

...we set off gaily ... the river was broad and shallow and the navigable channel very tricky ... nobody had any charts ... one of the steamers had fuel for only four hours ... we sent drum messages ahead to the natives to cut more fuel ... we also had two motor boats but never had both in service at one time...'

The film crew was recruited from America, France and England. The American cameraman was one Harry Jackson, on loan from MGM. He was very unhappy, largely because he was totally unsuited to the job. A genuine redneck, he hated the natives, calling them 'boogs' and mocking them unmercifully. The only European language spoken in the Congo was French and not a lot of that. Harry's second language was a few abusive expressions in Spanish which he may have picked up on some location in Mexico. Harry and I didn't see eye-to-eye from the word go; after a few weeks we managed a flimsy armed truce.

The others were good. Johnny Johnson, the production manager, was steady, wise and experienced in foreign locations, including Africa, but not the Congo. I had an English assistant director from Kenya who spoke Swahili and was a real help. The French assistant directors were first class. The camera operator, Lou Kunkel – always known as Uncle Kunkel – was from Hollywood and a genuine diamond, with a delightfully equable temperament which was a welcome buffer against the dreadful Jackson. The Technicolor camera crew, from England, were efficient as usual, but the man who did most to save us from complete disaster was Chick Kirk, the art director. He created the Mushenge village from nothing, handling the native labour with great skill and understanding. All these people quickly realised the seriousness of the problems we were facing.

One bright spot in the middle of this fandango was news from home, including the first news I'd had about *Don't Bother to Knock*. It had just been released and nearly all the critics, disregarding the implied advice, knocked Zanuck for the title. Several critics dismissed the film as unimportant, but there were also several who thought Marilyn Monroe showed some promise in her first opportunity to carry a leading role. But the over-riding factor was the reaction of the general public. They took to it in droves and it came into a million dollars profit after three weeks on release. I wasn't impressed by the money, in which I had no share anyway, but I was pleased that Marilyn had found an audience. It was a pity that I wasn't in LA to take a modest bow.

One other great comfort on the home front was the way Gary and Bette took so much trouble to look after my family, taking them on trips, inviting them to parties and constantly telephoning. Every week, contact was made at least twice.

Some aspects of the Congo were downright depressing. Some of the travelling was done in a chartered Dakota, but a lot was by car, driven by enthusiastic chauffeurs at hectic speeds along miles and miles of red, dusty, potholed roads. When the car swept through a tiny village, which was no more than straggling line of huts, the men would take off their hats and bow and the women made a curtsey. If one of the natives spoke French, he addressed you as 'vous' but you were expected to address him as 'tu'. If you wanted anything in a restaurant you shouted 'Boy!'

On one occasion we were staying the night at a resthouse and there was a sort of cabaret entertainment, given by a trio of musicians, white, Belgian. They sang satirical songs, mostly about the natives, which were well received by the few local whites. One song was especially cutting, about 'les évolués' – those natives who had tried to improve themselves by becoming clerks and so forth. All this in front of the native servants, who stared impassively ahead, understanding most of what was being sung.

Mind you, some of the administrators, especially M Schilling, were struggling hard for the betterment of the natives, but the majority of the colonials had given up. Typically, they had come on a five year contract, believing that they would put by enough money in that time to return to Belgium and buy a café. After ten years, fifteen years, they were still far short of the goal and well into the gin.

There is nothing more frustrating than trying to make bricks without straw. The prime instance of this was the native dances. A few months before this, MGM's *King Solomon's Mines* had been a huge success, featuring some marvellously exciting native dances. I didn't find out until far too late that MGM had used American choreographers and dancers to create routines that were far better than anything to be found anywhere in native Africa.

Still, we gathered a huge amount of material, some good, some bad, some indifferent: sound tracks galore and some good scenes at Paulis where there was a school for training elephants ... except that the African elephant doesn't respond to training like his Indian cousin. We found an okapi and built a huge compound for it. We discovered a small group of pygmies who are difficult to contact: they don't like paying taxes and when a white man appears they usually disappear up into the trees. We contrived a lot of long shots with doubles for Susan Hayward and Robert Mitchum which would fit into the scenes to be shot in the studios ... and so on.

At long last, after what seemed like years, we could pack our bags and say farewell to the Belgian Congo. I was away for four months, covering thousands of miles from Léopoldville in the west to Paulis in the north-east and Luluabourg in the far south. When I arrived back home I discovered how utterly exhausted I was. I had lost a good deal of weight, having started with only eight stone four (116lbs in American money), but I was cheered by a moderately enthusiastic welcome. I had accumulated some prestige from the success of *Don't Bother to Knock*.

Furthermore, I was pleasantly intrigued to find that Jay Lewis had made another Royal Navy picture after *Morning Departure*. This was *The Gift Horse*, directed by Compton Bennett. When the picture was shown, Jay's name was no longer on the credits. The producer was given as George Pollock. This must be one of the very few pictures where a producer has been fired off his own film. I confess to a certain *schadenfreude* and I admit having quietly mentioned the event to one or two people on the lot. Some years later Jay finally realised his ambition to direct and *Live Now, Pay Later* was good.

Some few more years after that, Jay sought me out again. I was living at Aston Clinton, so he came down and we gave him and his wife dinner at The Bell. When the two of us were alone, taking off our coats in the hallway, he murmured quietly: 'D'you remember, long time ago now ... that ... erm ... talk I had with ... Darryl Zanuck ... did it ... I mean, did you...?' I shut him up quickly. I'd be damned if I wanted an apology, or any reminder. 'No, not at all, no.'

Coinciding with my return from the Africa, Gary and Bette had decided to go to New York for six months to stage a revue there. The lease on my house was running out and so they gave us their house, a huge place in the old part of Hollywood, rent free for six months. And the use of Gary's car. All I had to pay for was the utilities and the ubiquitous Hollywood VIP – the Pool Man. A handsome gift.

I plunged into the studio preparation of *White Witch Doctor* with misgiving. At this time every studio was making an African film of the Jungle Jim variety. Zanuck was potty about Africa and fancied himself as an intrepid big game hunter. The more I read the script the more I worried. It bore no resemblance to the book and had none of its virtues; it only bore a resemblance to all the other Jungle Jim pictures.

It seems that Susan Hayward also had considerable doubts about the proposition, particularly the script. She wrote to Zanuck and he sent me a copy of a two page letter, marked 'Private and Confidential', which he had written to her in reply to her complaints. He assured her that he was ever watchful of her interests in finding only the best scripts. He pointed out that she was in a far better position in the industry than when she joined the studio and that this film would be one of the biggest and most expensive of that year. The letter resembles so many others written to unhappy actors which are quoted in *Memo from Darryl F Zanuck*. He could probably write them in his sleep.

Miss Hayward was still shooting another movie and she asked Otto Lang to come and see her in her caravan on the stage. I had never yet met the lady, so Otto took me along with him.

I shall never forget the look on her face as she greeted Otto. She looked over his shoulder and saw me. She whispered a quick word to him. He turned and walked me back to the door, explaining that she wanted to see him alone on some personal matter.

Well, if she had told me to my face that she didn't want me to direct the film, I am sure I would have shaken her warmly by the hand and thanked her profusely, but I was careful to keep this thought to myself. No wonder Julian had given me his unsolicited guarantee that I should complete the film. He had seen this sort of thing happen before.

Diplomatic relations now became quite ... delicate. I thought, I shall be cool and British, slightly confused and naturally disappointed, while allowing it to be known that my health had undoubtedly taken a knock after four months in the jungle. It all culminated in an interview with Lew Schreiber.

He was Zanuck's hatchet-man, dreaded by everyone on the lot. I had little to do with him so far; indeed I am not sure I had met him before. Now I come to think of it, I saw him when I came back to LA after *The House On The Square*. He wanted to know what I thought of their London office, how they operated, etc. Privately I thought they were a rather duff lot, a right little, tight little gang sitting pretty. Whenever somebody came over to make a picture, disturbing the even tenor of their ways, they bullshitted their way through it, getting away with murder. The only moments of sheer horror they had to endure happened first thing every morning, when they opened the regular sheaf of cables from Zanuck. Apart from that, it was a soft touch, bluffing their way through the rest of the day. People only bluff because they are stupid, but never forget – Bullshit Baffles Brains.

Publicly I made non-committal noises. I was sure a straighter answer would have come from Sol Siegel.

Lew Schreiber was small, neat and always fastidiously groomed and dressed. He proved to be absolutely charming. He sympathised fully with my physical state and the way things had turned out in Africa; everyone had been badly misled. I added no fuel to this fire by criticising Otto Lang; there was nothing I could tell Lew that he didn't know already. He went on, in view of my health...

I murmured my agreement.

...of course the studio was well aware of my great contribution to the success of *Don't Bother to Knock*. He suggested that the best thing for me would be to take a good rest. In the meantime they would look for a subject for me in the new year. They would not put me on twelve week's lay-off, which was due; also they would take up the third option on my contract straight away.

Well, you couldn't say fairer than that. Shortly afterwards, I was coming down the steps of the commissary after lunch when I met Henry Hathaway. He was the lucky man who had inherited *White Witch Doctor*. I wished him good day and he returned a grim smile: 'Next time, I'm going to get ill!'

I never saw the film, so I have no idea how much – if any – of my material was included in it. I threw the script away and blotted it out of my mind. I wish I could read it now and perhaps quote some of the joke dialogue. I had met Robert Mitchum at Dick Widmark's house and thought he was definitely all right, one of us; I can't believe he would have actually said some of that stuff, out loud, on camera.

THE ROBE – AND THE JACKET

Hollywood was now seriously worried about the inroads made by television on the box-offices. Every studio had top secret plans which – they hoped – would combat the menace and eventually put paid to it. Fat chance. Parallel to this was the determination in the industry that television production should be drawn away from New York, where it was growing strongly. If there was going to be any television production, it must be centred in Hollywood.

The 20th Century-Fox plan was based on the discovery in France by Spyros Skouras of the anamorphic lens. This device squeezed a widescreen image into a regular 35mm frame. With a similar lens on the projector the film could then be shown unsqueezed on a wide screen in the cinema. The result came out in the shape of a letter-box. Very quickly some wag invented the ideal scene for this system, to which I have ventured to add a few embellishments.

On one side of the hospital ward the heroine lies prostrate in bed. Way over on the opposite side of the room the door opens. Enter Jose Ferrer, giving us his Toulouse Lautrec number. Hastily he takes off his top-hat, there being no headroom for it. He has brought the girl's pet dog to cheer her up. He is leading an extra long dachshund.

Close-ups were unmanageable, though we all did our best by trying to balance a single character with a candlestick or some other prop filling (!) the other three quarters of the screen. This led a gleeful production department to point out that all scenes could now be played as three- or four-shots, saving time in shooting and editing. I asked Henry Hathaway what he was going to do with it: 'Same as I always do. Stick 'em in the middle of the frame.' I believe he always shot everything with the camera on an old-fashioned tripod. No crab dollies or cranes for him.

He had an excellent reputation as an action director, but he seemed to go berserk on the set, tough and ruthless and extremely rude. He fired people for the flimsiest of reasons. When he came to England, some of the crews didn't like him at all. There are many stories: one rather funny one was when shooting at Warwick Castle, some people not in costume wandered into the background of the set-up. Henry grabbed the loud-hailer and turned the air bright blue with four-letter words. He didn't know the intruders were the Earl and his weekend guests.

There was one film he was bitter about – *Fourteen Hours*. He put everything he had into making it a true-to-life drama, no action. It was good picture and he felt he never got proper credit for it. I had a long talk with him at one of Tyrone's parties and he was as quiet and charming as could be. Next day, I asked Eli Dunn, about this. 'Sure' says he, 'he's a great guy off the set but soon as he smells film it's like he smells pussy!'

It is amazing to remember that Zanuck managed to foist this idiotic CinemaScope shape on all the other major studios; he even sold some of them the equipment to do it. Furthermore it lasted for about seven years. Another one of its drawbacks was revealed when the time came to show these films on television. Now TV has adopted a wide screen but it has proportionate height as well.

The first vehicle chosen to demonstrate the wonders of CinemaScope was a grand biblical saga based on a book called *The Robe*. The entire studio was concentrated on it. But one of the other majors had decided that its salvo directed at TV was to be 3D – stereo photography. They cooked up an exploitation picture, rushed it out and made a fortune with it. Not to be outdone, Zanuck dragged his eyes away from *The Robe* and looked around for a stereo subject.

The firm of Blaustein and Bloom had the right article. It was called *The Waterhole*, which was good for a laugh to start with, though not after one had read it. It was a very good story indeed, written by Francis Cockerill as a long short story for one of the monthly magazines. During my period of R & R, I kept in touch with the Old Firm and allowed my interest in this property to be known. I had always had an ambition to make a picture in which the leading character spends long periods alone on the screen, where the interest would be in what he does, rather than what he says. A silent movie, a return to the most effective presentation that a film can offer. This script depended upon the fullest use of this element. Incidentally, an occasional visit to the ballet can be instructive as well as enjoyable, showing how a story can be told without dialogue.

The Waterhole is about a man who is exploring mining prospects 30 miles out in the Mojave desert, accompanied by his wife and a mining engineer. His horse stumbles, he falls off and breaks his ankle. He sees no problem. He is rich and has been thoroughly pampered all his life. He sends his wife and the engineer back to the nearest town to charter a helicopter to lift him out. What he doesn't know is that they are starting an affair, which is duly consummated on the journey back to town.

After 24 hours without result he realises that the lovers have abandoned him. He has very little food or water and only six shots in his revolver but he slowly develops the determination to survive, to patch his leg somehow and walk out of the desert. After survival, his second ambition is revenge. In the end he decides that revenge is worthless. There were of course a number of scenes of the man alone, battling with his predicament. Just what I had been looking for.

We looked at several desert locations, all reasonably close to LA, and eventually decided on Apple Valley, which is a small community on the edge of the Mojave desert. It was established after the First World War, for returning servicemen to start apple orchards. There is plenty of pure water but it is very deep down, so when it comes up it is almost freezing. In one scene, William Lundigan had to dive into a swimming pool which, surprisingly, was unheated. Not an enviable task. And then Zanuck complained that when Bill surfaced his hair was disarranged. I began to suspect that Zanuck and I were not sharing the same attitudes to filmmaking.

On the Sunday before shooting we awoke to find four inches of snow on the ground, a most unusual sight in those parts. Some of the natives had never seen snow before and there was a lot of sky-larking. On the Monday morning it had all disappeared and shooting started as planned.

The 3D process that we used was far and away the best, but, in the final stages, it was also impractical. The indispensable element in stereoscopy is that there must be two separate images of the subject, photographed by two cameras spaced three to four inches apart, roughly as the human eyes are set. No difficulty so far. However, in presenting these two images to the viewer they must still be kept separate, so that the left image is presented to his left eye and the right image to his right eye. In spite of all the bogus claims that have been made over many years, there is no other way of achieving the true 3D effect. Similarly, stereophonic sound can be plausibly presented by feeding two separate soundtracks into two loudspeakers spaced apart, but it is only an illusion. To obtain the true effect the two sound tracks must be heard separately through headphones, the left track to the left ear and the right track to the right ear.

Our method was quite simple: two cameras were bolted on to a large plate at right angles to each other and mounted on the usual dolly. A polar screen was placed in front of the lens of each camera and the two screens were set in opposition to each other. A two-way mirror was set in front of both cameras at 45 degrees: the right-hand camera shot straight through the mirror and the left-hand camera received the mirror image, which was then flopped in the processing so as to present it the right way round. Some compensation was made in exposure for the slight loss of light. The cameras were interlocked and run in synch. Thus we had two matching films, left eye and right eye.

Two perfectly balanced prints were required from the labs. In the cinema projection box two projectors were needed, running in synch, with the illuminant carefully balanced, also with polar screens over the lenses. For reel change-overs there had to be another similar pair of projectors – at least it was so in those days; modern projectors would obviate that problem.

At last we come to the audience. Each person must wear a pair of spectacles with polar lenses opposed in the same sense as those on the projectors. This caused some difficulty for people who habitually wear glasses. Again, in those days these specs were expensive; also, the customer was asked to leave a deposit on them, which was redeemable after use; then, the specs had to be hygienically cleaned for the next use.

One way or another, it wasn't going to work on general release, but under near perfect conditions in the big theatre at the studios it was a marvel, the effect was stunning. There you were, sitting in an ordinary cinema and when the proscenium curtains drew back, the house lights dimmed and the film appeared, it was as if the wall at the end of the hall had disappeared. The far end of the cinema no longer existed. Most of the movie takes place in the Mojave desert and from some of the high points you could see a range of mountains 90 miles away. You forgot you were in a cinema: you were looking 90 miles deep into the Mojave desert.

One pleasant aspect of the production was that we were miles away from the studio for the bulk of the work; everybody there was concentrating on *The Robe* and we were neglected. In contrast, William Bloom thought that our movie should be called *The Jacket*.

Robert Ryan, Rhonda Fleming and William Lundigan were the stars of *Inferno* and all did well, Ryan being outstanding and a good actor. Independent minded, too. He lived in the Valley and was dissatisfied with the local schools, so he and his wife set up a school of their own for their children. Soon some of the neighbours' children joined in. We were chatting one day about the collapse of the British Empire. Bob grinned at me and said, 'Oh, the Brits are all right. You just have to beware of their charm.' Diplomatic, was he. The same thing could be said of the Chicago Irish, I suppose.

At that time, Rhonda was one of three famous redheaded ladies. Susan Hayward (see above) was famously disagreeable and Lucille Ball was famously funny. Rhonda was the one I had and she was absolutely delightful. She was inclined to worry about her appearance; some lines on her neck bothered her. I assured her that Lucien Ballard and I would take care of that. In the mean time, let's talk about how we're going to play the scene. 'Oh, you take care of that too' she said. She was thrilled when she heard me call for 'Miss Fleming's feet to be marked'. She explained that over at Paramount, where she belonged, somebody just called 'Okay, bring on the girl' when she was wanted on the set. So we motored happily on. She came out quite well, too. The supporting cast were good, with the excellent Larry Keating giving a beautifully understated but truly effective performance. Henry Hull's appearance as a desert rat gave a big lift to the later scenes in the film.

When the rough cut was shown to Zanuck by the producers (directors were not allowed in to these showings) he was impressed and rather surprised, but he couldn't take the hero's renunciation of revenge; another difference of outlook. So a new ending had to be devised. As we originally had it, the engineer abandoned the wife in the desert and walked off toward Mexico. The husband picked up the wife and took her back to town and a divorce, but no more than that. A compromise was finally accepted by DFZ, whereby the engineer abandons the wife and then, on his long walk to Mexico, stumbles across the hero and tries to kill him, which culminates in a knock-down and drag-out fight in a desert hut. An oil-lamp is knocked over (after swinging wildly straight at the audience) and in the ensuing fire the roof collapses on the engineer and he is burnt to death. Next morning the hero picks up the wife, as written, with no further comment.

The fight sequence was arranged by the renowned Dick Talmadge – he was Norma Talmadges's brother – who had many years' experience. I learned so much from him; he used a simple set of dodges on which he played many variations, all of which have stood me in great stead ever afterward. He was most generous in explaining them and he had one vital characteristic: he understood the characters and the situation and he never sought to distort them for the sake of a gratuitous effect. This is an attitude not shared by all the fight arrangers and stunt men I have met since. Some of their suggestions border on lunacy and when denied them, their acceptance of a refusal is sometimes grudging indeed.

Obviously the title of the original story, *Waterhole*, had to be changed. Zanuck thought up *Inferno*, remembering that William Fox had made a version of Dante's *Inferno* in the silent days – yes, he did – so the studio had every right to use the title. Incidentally, Mr Fox's vision of the infernal regions incorporated lots of lovely ladies lightly clad in diaphanous chiffon and on that account – it was rumoured – it was one of the films than prompted the invention of the Breen Office.

Inferno was shown in 3D only in New York, Chicago and Los Angeles, also in London. The critics gave it unanimous applause, largely because it had a good story to which the process contributed greatly, as opposed to the usual stereo films which were simply exploitation stunts. However we did include a few of the clichés, at the behest of DFZ. I guess he was right, at that.

It is a pity that it could never be widely shown; it was certainly the best film I made for Fox. By dint of great persistence on the part of John Carpenter of the British Council, a 16mm black and white slash dupe was discovered, of the right eye only. It was shown at the Dinard Film Festival as part of the aforementioned retrospective of my work. Obviously it was a poor relation to the original, but it was nice to see it again, after 40-odd years, even in the flat. I subsequently discovered that a complete version, with both left and right reels intact, is held in Bob Furmanek's 3D archive in New Jersey, USA.

Viewing Carpenter's print in the flat, I saw that I had relied too much on the 3D effect in handling the cameras, which were unwieldy in the dusty desert, so the coverage looked very flat, if you see what I mean, but the story stood up well and the performances were okay. I thought we had used too much music – a common fault to this day; also the voice-overs of Robert Ryan's thoughts were inclined to explain the obvious and were too wordy. Generally the dubbing was sketchy: some of the dialogue scenes in the desert had been shot in a high wind. So much so, that the noise of the flapping of Rhonda's silk shirtsleeves drowned the synch dialogue, which had to be post-synched. That was all right, but the dubbing editor failed to put enough wind back in. It does look a bit silly, with the actors' clothes and hair flapping and dust and tumbleweed flying about. The dialogue is clear, but the actors sound like they are in a dubbing room. Well, they were.

Meanwhile, back in Hollywood, I had come to the same conclusion as the studio: the time had come for me to move on, back to England. Hollywood was on the brink of fundamental changes which would take some time to work out. I had seen the last of the old studio system; it was now breaking up. It was a brilliant system which had been tremendously successful for 40 years or more. Of course there were drawbacks: in my opinion the atmosphere was debilitating. Life for the director was conducive to idleness; there was so little for him to do. He was expected to know his place and stick to it, like everyone else.

One minor example was when I was preparing *Night Without Sleep*. I asked my assistant, Gerd Oswald, when we should go out to shoot back-projection plates for the car scenes. He explained gently that all such chores would be taken care of by the process department. Still I persisted in having a talk with Our Man in Process.

It was true; he had the plates all worked out, angles, backgrounds and all. No need for me to worry. It was the same story all over the lot: art department, editing, music, mardrobe, make-up – everywhere. As soon as they read the script, they went to work. The director only had to glance over it and nod agreement. When I went to see Alfred Newman about the music for *Don't Bother to Knock* he had it all doped out. He played me a short theme for the title music – 'Ah ha! – this is good' he said, 'now we extend it ... this gives it class!' He was delighted to give 'Manhattan' to Anne Bancroft to sing, because 20th owned the film rights and the charge to the production would be $25. After all, it is one of the great standards.

The only time a director could exercise any influence on a film was during discussions with the producer and the writers, though by the time he was called in the script would be in an advanced state and difficult to manoeuvre. Thus Zanuck imposed his personal blueprint on every script. I once bumped into one of the writers when he was emerging from Zanuck's office. I asked, how's it going? The reply was, 'A downhill fight all the way'.

As Eli Dunn said, 'Yuh can't fight City Hall!' The director was encouraged to wallow in the lap of luxury, but I enjoyed wandering about, talking to the heads of departments. I believe one or two of them rarely saw the director and enjoyed a chat with one. When some of the American directors came to England to shoot a picture they were sometimes at a loss when expected to participate actively. At Pinewood, for example, the departments started work as soon as they received a shooting script, in the same way as their Hollywood counterparts did, but they made no final commitment until the director laid down some guidelines. The Pinewood style has the advantage of flexibility: they can easily supply several different interpretations of a script which they may offer to the director, leaving it to him to make the final decisions. Of course, if they don't agree with him they may fall back on the time-honoured formula: 'Fine ... if that's the way you want it, Guv'.

The Hollywood system gave the production department the initiative and consequent control over all productions, with all departments working to long-established formulas. It was true: it was the studio that made the picture, not the individual. And so the films were formulaic.

The last three years had been a wonderful experience. In spite of a shaky start which had wasted a good deal of time and energy I had done some good work and it certainly turned me into a professional instead of a gifted amateur. I simply could not see myself spending the rest of my life in Los Angeles, with all its attractions. It was then and probably still is the best place on earth to make a film. Anything and anyone required can be supplied. It has the largest western audience. The outlook is international and not parochial because that's the way America is.

For the most part I had enjoyed it. I could leave without regret.

PINEWOOD

PASSAGE HOME

London, 1953. Another November. Another fog. Piccadilly was cold and quiet in the mid-evening. There was little traffic, moving slowly; sounds were muffled but somewhere in the distance I could hear a busker scraping away at his violin. The tune was the theme from Chaplin's *Limelight*. Wonderfully, plaintively nostalgic it sounded, but I doubt the fellow took much money on a night like that one.

It was good to be home. For the most part, the places I have seen, all over the wide world, were attractive, interesting, stimulating and sometimes fascinating; but the only place I feel comfortable and at ease is London.

After three years absence, little had changed, though my friends were going about their business in all different directions. William Fairchild, who wrote the script for *Morning Departure,* was working on another sea story of an entirely different kind. *Passage Home* it was called and it came from a novel that had been published the previous year, by Richard Armstrong. The picture was to be made by Rank at Pinewood and produced by Julian Wintle.

This tale was about a semi-mutinous crew and a martinet captain in a cargo steamer making a 30-day voyage from South America to England. The captain has been obliged by the local British consul to give a passage home to a young woman who has been stranded. Every man in the crew has problems with the captain and with each other, which are exacerbated by the presence of the woman.

Almost all the action takes place at sea and the process projection people at Pinewood seized on this film to demonstrate their brand new process, known locally as blue-backing, more correctly as travelling matte. They were ahead of everybody in developing it and very good it was. They got an Oscar for it. The general principle of the system was to use a blue cyclorama as background and light the foreground with yellow light. Thus the foreground could be separated from the background as part of the laboratory work, providing a moving matte behind which the desired background would be added later. The beauty of it was that it didn't matter how much the actors or – in this case the ship, which was built on hydraulic jacks – moved around. This method was streets ahead of back projection, which was clumsy, limiting and never looked truly convincing.

Of course the director has to specify what angles he intends to use on any given set in any given scene, so that the backgrounds can be photographed to fit, but if need arise a background plate could be shot after the scene had been covered and edited. In the present case, a camera crew were sent off in a cargo ship of appropriate size, to sail from England to the Mediterranean and back. The cameraman was Peter Henessy. We went through the script and the sets with Vetchinsky, who was again to be art director. Day scenes, night scenes, port, starboard etc were all covered. Peter went off while we were shooting and came back with the perfect set of plates, absolutely spot-on. We were all extremely grateful to him. So often a second unit comes back from location with a lot of splendid material which simply doesn't fit the purpose.

Obviously a lot depended – as it always does – on the lighting cameraman who was taking care of the main shooting. This was my first picture with Geoffrey Unsworth. He was just great. I cannot find words to express my feelings about him, as a man and as a professional. We struck up a firm friendship and a sympathetic and responsive working relationship. Not only that, but I also had David Harcourt as camera operator – my old friend and fellow traveller from the days of our youth at Gainsborough.

The lighting cameraman is the director's right hand. Some years later, in the sixties, I noticed a number of directors posing with a viewfinder hanging round their necks. Also, I was being invited by the camera operator to crawl round the set with a viewfinder looking for nifty set-ups. The idea was that once the angle, tracking, crane or whatever was chosen, the lighting cameraman would be invited to light it. Putting the cart before the horse, I'd say.

The casting of *Passage Home* was pure joy. Julian was determined to go all out for the best available actors and there were well over a dozen important parts to fill. Together we assembled an excellent group led by Peter Finch and Diane Cilento. Peter was cracking good company always. He had three different versions of his life story, not absolutely incompatible with each other and all of them riotous adventure stories. One day during the shooting we had an actor on stand-by until two o'clock and we called him. The second assistant, Kip Gowans, had some trouble contacting him but eventually got through. Peter and I were standing on the bridge of the ship, giving a full view of the studio door. It opened and our man entered, peering through the dim light, supported by an embarrassed girl on each arm. Peter's version of the story is that I took one look at the new arrival, turned to my first assistant, Peter Manley, and said matter of factly, 'He's pissed. We'll do those other scenes instead'. It turned out later that the young blade had decided that he wouldn't be called, so he took a couple of birds out to lunch. Probably Kip had to apologise for calling him and not using him.

Diane is also Australian, or rather Italian-Australian, formidably brainy and endowed with devastating sexual attraction; wilful and never going to be pushed around by anyone. She probably found stardom rather boring and ultimately stupid. She wasn't deeply impressed with the plot of the film; it was novelettish, but she and Peter buckled down to thoroughly professional performances which helped us over these weaknesses.

And then there was Geoffrey Keen, honest and powerful. Cyril Cusack was a master of subtle expressiveness. We also included some comparatively new (1954) people: Bryan Forbes, Patrick McGoohan, Michael Bryant etc. Michael impressed me with his sparky, cheeky midshipman; I have seen him several times since at the National Theatre and surprisingly, he always seems to be playing a gloomy Russian. I always enjoy working with new people. If you pick them well they come up fresh as a daisy and since the audience doesn't know them, they're all the more effective.

When shooting was finished and a fine cut was ready, we showed the picture to John Trevelyan, the secretary of the British Board of Film Censors. Only recently appointed to the job, he surely was full of himself. He picked on two scenes: there was a fight on the foredeck between two or three of the crew and the scene where the captain suddenly goes berserk and attempts to rape the girl.

The fight was very effective. I put all that I had learned from Dick Talmadge into it. It was crucial to the story. It took place on a dark night at sea, so the effect of it lay more in what you didn't see, than what you did. It was certainly no worse than the fight in *Inferno*. Trevelyan really slammed into it. We reached a compromise in the end, only after a lot of hard words.

The so-called rape scene never takes place. The captain and the girl are in the captain's cabin. Both are fully clothed throughout. The captain seizes the girl and pushes her back on to a bunk. Just as he is about to climb on top of her, the first mate appears, pulls the captain off the girl and floors him with an uppercut to the jaw. That's all. But you never heard such a fuss. It doesn't matter that the rape didn't happen – the intention was there. How we got over that one I forget; I suppose we shortened it a bit. Trevelyan was showing off, exercising his muscles, but it was all very tiresome.

There is no denying the fact that the subject didn't really justify the tremendous efforts put into it by all hands. From preparation to premiere took over fifteen months. Julian was a tower of strength, which is the right way to put it, because he suffered from serious illness all his life. He was a haemophiliac. Even to walk from his office to the restaurant was painful but he never once complained. He never even mentioned his disability. He was a great enthusiast for film; his methods were quiet, gentle and determined. We had a number of close associations over a number of years; we had our arguments but we worked well together.

The next venture was *A Grand Man*, which was a book by Catherine Cookson. It was re-titled *Jacqueline* because that was the name of the child who played the leading character, who was also called Jacqueline. The script was written by Patrick Kirwan with additional dialogue by Liam O'Flaherty. George Brown was the producer. I had met George quite a lot when I was working at Denham on *The October Man* and he was producing *School for Secrets* amongst others with Peter Ustinov. Tall, bi-lingual in Spanish, genial and seriously hard-working but always lighthearted about it, he kept a close eye on every nook and cranny of the production.

We set off for Liverpool, Belfast and Dublin, looking for locations. The story was about a scaffolder in a shipyard who has to work at dizzying heights. He develops vertigo and is losing his nerve. He takes to the booze which only makes matters worse. He is saved by his daughter, a saucy little brat, who finds a job for him away from the shipyard.

This was another opportunity to use travelling matte. Harland & Woolf in Belfast allowed us to shoot in their enormous shipyard, so we shot a lot of plates and some long-shots with doubles. A crane hoisted me up in a bucket. The view from up there was fantastic. I noticed from up there the tiny figures of the foremen on the ground below. They all wore bowler hats, this being before the builder's hard hat was invented. This was just in case somebody dropped a red-hot rivet. By accident, y'understand. They were all very helpful in spite of the inevitable disruption we caused, with so many people stopping work to goggle at the fillum people. Then the bowler hats shouted at them and rude words were exchanged. It seemed to me that industrial relations were a bit tense.

Meanwhile, back at Pinewood, one James Archibald arrived. He was an entirely new figure; no one seemed to know much about him or his experience of films. Young, very bright and energetic, he was to be John Davis' production representative. Earl St John continued as executive producer. It seemed that the new appointment was an attempt to unseat Earl. I remember Earl quietly mentioning that beside being on the board of Rank Productions Ltd, he was also on the board of the Rank parent company. The apportionment of responsibility and authority between the two men was never clearly defined, which probably suited Earl very well. After taking a quick look around, Archibald decided that the current system of contracting people for one film at a time would not build up a strong team that would last. Among other producers and directors, he offered me a three-year deal for at least three pictures, at increased fees, which was fine, but there was an uneasy time ahead of us.

To my delight the lighting cameraman on *Jacqueline* was again to be Geoff Unsworth. The art director was Jack Maxsted, who had not been in charge before. He put up some excellent sets and drew up a super storyboard for the TM sequences. The cast list looked like a Who's Who of the Irish Theatre: Cyril Cusack, Noel Purcell, Liam Redmond, Maire Kean, Maureen Delaney and many more. The Abbey Theatre and the Gate must have been closed at the time. Delaney was known simply as 'Delaney'. She was well on in years and she was the acknowledged *Grande Dame*. She was absolutely delightful. John Gregson played Mike the scaffolder and Kathleen Ryan was his wife Elizabeth. A newcomer – or new-ish – was Tony Wright in a minor rôle. He played Gregson's mate on the scaffolding and also had a very small love interest with Maureen Swanson. They had only two short scenes and little could be made out of that.

I have one regret about this film. Early in the story a tally-man calls at Mike's house and launches into a high-pressure sales talk, tempting Elizabeth to buy some of the goodies in his suitcase. It wasn't a very long scene but it was a showpiece for the actor who played the tally-man. Harry Towb seized it with both hands and gave a superb performance, complete with authentic Belfast accent. I was horrified when we got to the fine-cut stage and I was told the whole scene had to be cut out because the film was over length. To this day I can't understand it. Strangely, a similar thing later happened in *The Vampire Lovers*.

The casting of the character of Jacqueline had been decided before I started work on the film. While we were in Belfast looking for locations George took me down to Dublin to meet the little girl. She looked right and sounded right. Her mother was an actress, but the child had no acting experience at all, as far as I know. We chatted and I felt we were getting on well enough, but when she came to England she seemed frightened to death, not only of being in front of the camera, but terrified of everything and everybody around her. We all did our best but she never really relaxed. She didn't let the picture down; her performance was all right but with that leading part she should have made a name for herself. Somehow she didn't – or couldn't – take the opportunity. I am forever grateful to Noel Purcell, who shared several of her longest scenes. He took Jacqueline under his wing and was a great help to her and to all of us. Perhaps she didn't want to be a film star anyway.

Jacqueline was popular but it never came into profit; this was the first time I had a small share of the producer's profit, but nothing came of it. Apparently the film was well received at the premiere; Jacqueline herself got a round of applause at one point. I was elsewhere, at Dinard in Brittany, shooting locations for my next picture. Looking through my sketchy diaries I can see that during my seven years at Pinewood my feet hardly touched the ground.

Both these films were generally satisfactory by the standards of the time but the truth was, they could have been made before the war – which had ended ten years before this. By now, in the middle of 1956, change was in the air. I wasn't fully conscious of it at the time, but I could feel that there were fresh breezes blowing. People speak of the Swinging Sixties, but it was all beginning to happen as early as 1954, when Kingsley Amis published *Lucky Jim*. Commercial television had a lot to do with it, because there were now two channels instead of one. In the theatre, in '55 we had *Waiting for Godot* and *Cat On A Hot Tin Roof*. In '56 changes in attitudes were gathering momentum with *Look Back In Anger*.

And cinema attendances were falling rapidly. John Davis called a conference at Pinewood of all producers and directors. Every sort of idea was put up and discussed without any useful conclusion and by four o'clock in the afternoon we thought there was no more to be said, except that we should make good films that the public will want to see. By the way, nobody in the ensuing years has thought of a better idea. Still this was not enough for JD. He suddenly announced that he had arranged dinner for us at Pinewood and we might leave the room for a few minutes to phone home and explain. It felt like being kept in after school.

The most dramatic event of that dinner was when JD was called out to take an urgent phone call. He came back after only a minute or two, beaming broadly. We all stopped talking and looked up. Triumphantly he said: 'We're invading Suez!'

Dead silence, apart from one or two gasps of horror. JD looked round, puzzled. Somehow conversation picked up again. JD sat down with a shrug, dismissing this extraordinary reaction. Nobody displayed much inclination to continue bandying ideas about the future of film production at Pinewood.

In the second half of that year the next film gave me wider imaginative scope and was a real blessing – but a very mixed blessing.

Tiger in the Smoke was to be produced by Leslie Parkyn. I believe he had been a high-ranking civil servant at the Ministry of Food during the war. I noticed that although he was co-producer with Jay Lewis on *Morning Departure* he preferred to have 'Administrator' as his screen credit. He told me that in the civil service the administrative division is the senior one: it is the administrators who decide what is to be done; the executives are merely those who carry out the administrators instructions.

I first knew of him when he was managing director of a Rank company called piffle – PFFL, or Production Facilities (Films) Limited, which provided a range of services to the production side: a central story department, a meteorological department, a travel bureau for location shooting and so on. Then we met on *Morning Departure*. He was a man of extreme reserve and discretion. He was as straight as a gun barrel and you wouldn't meet anyone more charming. He was a widower. He almost never spoke about it but he was deeply bereaved and inclined to spiritualism. Throughout this new production he gave me total confidence and encouraged me to give my imagination full rein.

The script was from the book by Margery Allingham and I was one of her most devoted fans. I had read all her books – but boy!, are those stories difficult to convey to the screen. Socially, Miss Allingham and her husband, Pip Youngman Carter, gave only one party each year. This was held in midsummer at their house near Tiptree in Essex. Not only were you offered lunch, tea, dinner and supper, but also, the free use of a full-scale fairground in the fields around the house, complete with swings, roundabouts and all. Magnificent. Pip was an artist and his Christmas cards were a delight.

Tiger in the Smoke produced an extra problem, over and above the task of putting the story effectively on the screen. The screenwriter had got just over half way with it when he was offered the temptation of directing a television spectacular with Eartha Kitt. He found himself unable to resist it. This was Anthony Pelissier, one of the most talented men I ever met. Actor, playwright, screenwriter, director in theatre and film, he could do it all, with considerable success. Anyway, as good writers go, he went and Leslie decided it would be vain to pursue him. We had to complete the script as soon as possible: we were scheduled to shoot in June. Leslie also decided that I should complete the script. A new writer would want more time than we had; so I did it, taking no credit and no pay either.

That was only the first of the snags. The next one was more serious. The central character in the story is a villain, who has a tremendously menacing presence. He dominates a gang of broken-down ex-soldiers; his hold on them is positively mag-netic. This was a part for Jack Hawkins or Stanley Baker, if ever you saw one.

John Davis was now taking an ever-closer interest in production. He decided that Tony Wright should play this part. This was exactly the same situation as I'd had with poor Connie Smith and *Berkeley Square*. Tony was simply not good casting for this. He was perfectly all right in *Jacqueline* in spite of having very little to do. But for this he was too good looking, too young and too charming: he was a really nice fellow. Also, he had appeared in one or two pictures in France but hadn't the long experience required for a job like this. JD wouldn't budge. He insisted and after all the arguing and pleading we had to accept his decision. It seriously weakened the film and of course it did no favours for Tony. Heaven knows he really did his best. I think in his heart he knew this so-called big break would come to no good. It pret-ty well ruined his chances as an actor.

I had a strong cast (see the appendix). Bernard Miles was at this time collecting the money to build the Mermaid Theatre. Gerald Harper was excellent as Duds Morrison, his first time on film. I decided to shoot the whole film with the camera set up on a baby crane, so that I could keep the camera on the move, in any direc-tion, throughout the action. In some cases, close-ups for instance, the movement was slight. Nobody ever commented on it, so perhaps I didn't carry the idea through boldly enough. Still I think it may have imparted a feeling of unease to the audience.

I said this assignment was a mixed blessing. The icing on the cake came when Malcolm Arnold composed the music for us, which was very effective indeed. It was intensely dramatic over the murder of 'Duds' Morrison and I do believe it had some-thing to do with the censor's objections to that sequence. After our first encounter over *Passage Home* this put the kibosh on our relationship. Trevelyan had that schoolmasterly habit of pigeon-holing people. If you were in the box marked 'art cinema' you could tackle anything, however controversial: sex, violence, politics, religion – anything. If you were in 'commercial cinema' you faced obstruction and nit-picking all the way. He chose these categories and allocated everyone according to his estimation of them. He was a sinister, mean hypocrite, treating his favourites with nauseating unctuousness. At one time he convinced some of the directors to submit their scripts before shooting, so that he could guide them in 'How to present a censorable scene in such a way as to avoid censorship'. He certainly had the idea that he was running the British film industry. I am quite conversant with the 50 OK artsy-fartsy words so dear to the liberal arts establishment but, as was the case with Marilyn Monroe, I don't use them; they may be misleading, they may create a fog in the mind. It was one of those cases where the killing wasn't shown at all, so it was difficult to cut out anything objectionable, because there wasn't anything objection-able – and all the more powerful for that. I can't remember the details now, but I think I shortened the scene by a few feet and a certificate was issued.

At the end-of-picture party my invaluable first assistant, Peter Manley, told me that he had been keeping a secret from me ever since we started shooting. I noticed that as he spoke several other members of the crew joined us. John Guthridge, the editor, Penny Daniels, the continuity girl and Jack Maxsted. The secret was that Penny had never worked as continuity girl on a film before. She may have spent some time assisting the more experienced girls at odd times, but this was her first picture in charge. I never had the faintest idea that she was new to the job. Whenever I referred to her she came up with the answer without any fuss. She never put a foot wrong, was quietly efficient and charming with it and never nagged. Some of them do turn out to be naggers. She stayed with me for my next four pictures. I couldn't be more grateful. Here's why:

The production of a film is a complicated affair. The director has 80 or 90 people advising him, putting up suggestions, asking for clarifications and so forth. All these discussions demand decisions, for which the director bears the final responsibility. Most of these talks take place before shooting starts and the director will take part in them personally. Once photography starts the information flows in the opposite direction and the director is very busy indeed with the cameraman and the actors. Personal communication with each member of the crew is well nigh impossible, but simple links can keep the lines open. On one's right hand is the cameraman. For obvious reasons he is the kingpin of the shooting process. On one's left hand are the first assistant director and the continuity girl. The 'first' is leader of the floor crew and will be in constant touch with the production department and the art department. The continuity girl will keep close contact with the editor. Through them all the other departments will get the current information they need. In any case the producer will be keeping a supervisory eye on everything. The simpler the chain of command the easier life will be for the director, who can concentrate on his main task: putting the script on to the screen.

So you see, her as does the continuity is a Very Important Lady indeed.

REALISM

In London, you'll never be short of a book shop. The one I took to was the Piccadilly Bookshop, at the top end of the Piccadilly Arcade, next door to Hatchard's. I was told about it by Stephen Watts. The reason I liked it was the man who owned it, Frank. I never knew his other name. He was a walking encyclopedia of the modern book trade and forthright in his comments. One day I mentioned the extraordinary flood of reprints that were appearing of every single sentence ever written by W Somerset Maugham. Frank was grim: 'They'll be bottling his piddle shortly and selling that!'

He turned to the shelves and grabbed two books. 'Here, I've got something for you'. Although all the stock in the shop was brand new, he had the habit of blowing imaginary dust off the top of the book and slapping it hard on his left hand before handing it to the customer. Following this ritual he gave me two books: *The*

One That Got Away by Kendall Burt and James Leasor and *A Night to Remember* by Walter Lord. 'There you are' said Frank, 'read those. You could make a couple of decent films for a change'. I had not heard about them or read a review but to my lasting benefit I took Frank's advice.

John Davis had now established a meeting every Thursday at Pinewood, convening producers and directors to discuss production over lunch in the flat. Regular attenders were Earl St John and Mrs Olive Dodds. She was head of casting and had her being at South Street. I put myself down for the next meeting and when I got there I was surprised to find that none of the others had turned up. JD and I were alone. He gave me the John Davis stare. 'Well come on, what do you want to do?'

Safe from interruption I enthused about the two books. JD said nothing, but I felt it was going down well. I completed my speech with a plea that both should be made and the rights should be bought. The man grinned. 'We've already bought them. Julian Wintle is going to produce *The One That Got Away* and William McQuitty the Titanic story.' Julian I knew, as above; I had met Bill only once before, some time before this, when he had asked me to direct *Above Us The Waves*. It was a good script but I turned the offer down for the stupid reason that I had already made a submarine story. I was devoted to the idea that I should try something different with every film I made. I should have decided to specialise, in sea stories at that; there is plenty of variety in that field and it's one of the things I'm good at.

If there was one sort of person John Davis liked – and there weren't many – it was one who declared what he wanted to do and was prepared to carry it through straight away. Three days later I was at South Street with William McQuitty and Eric Ambler, who was writing the script of *A Night to Remember*. After general discussion, casting was the big issue. There were dozens of important speaking parts but only one character stood out: Second Officer Lightoller. Could we get a star to play it? It could be said to be the central character but it was not a star part; *primus inter pares* at best. The obvious ideal casting for this was Kenneth More, but would he do it?

It was decided that I should go and see Kenny. 'Right', said I, 'I'll do that.' John Davis asked, 'By the way, where is he?' Quietly I broke the news, 'He's in Bermuda. He's doing *The Admirable Crichton* with Lewis Gilbert.' JD hesitated for a split second. 'Er, well, all right. You'd better go out there and talk him into it.'

Two days later there was another meeting with JD, this time at Pinewood, with Julian Wintle on *The One That Got Away*. Casting was again the main topic. JD was adamant that he would not play a German actor in the part. In any case he thought Dirk Bogarde was ideal. I didn't twig until later, but it seems JD was suggesting Dirk for everything: Dirk's contract was nearing its end, he was a big box-office star and there was already some anxiety that Rank would lose him. In fact they had no chance of keeping him.

Julian and I were very doubtful but no decision was taken because we considered that a lot of work was needed on the script. The one we had was written as an old-fashioned Hollywood style adventure picture with no reality about it at all. The

German air ace was shown as charming and heroic. Probably a part for Errol Flynn. After liberating Burma single-handed, why not? The whole point of our approach was that, although the story sounded like fiction, it was true. This airman was to be tough, cunning and arrogant. Incidentally, not a bit like our own dear Dirk.

Next week I was landing in Bermuda in a tropical rainstorm. As the aircraft touched down it went into an almighty skid. Thanks to brilliant work by the pilot he instantly took off again, made a long circuit and this time landed safe and sound. I had a few days rest and recreation while Kenny read the script of *A Night to Remember*. He agreed to do it; in fact he very much wanted to do it.

Back home, there wasn't much time to retrieve the script of *The One That Got Away*. We were scheduled to shoot early in the new year and it was in our own interest to do so because the action took place in deepest winter, with plenty of snow.

Julian now pulled off an inspired move. He sent the book to Howard Clewes, who took to it like a duck to water. He turned in a first class script in less than three weeks and really saved our bacon in that department.

We had another piece of luck. Rank had convened a conference in London for their overseas distribution managers. At that time there were eight offices in Europe, seven in the Far East and so on. They were given a lunch at Pinewood and I buttonholed the manager for Germany, an Englishman, whose office was in Hamburg. I told him the story and my predicament about casting the Luftwaffe pilot. He promised to make some enquiries for a suitable actor in Germany.

I have no idea if Dirk Bogarde was approached about the film. Anyway, I was prepared to bet he would turn it down. Most actors believe they can play any character; they are most anxious to prove there is no such thing as type-casting. Dirk was one of the bright ones. He would know he wasn't right for it. Also there was already a hint of criticism floating round the studio about the wisdom of making the film at all. At any rate, JD's insistence about having Dirk play it seemed to be weakening slightly.

At this time, there was a picture called *Whirlpool* shooting at Pinewood. It starred a German actor called OW Fischer, who had managed to clear himself of any taint of Nazism and had gained acceptance thereby. I was deputed to talk to him about taking the part of our pilot, Franz von Werra.

Fischer was utterly wrong for the part. He was pushing 60, or looked as if he was. He was unbelievably vain and grand. Haughty is the word. I felt sure he wasn't an actor at all; he was a poseur. For his appearance in this other picture he had demanded a special moustache to be made. He was a great one for demanding and in a short time he had managed to upset everyone around him. The make-up department was headed by Billy Partleton, that old friend of mine from the pre-war days at Gainsborough. Billy saw an irresistible opportunity. He organised a collection of pubic hairs from everybody round the studio and made up the 'tache from them. Fischer was delighted with it. I found no difficulty in presenting the case to him in such a way that he felt obliged to refuse the part. We exchanged the usual compliments and that was that.

Sadly I reported that he was unable to accept. Just at the right moment my Hamburg friend came through with the goods. He had three possible actors; two in Hamburg and one in Munich. The associate producer was David Deutsch and together we shot off to Munich. We put up at the Vier Jahreszeiten, interviewed our first candidate and decided he wasn't right for the part. Back in Hamburg, we found the ideal casting in Hardy Kruger. He came over to London and we made a test of him. JD finally capitulated. We all owe a great debt to Our Man In Hamburg.

We now had a first rate script and ideal casting for the lead, but a serious problem had to be solved. Every effort must be made to convey the authenticity of the story and therefore the locations had to be right. This character's adventures in England were fairly simple. The airfield at Hucknall could be shot at Northolt. Some interior sets were built at the studio, designed on the basis of the originals. The only genuine setting was Grizedale Hall in the Lake District. This was a baronial monster, looking as grim and sinister as it sounded. During the war it was used as a POW camp for German officers, the very one from which Werra made his first escape and was soon recaptured. The place had just been sold but fortunately we were able to negotiate a stay of execution long enough to do our shooting.

After that, the other locations were more difficult. Werra had been sent with a ship-load of other POWs to Canada, where they would be safe from the horrors of war. Here he jumped out of a train and fell into a snowdrift, walked to the St Lawrence river and rowed across it into the United States, still at that time neutral. The Americans were persuaded by the German Embassy in Washington to repatriate him to Germany. He got a great reception from Hitler, who pinned an Iron Cross on him. He was later killed in a flying accident over the Channel.

The crossing of the St Lawrence was obviously going to be difficult to realise. Julian wisely decided to send me with a small team to Canada to investigate the possibilities there.

Driving through rural Canada in mid-winter was a strange experience: there was no sign of life anywhere, except for the occasional plume of smoke from a chimney. The inhabitants have brought hibernation to a fine art. We persevered in our search and finally found a spot where Werra had probably made his crossing.

However, this use of dollars was not permitted by the Bank of England, so we transferred our search to Sweden. Here we found everything we needed, including a huge lake near Falun, which doubled for the St Lawrence. The Swedish Army carefully monitored our work on the lake, taking cores from the ice from which they calculated how much weight it would bear. This included a huge generator. The noise of the ice cracking under its weight was frightening, but it didn't break through.

When we planned the Lake District locations we were happy to discover that we had some good weather scenes and some bad weather ones, all in different places. So, we thought, we'll have no trouble with the weather. In practice, we soon found that the moment we set up for a wet weather scene, the sun would come out. We then packed up and hared over to a fine weather spot – and down came the rain.

Other countries have climates; in England we have weather. In the Lake District they change it every 20 minutes.

Julian had to remain back at the studios, simply because of his physical inability, which must have been very frustrating. He was increasingly worried about progress, for which I don't blame him. Indeed, I was summoned to visit Earl St John at his house near Pinewood, on a Sunday when there was no shooting. We talked for several hours about all aspects of the production, especially the weather. Earl was also worried that I was making too much of a hero of Werra. I assured him I had no intention of doing that, but we had to remember that Werra was the central character of the film and never off the screen, so there was no way of distracting attention from him. He simply had to do the things he did in fact do.

I pointed out that if the treatment of the prisoners seemed easygoing, we were simply showing our adherence to the Geneva Convention; this was not weakness. We had seen several stories showing British prisoners in German POW camps; now we were showing the other side of the medal. Audiences would make up their own minds as to which was the most humane. Dear old Earl was yearning for more slam-bang action scenes.

But he was apparently satisfied and I motored back to the Lakes. I heard later that the unit didn't expect me to reappear on the Monday. It had never occurred to me that I might be replaced. From then on everybody had the sense to realise that we were more than half way through shooting, the picture was looking good and the prospects of commercial success were fine. By virtue of the story we were trying to tell, we were at the mercy of the weather and if we didn't get it right we'd have no picture at all.

One thing gave me confidence: Julian had selected a cameraman for this picture who turned out to be ideal casting. He did a brilliant job. His name is Eric Cross and I can't speak too highly of him. He was a joy to work with and one of his great strengths was his implacable determination that all the conditions – particularly the weather – should be absolutely right for every scene: the snow in Canada, especially when falling; the pouring rain and high winds in a huge marsh in the Lake District, and so on. We both had to withstand heavy pressure from the studio about the schedule and the budget and without his indomitable backing I might well have caved in. Let me repeat, if ever a film depended on what it looked like on the screen, this was it – and Eric Cross delivered the goods.

Hardy gave a superb performance, absolutely right in every detail. I had never before and have not since worked in such complete accord with a leading actor. In spite of the discomfort we all had to bear in the location conditions, all the actors and especially the crew drove the thing on with tremendous enthusiasm. Incidentally, I used another atmospheric trick in this picture, which no one noticed; they weren't supposed to notice. Remembering that, at least in Europe, people read from left to right, I staged everything so that Werra always moves in the opposite direction, from right to left; all other characters move conventionally from left to right.

This was also one of the happiest pictures I have made. I was on the top of my form and sure as I could be that it would be a good film and that a lot of people would want to see it. We got good notices, with only one or two expressing doubts about the wisdom of making a film about a German airman, so soon after the War. Twelve years after, in fact.

As the film developed into a box-office hit the doubts began to be more widely expressed. Basil Dearden accused me of glorifying the Germans and depicting the British as cripples. He was apparently unaware that the people conducting the inter-rogations and running the prisoner of war camps were selected for their experience of combat conditions and in many cases had been severely wounded and were therefore no longer fit for active service. Their attitude to the captives was scrupu-lously correct, which may have been misinterpreted by some as indulgence. The Germans were inclined to execute escapees if they caught them. The Japanese apparently thought we were insane and it seems they still do. Those of us writing, producing and directing the film believed that the story was a feather of the caps of the British, who were clearly seen to handle their prisoners firmly but properly and above all, Werra was the only one who escaped and got back to the Fatherland. Nor did he escape from England; he hopped the twig in Canada.

I have never been the sort of director who deliberately makes films with a mes-sage but I came close to it with *The One That Got Away*. From the early 1940s, which meant a period of 15 years or more, I became more and more irritated by the depic-tion of Germans as homosexual Prussian officers, Gestapo torturers or beer-swilling Bavarians, all presented in ridiculously hammy performances. I had no doubt at all that these characteristics could be proved to exist in Germans – and possibly other nations – but in my opinion these cartoon caricatures were dangerously misleading. Just the sort of thing to get the filmmakers a bad name and give the audiences a wrong impression. On at least three occasions during the war the Germans had come close to winning it. By 1957, the year the film was shown, they had already shown clear signs of a formidable industrial recovery, heading for leadership in Europe.

Always excepting Hardy Kruger, who is an exceptional man anyway, I have met very few Germans. Hitler and his gang took six years out of my young life; I have no reason to like them. Neither do I fear them, but their possible domination of Europe is nothing to look forward to. In general they were not the joke characters as shown in the forties and fifties and they certainly aren't now. They were the first to discover that wars are no longer waged or won by guns; except for tribal wars like the Balkans, wars are now fought with money. As witness the long undeclared war with Russia which ended at last with the threat of 'Star Wars'. Russia went broke and the Berlin Wall came down.

Before we started shooting Julian had mentioned the director's share of the pro-ducer's (his) profits and his intention to abide by this unwritten convention, always provided that there were any profits to share. I thought no more about it until a couple of months after the picture was in distribution. Julian called me into his office and told me that profits were now coming in, surprisingly soon after the release. He then said that he felt that we should share the profits half and half, thus increasing my percentage considerably. He was under no obligation at all to do this; it was a most generous gesture and typical of the man.

On the 30 September 1957 Pinewood Studios came of age, being 21-years-old, as the qualifying age then was. A magnificent luncheon party was organised for five or six hundred of Rank's most intimate friends. It was extremely well done and a good time was had by all until we came to the speeches. There were 14 dignitaries seated at the top table and the awful prospect dawned on us that each and every one of them was going to say his piece and at some length too. It must have been well after half past three when Our Man From The Canadian Odeon took the lectern, on which he placed a thick sheaf of foolscap. He began to drone through it, steadily, page after page.

Two tables away from where I was sitting, one of the most famous actors of all the celebrated names in that distinguished gathering was AE Matthews, who was well-known for his mordant wit and shortly to celebrate his 88th birthday. He had already shown signs of restlessness. He shifted once more in his chair and said in a loud voice: 'Doesn't this fellow know that I haven't much longer to live?'

A Night to Remember presented another challenge of authenticity. There was a considerable amount of historical evidence, mostly undisputed but some of it questionable, all of it to be sifted. There were a number of myths and fantasies which had to be carefully evaluated. There were the reports of two inquiries, one by the US Congress and the other by the British Board of Trade. Any survivors within reach were asked for their experiences and comments. We had considerable help from Commander Charles Lightoller's family. All this ground had been thoroughly scrutinised by Walter Lord and his book was the basis of all our work. All the information was triple-distilled by Eric Ambler, who wrote the script. The balance that he achieved between so many disparate elements was superb, bearing in mind that it all had to be compressed into a reasonable length for a film. In the first draft version the steerage passengers got hardly a mention at all. I pressed hard for this aspect to be given the weight it merited, as part of the balanced story we were aiming for. My colleagues were doubtful, thinking we might be criticised by higher authority. This never happened, apart from a letter John Davis told me he had received from the shipping line. They accused him of making money out of the tragic fate of over a thousand people.

In the end the film ran just over two hours, which was long for a film in those days. Quite long enough for any film in any day. How can any filmmaker expect audiences to sit in a confining chair with poor leg room, in the dark, staring in one direction, for much more than 90 minutes. Any longer than that and they'd run out of popcorn. No wonder the double seats they used to have at the back of the cinema were always full; but then, their occupants weren't much interested in the cavortings on the screen.

A Night to Remember was a truly enormous undertaking, entirely financed by Rank. It cost nearly £9 million in present day money. All the settings were faithful reproductions of the originals. Some were very big and in addition had to be built on platforms which were supported by hydraulic jacks, so that they could be tilted at various angles according with the progress of the sinking. Some had to be flooded at various levels. All this was under Vetchinsky and a number of assistant art directors, headed by Harry Pottle. Their scrupulous attention to detail brought the whole thing to life. The grand staircase was marvellous and the first class dining-room was exactly like the original. During the scene of lunch at the captain's table we served the same menu as on the fatal day. There was no need to do this, but some food had to be eaten and it might as well be correct. It all helped the atmosphere, which, as I have said before, helps the actors.

The principal exterior set was a long section of the port side of the promenade deck, together with the boat deck above it. This included lifeboats slung in davits which could be swung outboard and lowered, with 60 people in them. Some people of experience in the necessary engineering were recruited from London Docks. Most of these scenes took place on the port side, but there were one or two smaller actions which came about on the starboard side. It would be economically impossible to build a set especially for such short screen time.

I suggested to Geoff Unsworth that we stage the starboard scenes on the port side but by shooting them through a mirror. Only a few characters were involved. The gentlemen were wearing double-breasted suits and could button them the wrong way round. Buttonholes would be transferred to the right lapel. The ladies looked the same both sides with minor modifications of brooches, etc. The officers' cap-badges and the crewmen's cap-ribbons were a problem. Yvonne Caffyn, the redoubtable costume supervisor who was never fazed by any difficulty, ordered the necessary badges and ribbons to be made mirror-fashion.

It worked. The officers saluted with their left arms and the gentlemen exchanged left-handed handshakes. I gather that this wheeze has also been used elsewhere; I have no copyright in it.

Throughout the film, Yvonne's presentation of 92 speaking parts was perfect and made an enormous contribution to the final effect. She had some wonderfully grand ladies' hats designed and made by some famous milliner. He seemed reluctant to hand them over: she thought perhaps he wanted to wear them himself. All this with Biddy Chrystal doing the complicated hairdos of 1912 and Billy Partleton in charge of make-up. As I said, Billy was a comrade and greyhound racing fanatic during the pre-war days at Gainsborough.

David Harcourt was again camera operator and by all odds one of the finest. We met at Islington, where he was a focus puller. In 1938 we both had a couple of weeks off and decided we would drive to Nice. We chose to go over the mountain route, by Barcelonette, which was recommended to us for its scenic values by Marcel Varnel. On the way I nearly put the car over the edge, but was saved by bumping into a roadside pile of grit. There was no guard rail. I quickly removed my gaze from the stunning view. Then, the front spring of the car broke. David patched it up with a bough of a nearby tree. Next, as soon as we arrived at Nice, I dashed joyfully into the sea, got out of my depth and had to be fished out by a lifeguard. David took it all without reproach. Unflappable, is he.

Every problem has a solution, otherwise it wouldn't be a problem. All the preparations for shooting were thorough and carefully planned for everything that happened on board and on the sea, but there was one piece missing in the jigsaw. This was, how to connect the scenes on board with the scenes on the water. We discovered an ancient ocean liner which was lying in the Gareloch, in Scotland, about to be broken up. She wasn't as big as *Titanic* but she had the same straight sides and the drop from the boat deck to the water was nearly right. There were lifeboats in davits that could be used. Once again, a stay of execution was arranged with the breakers, Thomas W Ward & Co, who were extremely co-operative.

So, in the middle of October 1957 we embarked on a daunting schedule of 20 weeks, ten of those weeks being devoted to night shooting. We all assembled at Ruislip Lido, to shoot scenes with people in the icy water and in lifeboats. The Atlantic Ocean on 12 April 1912 was as calm as a millpond; there was no moon, but the sky was full of stars; the air was bitterly cold. Thirty-five years later the conditions at the lake at Ruislip were exactly right. A pitch black night. The temperature of the water was realistic and you could see the people's breath condensing in the air. All this gave everybody a clear idea of the tragic events we were recreating. Another help to the actors.

The editor on *The One That Got Away* was Sydney Hayers, a man of long experience. I was delighted that he was available to do *A Night to Remember*. I suggested that he go up to the Gareloch with a second unit to shoot the vital linking scenes between the boat deck and the water. He covered it well and his final edit of the film was excellent. However we lost a fine editor because he now developed a taste for direction. He made a few pictures – one very good one – before going off to Hollywood to direct a couple of episodes for one of their television series. This went well, but he was surprised and appalled at the ramshackle methods the locals were using. They were all wildly enthusiastic and hopelessly undisciplined. Never one to let things slide – a truly outspoken John Blunt – he explained how order might be brought out of chaos. They thereupon told him to take over as producer, which he did, with success.

If ever a picture was a team effort *A Night to Remember* was the example and this has prompted me to introduce some members of the team. I owe them all a great debt for their unstinting support. There is no doubt they were inspired by the subject. It was punishingly hard work but they took it in their stride. Among the actors, almost everyone who was available was begging to be in it, however small the part. The special effects unit was an enterprise in itself under Bill Warrington and the cameraman Skeets Kelly. They performed miracles with the techniques that were available to them at that time.

Jack Hanbury was production manager. Unflappable and urbane in the best sense of the word. He was a joy to work with and we soldiered on together until my contract ended in 1961. The first assistant, Bob Asher, was a gem. We had worked together before, so I was familiar with his manner. He looked like an extremely mournful bloodhound with huge dark eyes staring dolefully at life. Underneath all this was a very sharp wit. He had long experience and if he didn't suffer fools gladly he never showed it, always showing patience. He had perfect manners, never wasted time in gossip, was always business-like.

My fondest memory of Bob was the occasion of the retirement of Arthur Alcott, the studio manager at Pinewood. A special lunch was arranged in the Green Room. The wine flowed like Niagara and everyone was getting sentimental. Earl St John made a sentimental speech, almost in tears. Everyone applauded Good Old Arthur. Staggering back to our office, Bob suddenly stopped dead. 'I just remembered' he said. 'Good Ol' Arthur. A couple of weeks ago I asked him for rise – only a fiver a week – and he turned me down flat!' Good Old Arthur, having retired last Friday, turned up again next week – as studio manager at Beaconsfield.

I admired Bob so much; he had the gift of cutting away the cant and the sentimentality. When we were shooting *Jacqueline* we had an actor who couldn't remember his lines, thankfully in a small part. Bob was quite annoyed: 'He's a fluffer, that's what. He has no right to call himself an actor.' He was content to remain a first assistant for many years, steadfastly refusing promotion until he finally became a director, mainly of Norman Wisdom's films. He was a lonely man, a bachelor and I believe deeply religious. He died some years ago, at no great age.

Pinewood was by far and away the best studio in Britain with some of the finest technicians, but there was one aspect of it which irked me: the general attitude of the departmental heads. No matter what you asked for, their initial response was a sharp intake of breath, sucked through the teeth, the head nodding slowly from side to side. I suppose my approach must have been wrong but I just couldn't stand their lack of enthusiasm. Of course they supplied the goods in the end, after some wrangling. I coined a phrase for them. I called them 'The Abominable No Men'. Some time later I was delighted when President Kennedy used this phrase. Surely he couldn't have got it indirectly from me? Or perhaps it was just a case of great minds thinking alike.

Kip Herren was assistant studio manager, and when Arthur Alcott left, he took over. He really stirred things up, giving everybody self-confidence, revolutionising their attitudes and methods. He was a born leader and his sudden death long before retirement age was a tremendous loss. At his funeral there was a great crowd; as many people outside the chapel as were in it.

At last the long schedule was completed, the final cut agreed and Muir Mathieson and William Alwyn came in to add the music. Muir at once declared that there should be no music – apart from that heard incidentally from the ship's orchestra – until the ship started its final plunge. My own view precisely. It comes in at the right moment with tremendous effect. We discussed the inconclusive evidence about the last number played by the ship's orchestra: it could have been any one of three tunes. This was not the only instance of conflicting evidence sworn by eye-witnesses. We decided on 'Nearer My God to Thee'.

It was about this time that Eric decided to move to Hollywood. He had recently bought a new car, a Porsche 356B, then a rare one in England. He made up his mind that I should sell my Jaguar and buy the Porsche and after some hesitation I did. This may have added another blot to my patriotism, in some quarters. Even Vetch said, 'But it's German, isn't it'. Now there are hundreds of Porsches.

The notices for *A Night to Remember* were even better than *The One That Got Away* and more importantly gave the Rank Organisation considerable credit for making it. This was something new for the Org, which rightly gained considerable prestige. For years there had been nothing but criticism and downright barracking of all Rank's efforts. Of course they had made some bad pictures. Of course they were becoming more and more old-fashioned; the world around them was changing fast and they were too slow in responding. However, I put a lot of the trouble at John Davis' door. He had no talent at all for public relations, no idea how to get on terms with the media. When you remember how Korda had them eating out of his hand ... but he was a film-maker, John Davis was not. He had one set speech on The Way and Purpose of the Rank Organisation which wasn't bad, but it was a businessman's speech.

Nevertheless he should not be dismissed simply as a narrow-minded accountant. He had drive and ambition and he was capable of keeping Rank on an even keel with all its ramifications. And that stability was vital to the consistent production of a lot of films over a number of years. Any industry needs a core, a focal point, if only for the continuing development of ideas and fresh talent. Rank's withdrawal from production was considered no loss at the time, but it was a devastating blow to the stability of the industry as a whole. It also freed the G-B/Odeon circuit from showing Rank productions because there would no longer be any.

As executive producer, Earl St John was no great help; he wasn't a filmmaker either. He was an exhibitor, fully conversant with the cinema side and it wasn't enough. People who claim to know what the public wants are often wrong, because the public doesn't know what it wants – until it sees it; the filmmaker must use his imagination in stimulating the public's imagination. Sadly it is not likely that his guess will be right every time.

It always seemed to me that Earl spent most of his time in protecting his own job. This seems to be a common fault among men who rise to high command in a company. Some of the gossip in the business pages of the newspapers is alarming. Cutting the throats of rivals, or those assumed to be rivals, is more important to them than actually running the gaff. As was said of President Mitterand: 'He will take more satisfaction in dividing a majority against him than in commanding one of his own.' Earl was surely thinking on these lines around the time James Archibald appeared on the scene.

After James Archibald left, Earl brought in Connery Chapple. He had been editor of the trade paper *Kinematograph Weekly*, which leaned toward Wardour Street, with its distributors and exhibitors. I still don't know what his function was supposed to be. Protecting Earl's back, I suppose.

Earl's comments on scripts were always guarded and could be easily modified or withdrawn at any time. I suspect they had been prompted by some reader or other tame acolyte. He wallowed in nostalgia, mooning over the great days of thirties Hollywood. He told me he longed for leading men who had developed gravel-toned voices by smoking too many cigarettes. The English actors were too light-weight, bordering on the effeminate. Most of them were too short and they all spoke with a broad 'a'.

The opening night of *A Night to Remember* was certainly memorable. Bette Davis was in London so she came along, which gave me great pleasure. JD gave a great dinner at the Dorchester after the premiere. He received the guests and was delight-ed to meet Bette. As we moved on toward the restaurant he held me back, allow-ing Bette and my wife to go ahead. He gave a quick look round the lobby. We were alone except for a few photographers. He waved them all away and suddenly took my hand and knelt down on one knee, murmuring thanks with a broad grin. I was stunned. I too knelt on the floor, pretending we were looking for a lost half-crown. As we stood up, I couldn't think what to say. I started 'Mr Davis, I – ' He interrupted: 'Call me John' he said.

Now for the hard luck story to end them all. The New York critics gave the picture rave notices and included it in their best ten films of the year. This was tremendous news, except for the fact that all the newspaper publishing departments were on strike, so the papers were never distributed and the public never saw them. Ah well...

Cheer up! We got a Golden Globe from the foreign press in Los Angeles and I was awarded a Christopher from the Catholic Film Guild in New York. In England, I got a Certificate of Merit for craftsmanship from *Picturegoer* magazine. In England, you see, the director was still an expensive technician.

THE DEEP END

Success brings as many problems as failure does. Treat those two imposters just the same. Well, yes. Everything depends on how one copes with them and what natu-ral handicaps one brings to the coping. Mine is an obsession about 'going it alone', combined with a compulsive drive for firm, clear decisions, to be arrived at as soon as possible. A determined autodidact since leaving school, my life-long dream was to be an 'intellectual', believing that all decisions should be made by rational thought; but beneath all that there lies a deeper belief that natural instinct is the stronger impulse and will prevail. The essential counter-balance is common sense, but in some strange way it is not always available. Anyway, Horace is my middle name and he was the one who said, *Naturam expelles furca, tamen usque recurret.*

I had several offers at this time, but none of them included a specific script. In any case I still had one more film to do under my existing contract with Rank, so I was not able to wander far from the fold. John Davis simply said, 'What do you want? You can have the top brick off the chimney.' Thereupon we agreed on a new contract for three films as producer/director over three years. I wanted the rank of producer, which would give greater control and access to properties, but I did not want to 'produce'. I persuaded Jack Hanbury to come along with me with the intention that he would be the producer. I asked Earl to give Jack the title on the screen but he refused. Anyway Jack did look after the production work, which he did excellently well for the next two films.

The search was now on for a story. Studio policy was much in favour of choosing vehicles for contract stars. There are advantages in having big box-office draws under contract but the search for stories to fit them soon becomes frantic and usually leads to disagreement between the actor and the studio. Earl asked me to look out for leading parts for Kenneth More and Dirk Bogarde.

Earl handed me a novel: *The Singer Not the Song*, by Audrey Erskine Lindop, published in 1953. A great subject for Dirk, he said. Two of Miss Lindop's other books had been filmed successfully. This one was set in Mexico in the late 1920s, after the revolution. It concerns an Irish priest who is drafted to a remote village which is dominated by the local bandit and his gang. Despite this dangerous opposition, the priest is able to exercise considerable influence with the peasants. The bandit, after his initial hostility, is deeply intrigued with the priest, who almost succeeds in reforming him. They both find the relationship disturbing.

Now the young daughter of the local landowner falls in love with the priest, causing him difficulty with the inevitable misunderstandings amongst the villagers. The bandit cannot resist the chance to discredit the priest and oust him for good and all. This would have been a waste of time, because the bishop would simply send in another priest. Anyway, it all ends in a gun-battle in which the bandit is shot accidentally by one of his own men who is trying to shoot the priest and the priest is shot while trying to persuade the bandit to say an act of contrition.

There was not one single element in this story which appealed to me. I was not interested in any way and the situation of the girl falling in love with the priest had been done to death, as it has again since. I discussed it at great length with Earl. I couldn't understand why the Rank Organisation wanted to make an entirely Catholic film, with J Arthur himself being an eminent Methodist, especially since a lot of it would inevitably be critical of Catholicism, despite the devout efforts of the author. Some of the speeches she put into the mouth of the bandit were contemptuous of the religion and were susceptible of misinterpretation. I had no desire to offend the followers of any religion. There were also the obvious production problems. The whole thing would have to be shot in Spain or if possible Mexico. I suggested that the film should be an Italian or Spanish production and Luis Buñuel should direct it. Earl said,

'Who?' – but I think he was pulling my leg. He agreed to lay the project aside.

I had two other projects in development. I was much intrigued with a novel called *The Visitors* by Mary MacMinnies. It was a Cold War story, topical and completely different from the usual Iron Curtain thrillers. In Cracow in the late fifties the Poles are making the best of a miserable and frightening existence under Russian occupation. The wife of an English press attaché is beautiful, scatty and acquisitive. Soon she is entangled in the black market in food and antiques, involving her husband and the American press attaché – without their knowledge – and several hapless Poles. The Russians move in and the foreigners' diplomatic status is withdrawn. All that happens to them is that they are asked to leave the country, politely but firmly. The Poles are left behind to face the music. Hence the title.

John Mortimer wrote two treatments of the book which were most encouraging. I went to Klosters to see Deborah Kerr, who was ideal casting for the wife. It was a very long shot because she would have wanted to be sure of a proper release in America; of course her presence would have helped us to negotiate an American release. She liked the idea and couldn't have been more charming. Everything would depend on the script. Irwin Shaw also lived in Klosters and we were invited to dinner. Shaw told me the story of how John F Kennedy was visiting Paris and had asked him to come to Paris to see him. Naturally Shaw was flattered and curious as to why Kennedy had made the invitation. So he packed his bag, went to Paris and presented himself. After the usual greetings Kennedy said: 'Now, you know this town. Tell me, where are the broads?' And that was the end of the meeting.

Zanuck was also in Klosters and I saw more of him there than I had during all the time I was in Hollywood; not the most stimulating talker, but pleasant enough. Juliette Greco was with him and she was charming, bright as a grenadier's button and fun.

However I couldn't persuade Earl to go ahead with a full script and the project gradually faded away.

The Progress of a Crime, a novel by Julian Symons, also had an interesting angle. On the surface it is a crime story about two teenage tearaways who commit a murder, but the focus of the book is on the general effect of the involvement of the press. The book was well reviewed and was Best Crime Novel of the Year in America. The usual objections came up: surely we've had enough of teenage tearaways? Will the press object? Earl agreed to Julian writing a treatment but wouldn't go on to a script. We can't have anything controversial, you see.

The long-awaited end of my seven-year contract with MCA Hollywood had at last arrived. Nothing was heard from them, so I was able to take advantage of the law in California which laid down that no contract was allowed to last longer than seven years. I rang up Jack Dunfee and invited him to lunch at the Dorchester.

Jack's reaction when I told him that I had decided to quit MCA was completely unexpected. He exploded with rage. How could I do such a thing? There would be terrible trouble. What could he say to the headmaster? – presumably he meant Jules Stein or Lew Wasserman.

I was astonished, absolutely amazed. At that time MCA was the dominant agency with dozens of highly paid clients, of whom I was one of the least important and lower paid. I simply couldn't understand why Jack was making such a fuss. Surely I wouldn't be missed? It may be that this was another instance of my under-rating my own value. But if they were so keen to pick the fruits of my recent success, why didn't Jack take the initiative and approach JD for a new deal? During the previous 12 years O'Brien, Linnit & Dunfee had found only one film for me: *Paper Orchid*.

If it was all so important, why didn't Jack try to persuade me to change my mind? Without further ado he suddenly stood up and marched out of the restaurant.

Of course, I should have negotiated a new contract with MCA London, this time on proper terms; either that, or gone to another agent. Alan Grogan of Christopher Mann's office had been serenading me for a long time. But I had already agreed a satisfactory arrangement with John Davis for the next three years – and ten per cent is quite lot of money and, like a lot of clients, I wasn't impressed by the services provided. For one thing, I always had a feeling that Jack Dunfee never had proper confidence in me. Any success was put down to luck. My father had taught me that a salesman can't operate well unless he has confidence in the product he is selling.

Nevertheless a good agent who was interested enough in furthering my work would have been of help during the next period. I was dealing with matters outside my experience. I remembered Sol Siegel's remark to me: 'You're doing all right – but you've got to learn to protect yourself in the clinches.'

Personal relations were going so well at Pinewood that I decided to invite JD to dinner. My house was at Aston Clinton in leafy Buckinghamshire and I wasn't sure he'd want to make the journey. I was pleasantly surprised when he accepted. He duly arrived at the appointed time, driving his Bentley with his wife Dinah Sheridan at his side. With considerable embarrassment I had to break the news that, at the last minute, we couldn't have dinner at home for domestic reasons, so I had booked a table at the Bell Inn instead. Whatever plan I had for a conversation at a private dinner, however sketchy and fragile it might be, was thrown off course.

As we sat down, John threw out an odd conversational gambit. He said he had recently been accused of being too ambitious. What did I think of ambition? Was it really a bad thing?

I floundered. I murmured a few platitudes and stuck my nose in the menu. Was he offering me an opening? – to put forward an outlandish idea? Like everyone else I had been following the politics of Pinewood and Earl St John for the last two years or more. I felt strongly that the place needed a new head of production. James Archibald had been brought in to ginger things up, which he had done, but after a couple of years or so I guess he fell out with John and he left. He went to the advertising agency J Walter Thompson and pursuing his interest in films made a string of first class TV commercials.

Well, what about ambition? I had never thought in those terms. I had hopes that I would make more films with increased imagination and scope, but I realised that

I hadn't thought this somewhat different idea through properly. Should I voice the nagging ideas that were in the back of my head? I wondered if John had sensed that I was getting ideas, else why had I asked him to dinner? It wouldn't be to discuss the weather. Why had John bothered to accept the invitation? It couldn't just be curiosity, to see how I lived. There must be something in his mind. Suppose he opened the door a little further. He was just the man to be amused and interested in a bold proposal. Suppose he might just possibly agree? – because he would delight in putting the cat among the pigeons, just to see the result.

Suppose, suppose ... What about Earl? But above all, what would I actually do? Suddenly I knew I was not well enough prepared. I hadn't worked out a plan of action to put forward. The moment passed and we ordered our food. Typically John had caught me on the hop before we had time to settle into a conversation. I shall never know whether I missed a great opportunity or a disastrous failure. I am sure of one thing: if my next picture had been another smash hit, this 'ambition' would have come up again.

Apart from this diversion I had assembled three possibilities for subjects. The first was a play written by Hugh Williams and his wife Margaret called *The Grass Is Greener* which offered a vehicle for Kenny More.

The second was a play at the Royal Court which Earl St John asked the producer Hugh Stewart and me to see. Earl never went to the theatre or cinema himself, except for premieres. He always sent an emissary. The idea was that Hugh and I should team up for this project, which we were both willing to do. The play was *The Long and the Short and the Tall*. We both wanted to do it and were also convinced it would be a success. There was a marvellous new actor in it – Peter O'Toole.

The third was *Saturday Night and Sunday Morning* by Alan Sillitoe, who came to lunch at my house, when we had a most agreeable discussion. This came about through a friend, Clarence Paget, of Pan Books. He had bought the paperback rights of the book from the publisher, WH Allen & Co, whose principal was Jeffrey Simmons, who gave his permission for Clarence to show the book to me. I saw it at once as an absolute winner. I mentioned the book to Earl, but I knew nothing of the fact that the Rank Org promptly bought the film rights, at my instigation I suppose.

The next twist in the story came with a phone call to Jeffrey Simmons from J Arthur Rank in person. He begged Jeffrey to help him with a problem. In short, the Org had bought the book before J Arthur had read it. Having done so, he wanted to return the rights to Mr Sillitoe and would certainly not want him to return the purchase money. With apologies to the author, the problem was simply that the Rank Org made films for the family audience and this book was not suitable.

The first I heard of all this was when I approached Jeffrey, now a prominent literary agent, asking him to read the manuscript of this book, the one you are now reading, with a view to finding a publisher for it. He told me the whole story about *Saturday Night and Sunday Morning* only last week, forty years later.

On 2 December 1958 I put my proposals before the production committee, which consisted of John Davis, Earl St John, Mrs Dodds and one or two others I can't remember. All three stories were turned down. *The Grass Is Greener* was condemned as immoral; *The Long and the Short and the Tall* had so many swear words in it that if they were all taken out there would be nothing left; *Saturday Night and Sunday Morning* was sordid and 'common'.

It is true that in all probability Columbia would outbid us by a mile for *The Grass Is Greener* and they did. It was made with Cary Grant. Nobody said it was immoral. Elstree were in the field for *The Long and the Short and the Tall* and there was by now another group pursuing *Saturday Night and Sunday Morning*. Of course I knew nothing of J Arthur's intervention on that. The business of getting the rights for either one of them was going to be difficult but was possible with one and maybe two of these stories. Now I was spared the effort. Worst of all, I was left without a subject.

...and the consequence was:

JD revived *The Singer Not the Song*.

The two of us must have lunch. We did. John repeated his belief in *The Singer*. I repeated my doubts. He had no doubts: it would be a great film, I was the man to direct it, it will be a great vehicle for Dirk, etc. It would be his last film under his Rank contract and no effort or expense was to be spared in order to persuade him to continue with Rank. He was already in Hollywood, making a picture about Franz Liszt and JD was afraid he would never come back to Pinewood. Fifteen months had gone by and I hadn't produced a subject on which we could all agree and the prospect was that we never would. After further long discussion, in the end I had no option but to accept the situation. Now I must go to Hollywood at once to sell the proposition to Dirk.

As I outlined the story he listened courteously, but cautiously because he knew very little about the project – there was no script and he was up to his eyes in the Liszt picture, which was still shooting. He put his finger straightaway on the most important decision to be made, apart from the script: that was, the casting of the priest. I explained that we were going for someone who had a track record in the American market, which would pair up with the impact he would make there with the Liszt picture. I'd had no dealings with Dirk before this and didn't know him at all. He impressed me at once with his undoubted charm and humour and the sheer speed of his sardonic wit. He certainly had the fastest brain of anyone I've ever met. As it turned out later, he was a man of many talents and I don't mean a jack-of-all-trades. Whatever he took on, he made sure that he was simply good at it. Gardener, aviculturist, interior decorator, painter, writer and actor. I promised to keep him posted with developments and we would meet again as soon as he returned to Europe.

I contacted Hugh French, the agent, a true Hollywood Brit, about Richard Burton to play the priest, Father Keogh. He was interested but everything depended on the script. Then Hugh suggested Nigel Balchin to write it. Apart from the success of his books he had written some good screenplays. He had recently extricated himself from the complications of *Cleopatra* and several other writers and directors. I cabled

Earl, who was delighted – provided the price was right, of course.

I spent far too much time in Hollywood following up star actors, most of whom were wrong for the part and anyone who was right for it was not available. After reading the book Burton suggested that he would be better for the bandit than the priest. Of course he was right but that part was not available. There was no question of persuading Dirk to change over to the part of the priest.

I enjoyed a talk with Sol Siegel who was now in charge of production at MGM. I also called on Lew Schreiber at Fox, who insisted that I come to lunch. He mentioned that only a short while ago he had contacted Rank in London to ask about my availability to direct, but was told that I was not free. This must have been the work of JD or Earl. Pity they didn't accept it: it would have increased my prestige and therefore my value to the company. It was disappointing, but it was gratifying to know Fox were still interested in me.

Returning to Pinewood, I spent two days reporting progress – such as it was. Then off again to stay with Balchin at his villa in Tuscany, just outside Florence. Discussions went well and two or three more of these trips were necessary because Nigel was a tax exile. Certainly, that was no hardship. When Dirk came back to Europe, indeed to Rome, the three of us met there to talk over script, which went happily enough.

As soon as we had a semi-final script, casting could start. Earl was in favour of John Mills for the priest, to which I had no objection at all. However I did hanker after trying to get Paul Scofield, although I had no hope that he would want to do it; Earl wouldn't have it anyway, so the approach was never made. Dirk had already said to me that he did not want to see John Mills as the priest. Earl dismissed this out of hand. I thought they were supposed to be bending over backwards to please Dirk.

What Dirk had against Johnnie he never explained. As far as I know, they had never played together. Whatever personal reasons there may have been for this attitude, Johnny is a scrupulously professional actor of vast experience and has been a star since the early thirties. Later, when I told Dirk that Johnny had agreed to appear, Dirk declared, 'I promise you, if Johnny plays the priest I will make life unbearable for everyone concerned.'

Well, he was as good as his word and he succeeded. There is nothing more to be said on that score. It was also clear that whatever we did and whatever the outcome of this picture, nothing would induce Dirk to continue with the Rank Organisation, so from that point of view the whole operation was a waste of time.

Johnny naturally turned in a fine performance despite the difficulties. He bore no animosity toward Dirk, but he certainly thought his behaviour was strange. Of course there were irritations which came about in the natural order of things and couldn't be helped: for instance, Sir John was a polo player and rode very well, whereas Dirk didn't; riding was not one of Sir Dirk's many talents.

Incidentally, not in connection with the above, I have long thought that all actors should be competent riders, able to drive a car, swim, dance a few steps, sing a few notes, play a ball game and handle a gun as if it belongs to them. Not a lot to ask; most people can do all these things. Surprisingly, too many actors are deficient in these abilities. Tap-dancing and skating would come as optional extras.

Another of my difficulties was with the Catholic Information Office whose co-operation I needed for procedures, costuming, etc. They tried hard indeed to be helpful but were anxious to discuss every smallest detail of the script at length, including the moral values involved. We had deviated hardly at all from the original book, but parsing the script took a lot of time, especially when we came to what became known as 'the scene in which the priest kisses the girl'. In fact he doesn't: the girl kisses him and he doesn't respond. The author also took a hand in this declaring that this incident was not in the book. But it is. In fact the girl does it twice in my copy of the 3rd edition reprint, pages 339 and 347. So that is what the girl does in the film. When we shot this scene I prohibited the taking of any stills, much to the dismay of the publicity department. I felt sure that the distribution of such a photograph, divorced from the context of the film, would give a wrong impression.

Most of the film was to be shot in Spain, so there was a long-drawn out flamenco with the censor's office in Madrid. General Franco was still in charge. Jack Hanbury did excellent diplomatic work, together with Mr Sargison, who was Rank's Man in Madrid.

I must also mention another great supporter in all this turmoil: the excellent lighting cameraman Otto Heller. He had a magical control over colour values, in the customary changing conditions. He had a large box full of gadgets which he kept exclusively to himself. No one was allowed to poke his nose into it. He would surreptitiously slip filters into the matte box on the camera; sometimes his own crew didn't know what he was doing. He was a wizard. We were shooting in Eastmancolor and the obligatory CinemaScope. The result was first class.

As we went struggling on I became more and more convinced that this picture would be a turkey. I remembered Brian Desmond Hurst, when he was making a right corker. I asked him how it was going and he said cheerfully, 'Oh it's a bag of shit – but it's going to be the most beautiful bag of shit ever made'. So I resolved to do all I could to make the thing look good. Indeed, when I showed the final cut to JD he said, 'I'm not sure what it is, but it is certainly beautiful.'

Well, the critics had a field day. They tore the picture to pieces, every one of them. They all had a go at Dirk for wearing tight-fitting black leather trousers. It never struck me that there was anything special about these trousers; after all, Hardy Kruger had worn black leather trousers as part of Luftwaffe uniform in *The One That Got Away*. They really got carried away. David Lewin of the *Daily Express* called in somebody called Clancy Segal, not one of his staff men, just to review this one film. To take that sort of action Lewin surely must have had some prior information about the film. Somewhat odd, that.

The *Times* man, anonymous, had a go at me, demanding 'What can you expect of a man who could cast Marilyn Monroe as a psychopathic baby-sitter?' That one must be laid at the door of Zanuck or more likely Joe Schenk. I wrote to the editor and got the usual 'lack of space' letter. I don't know why I bothered. The irony of the whole affair is that I didn't like the damned film either.

Forget it. There is no redress for this sort of thing. They threw the book at the film and at me, wrecking a promising career. My self-confidence was severely dented and it took me four years to get myself back on an even keel. I have never to this day fully regained the professional status I had at that time – which, I will say, was merited.

I thank my stars about one thing. Just before the film was to be released the BBC ran a short series of half-hour profiles of contemporary film directors. I was invited to be one of them. All went well until near the end of it when the interviewer asked about *The Singer Not the Song*. I had no intention of putting in a puff for the film: I merely said that it was now finished, it would be released soon and the verdict lay with the audience. If I had tried to boost it I would have looked very silly in a few weeks time. Television is a licence to make a complete ass of yourself in three short minutes. Incidentally, I discovered the impact television exercised even in those early days. I received a couple of dozen letters from friends and colleagues. (They liked it.)

A further irony was this: *The Singer* has taken over four times as much money overseas as it did in the UK. After 23 years on release it came into profit and is still paying royalties – to me, as the producer – after 36 years. So some people must like it, which is some consolation. When it was shown during the retrospective at Dinard I refused to introduce it to the audience, who loved it. I loathe it and couldn't bear to see it again. The simple truth is that I should never have allowed myself to be manoeuvred into a position from which there was no escape. I hadn't learned to protect myself in the clinches.

When the balloon went up, or rather came down with a bump, I was in the middle of shooting *Flame in the Streets*, which helped to take my mind off my troubles. This was a play by Ted Willis called *Hot Summer Night*, and he wrote the script. It was set in the present day, 1960, in somewhere like Ladbroke Grove/Notting Hill. Sylvia Syms plays a blonde schoolteacher who falls in love with a visiting supply teacher from the Caribbean, played by Johnny Sekka. They decide they want to marry. Johnny Mills was the girl's father, completely absorbed in his work as convenor of the local carpenter's union; he was dedicated as usual and revelled in the character. Sylvia was utterly sincere and not just pretty – truly a beautiful woman is more like it. Also a proper actress who has never had the recognition she fully merits. She was under contract to ABPC, who loaned her out to us, charging a fortune for her and paying her a pittance. Pinewood was new to her and she was uncomfortable for a day or two but we quickly got on terms and all was plain sailing. She is a darling. We met again later but I wish we had made more pictures together.

Brenda de Banzie was the mother. I never found out why, but it seemed she was disliked by many of her profession. She was condescending sometimes and looked down her nose rather a lot, but as far as I was concerned she played beautifully all through, and in particular she had one set-piece scene which she carried off exquisitely. At the end of it you could have heard a pin drop in that studio. Superb.

Ann Lynn gave excellent support as a girl who has married into the black community showing the problems she and her husband, played by Earl Cameron, both had to face. Earl is a nice man and was a great help to me, advising me on social customs. The film shows a true picture of life as it was in that community at that time. Vetchinsky and his set dresser Arthur Taksen provided settings that were absolutely true to life. The proof of this appeared only a few months ago, at the Black Film Festival at the Ritzy in Brixton. The festival was to mark the 50th anniversary of the arrival in Britain of the steamer Windrush, bringing Caribbeans to work here. The audience was entirely Caribbean and they were extremely complimentary. Some of the older ones testified that it was a true picture of the conditions the incomers faced and in some areas they still do face.

I had two other interesting projects in development at that time. Graham Greene's book *England Made Me* was an intriguing story about a brother and sister, for which ideal casting would have been Dirk Bogarde and Jean Simmons. A meeting with Mr Greene over dinner was arranged by a mutual friend, the producer John Stafford. It all came to nothing. I wondered why Mr Greene had bothered to come, since he hardly listened to what I had to say. He spent most of the time regaling John with the story of his recent trip abroad and a couple of remarkable brothels he had discovered. One woman was exceptional: apparently she could keep it going all day. What – no lunch break? I had nothing to contribute to this conversation, so I nodded politely from time to time and can't remember a word of it.

The other interesting aspect of this venture came when I was discussing casting with Mr Greene's agent, who warned me that I should be aware of a condition in the contract for the script, which was that the sister must be played by Miss Anita Bjork, a Norwegian actress, otherwise there would be no deal. Farcical.

Another proposal was on the tapis at this time: I had persuaded Kingsley Amis to write a film treatment of his *Take A Girl Like You*. Now here was a really stimulating author to work with, an absolute joy. We got on like a house on fire. I was particularly intrigued by this relationship. Kingsley was only five or six years younger than me, but our outlooks were different. The basics were exactly the same but the angle of view was different. I concluded that Kingsley was clearly a post-war man, whereas I am a pre-war man. A good combination, I thought.

One small incident – or accident – sticks in my mind. Kingsley and I had lunch at the Caprice and were walking up Arlington Street toward Piccadilly, which took us past the door of the Ritz. The tall, imposing linkman saluted me smartly and said, 'Good afternoon, Mr Baker'. I promise you, I hadn't arranged this. We exchanged greetings, and passed grandly on. I was at fault, because I couldn't remember the man at all. Kingsley wrote two treatments of the book, or rather a treatment and a revision of it, but Earl wouldn't go any farther; perhaps he couldn't anyhow.

John Davis had now – February 1961 – decided to give up film production. Bowling alleys and bingo halls were to be the main interest. Some time later Xerox came along, saving JD's bacon and the Rank Org's eggs and that was the end of regular, consistent film production in this country. Falling attendances and the rise of television were the reasons given.

The demise of Rank production was not mourned by everyone, however. The attitude of the liberal arts establishment to the Rank Organisation had always been one of lofty contempt. Politically, there was justifiable criticism of the so-called duopoly, which was the word for the system run by Rank and ABPC, each of whom controlled means of production, distribution and exhibition. This gave them almost complete power over UK releases, which they should have exercised with greater flexibility and discretion. Both distribution and exhibition had got themselves tied in with American companies and far too many weeks in the year were set aside for their product. Wait 'til I tell you about my picture *Two Left Feet*. However, I for one – and I may be the only one – cannot see any other system working in this country to the greater advantage of either the producers, the distributors or the exhibitors. The UK is too small to be a workable territory without mutual support between all three branches, but there was little love lost between Rank production and the other two. They had a low opinion of our work in general and their efforts to promote our films were poor. They issued the usual Rank poster, ran the trade show and set up the London premiere, the latter being regarded as a waste of time and money, held simply to indulge the egos of those maniacs at Pinewood. They didn't release the films, they allowed them to escape.

I am haunted by a scene described to me by my father. Through his friendship with somebody at Warner Bros' London office he was invited to a private showing of one of their films. This was in the early thirties, in a small theatre and the representatives of the Warner sales force were the audience. The show was run by one Jimmy Bryson, the manager of the outfit. He opened the proceedings with a short pitch about the film they were going to see, full of promise and excitement. About half way through the second reel he jumped up in front of the screen waving his arms madly, shouting 'Stop the picture! Stop the picture!' He then harangued the audience: 'Did you see that? Did you see that great scene? This lovely girl – she loves him, she's crazy for him but he can't see it and she knows the mob is going to kill him. We've got to tell the people this is one movie they can't miss – you've got these great stars...' and so on. The film continued with further interruptions but when the lights went up at the end, all those salesmen were fired up with enthusiasm, determined to do their utmost for the picture. This was my father's dictum: you've got to sell the product to the salesmen before you try to sell it to the buyer.

ABPC's production effort was desultory, to say the best of it. Rank made more films which, it was said, were dull, unenterprising, unadventurous, boring. I have noted the changes in taste that were taking place in 1954/1956 and although the reaction to them was not fast enough, there was some broadening of the horizons. The range of stories was widened and much bigger budgets were sanctioned. Still there was not enough imagination at the top and a reluctance to take risks, not only with money, but with audience appeal as well. Anything remotely controversial was a non-starter. By the time we come to the Swinging Sixties, the battle was lost. John Davis retired hurt, everyone's contract ran out and Earl St John um'd and ah'd until James Bond came to save Pinewood from extinction.

There were a number of stunning films being made during the new period and Rank – JD and Earl – should have been persuading independent producers and directors to come under the Rank umbrella, offering a large proportion of their budget, facilities at Pinewood, distribution, exhibition – the whole package. At that time they still had a lot to offer. It could have been an arm's length arrangement, to preserve the Org's attitude to controversy, if that were ever necessary. True, some of the independents were reluctant to risk the Rank embrace and could find support elsewhere anyway. On the other hand there were several big hits that Rank are known to have turned down.

Leaving Pinewood I was floundering and soon found myself in a choppy sea, commander of *The Valiant*. This film had a number of good points: the cast, led by John Mills and Robert Shaw, and the screenplay by Keith Waterhouse and Willis Hall. But it was based on a dubious French play which described the adventures of two Italian frogmen during the war and their treatment as POWs when captured by the Royal Navy. It was dodgy and we should never have made it. It was an Anglo-Italian production and the location facilities in Italy were lamentably insufficient. The necessary battleship was a rusting hulk in dry dock and I could only shoot on a section of one side of it. The Royal Marines Band as presented by the local talent in Taranto was hilarious, but not a bit funny at the time. Despite everyone's noblest efforts, it was a turkey.

Another one of Clarence Paget's publications intrigued me and I wrote a script on it; *In My Solitude* by David Stuart Leslie. I called it *Two Left Feet*, forgetting that PG Wodehouse had already used the title. It was a good title for the story and in the end I stuck to it. It was a simple comedy of teenaged boys having trouble with girls – and *vice versa*, come to that. The setting was bang up to date London in 1962. I took it to British Lion: David Kingsley, John and Roy Boulting, Frank Launder and Sydney Gilliatt. All dyed-in-the-wool filmmakers of long experience. What a pleasure it was to be with proper people all talking the same language. They were cautious but after long discussions they liked it and agreed to set it up. Leslie Gilliatt agreed to produce. The script needed some work so I roped in John Hopkins, who straightened out the construction, shortened it and gave it a fine polish.

Just when we were all set to start serious preparation, casting and so on, there was a hitch. I can't remember what the problem was, probably studio space, but we had to postpone shooting for six months. The picture would not now be shown until the next year and I was afraid that by that time it would no longer be topical. Also I knew there were other people in the field with pictures about young people in the sixties. If I had been really brave I would have suggested abandoning the project, but I wasn't and we waited.

When at last it came to casting we laid down one qualification: everyone must be under 21. This we achieved with only one exception and that one was only three or four years over the limit and didn't look it. It wasn't as easy then as it is now to gather a cast of young people who can play their parts well; in either case they will lack experience. This cast turned out to be one of the best I've ever had: Michael Crawford, Nyree Dawn Porter, Julia Foster, David Hemmings and Deborah Watling. They were all terrific and the picture turned out well. At least, I thought so, especially at a sneak preview one evening at a cinema in King's Cross. The audience laughed their heads off. There was no prior publicity or advertising to guide them and they had probably never seen any of the actors before. However, the circuit bookers who had been present throughout took no notice of the audience reaction. They turned us down. No general – or even limited – release for this film.

Thus I learned that so many weeks in next year's schedule were already allocated. Also we had no star names. Furthermore the censor, the egregious John Trevelyan, had barged in again and insisted on an X certificate. In those days the circuits would not show an X picture during the school holidays, which ruled out at least twelve of the remaining weeks. After a lot of pleading and bargaining by Frank and Sydney and the Boultings we were given a very limited showing in a double bill shared with another film none of us had ever heard of.

Harold Wilson was President of the Board of Trade in the post-war Labour government. He took a keen interest in British films and was instrumental in setting up the National Film Finance Corporation as a form of loan bank to prime the pump of film production. Here is an extract from a speech he made in 1949:

'I start from the proposition that all film finance whether private or through NFFC depends ultimately not only on production and distribution guarantees, but, so far as the end money is concerned, on a guarantee or high prospect of circuit release. The decision on a film's prospect of circuit release is taken in effect by two men – the appropriate authorities for the Gaumont-Odeon circuits and the ABC circuits respectively. However much work NFFC may do on the financial standing or even the quality and prospects of scripts etc, in the last resort their action is largely conditioned by the decision of one or both of these two gentlemen.

'These two are therefore dictators in the matter of deciding which films are made and by whom; the whole prosperity and also reputation and prestige of British films therefore depends on their judgement. As the department responsible for films most of the effectiveness of our long term policy in the end depends on the rightness and wrongness of their decisions. There is the additional argument that on the general question of censorship I am not satisfied that the decision as to which films are made should rest in the hands of two irresponsible Eastern autocrats. I am also pretty well convinced that in the case of one of them the decisions taken are made on the personal likes and dislikes of individual producers. You and I have heard statements by authoritative people in the industry on this point. One possible and radical solution would be to bust up the circuits. This may come in the fullness of time.

I hope it will, but I do not consider it a likely development in the immediate future and although I think we should keep it in our minds as a long term objective I am not sure that we ought to pursue as it as national policy in the months that lie immediately ahead. Apart from anything else some proportion of the losses on production are still being made up by circuit profits and to bust up the circuits or to divorce them from production (as in America) might lead to a drying up of such sources of finance as are at present available. But the time has come when we cannot allow national film policy, economically, morally or artistically to be dictated by these two Oriental potentates. The power of the circuits must be broken, or at least severely limited. This is not an undue interference with private enterprise or the rights of shareholders. Individual shareholders, I suspect, have no control whatsoever on at least one of the two gentlemen to whom I have referred, and in any case once a private undertaking has reached the size of these organisations and has assumed power of a quasi-monopolistic character, it is quite appropriate that that power, if the state permits it to be continued to be exercised, should be circumscribed by such safeguards for the public interest as the state may decide.'

I have taken this quotation in full from the Journal of ACCT. It is a clear statement of the position of the circuits; it is also clear that there seemed to be no solution to the problem. Nationalisation surely wouldn't have worked. In almost 50 years since then the circuit organisations have become more complex but they remain at the heart of any proposal for the promotion of film production. There are many more overseas markets now open to producers, TV, video and all, but a sound domestic cinema market is still essential to a healthy film industry. It leads all the other markets. In 1997 we were told that since 1994 70 British films have failed to find a circuit release. In the coming year, 1998, a further 150 films would also seek release. A daunting prospect. I still happily remember that audience in the cinema at King's Cross. Listening to a crowd laughing at one's jokes is a great experience. Some years later the film had one good outing. It was included in a series of *Films of the Sixties* on BBC 2.

So I was at a loose end, a decidedly loose end. After diving in at the deep end I confess to feeling a little bit tired as I walked slowly up the steps at the shallow end. Then a new approach came from an unexpected quarter, which resulted in five years of frenzied activity.

TELEVISION

FEEDING THE MONSTER

The television companies were beginning to realise that something must be done to provide the huge quantity of material they required. Good news for the production side. Filming motion picture-style was the chosen medium; for one thing, it gives flexibility in foreign markets which have differing technical standards. American television would only accept a 35mm negative. Lew Grade was the man of the hour – and of the half hour, as well. He embarked on a massive production effort, sometimes with five or more series shooting simultaneously. One of the first shows in work was *The Saint*, produced by Robert S Baker and Monty Berman at Elstree Studios. They offered me a script and it turned out to be quite a challenge. The daily screen time had to be six minutes or more, but as the scripts became more elaborate the schedules were lengthened. Even so, the screen time was over five minutes a day. The photography was black and white, shooting almost everything in studio built sets or on the back lot; rarely on location except for run-bys and long shots with doubles.

It wasn't as difficult as it seemed. The organisation behind it all was superb. It started as always with the scripts, which were usually available in good time before shooting and were tailored to revamps of the existing studio sets. They were also carefully timed to run the statutory 54min 20sec for a one hour presentation. At the end of each scene its estimated running time was shown in brackets. In those early days all the writers were long experienced professionals who handled these strictures well, but latterly I have had two or three scripts which would have run ninety minutes or more. Will you pass me that blue pencil, please? There were occasional hiccups but generally the whole thing ran on wheels. However, all this rigidly controlled super-production meant that there wasn't much a director could contribute. I kept up my interest by concentrating on the supporting actors, which did some good I think.

Television requires a high number of set-ups because the audience's eye tires easily and the attention span is short, compared to a big screen cinema presentation, where a long shot may be held for some time. With an eight day schedule it was hard enough to get adequate coverage. Finding time for rehearsals was even more difficult.

This was the first time I had ever bothered about the schedule. The fact is, every script dictates its own schedule and any production manager will forecast the shooting period with common sense. If that produces a schedule which is too long for the budget, you either increase the budget or re-write some part of the script. In most cases the script will turn out to be over length anyway. Sadly, few people are prepared to abide by the old adage – When in doubt, cut it out.

In my earlier days as a director I indulged myself in the affectation of not wearing a watch; in truth, the one I had wasn't reliable. I had damaged it when learning to ride a motorcycle during the war. So I would leave it to the first assistant to keep an eye on progress and tell me occasionally if we were ahead or behind. My own instinct was usually right. Suddenly a body blow came when the union reduced the working day. Instead of wrapping up at 5.50 pm we must now stop at 5.20 pm. Thirty minutes meant losing one set-up, possibly two, probably a dozen over an eight day schedule. In television, set-ups are vital; you cannot hold two pages of dialogue in a Tom Walls tight 15. It may be that the producers were compelled by reasons of their own to accept this diktat; I doubt anybody consulted the directors about it. Nobody would have listened to them if they had. The union looked on directors as just another form of technician and for that reason insisted on them being members of the union.

Up to this time zoom lenses were poor and could only be used for sports events and sometimes for the occasional crash zoom for effect. Monty Berman, being a cameraman himself, discovered a much improved zoom lens and was one of the first to introduce it. It was accepted with reluctance by the cameramen; admittedly it had been improved but it was still not as good as prime lenses. There were considerable benefits, which I for one soon discovered – albeit with certain provisos. It should never be used for zooming, except for the occasional crash effect as before. It should always be used in combination with a tracking or crane movement, a panning shot or bold movement of actors. The object is to disguise the zoom movement which will be all the more effective. A zoom movement on its own simply brings the picture closer to the viewer or makes it recede from him. There is no feeling of the viewer moving into or out of the scene, or going along with it. If you carry two characters walking along a corridor, they will appear to be running on the spot while the setting moves away from them.

In the case of *The Saint*, there was one other important factor: Roger Moore. He fitted the part perfectly, indeed he made the character entirely his own, but on top of that his enthusiasm and drive were infectious. He was the first one in the studio in the morning and often the last to leave at night. His sense of humour never failed. Superficially, it looked as if he never took any of it seriously, but this was professionalism made to look unprofessional, the object being to achieve a lighthearted style which was one of the most attractive and entertaining aspects of the series, contributing greatly to its success.

He is an extraordinarily quick study, taking in a page or two of dialogue at a glance. I asked him how he did it. He said airily, 'Oh I don't learn it. I just listen to the other actors and my words come automatically.' Hm. He makes it sound so easy.

Yet there is more to it than that: '...listen to the other actors...' Sometimes, in a group scene with three or four actors, it can be seen that one of them may be talking but the others are not listening to him; they look like they are simply waiting until it's their turn to speak. This is slovenly acting. Cutting away from the speaker to the listener to show his reaction enhances the effect of the scene enormously. Roger understands the value of all this and he is a good actor, yet he must not be described as an actor – he will deny it. 'No no, don't know a thing about it, acting'. Nearly all of the *Saint* stories featured a damsel in distress who told her troubles to him. Roger, listening sympathetically and faintly sceptically, was fascinating.

After a long and productive stint shooting features at Beaconsfield, in partnership with Leslie Parkyn, Julian Wintle took the plunge into filmed TV. He surfaced at Elstree with a series about a psychiatrist: *The Human Jungle*. Herbert Lom played the lead, with reams of dialogue to spout as he analysed the mental problems of each patient. He said once that when he went out to dinner and the waiter handed him the menu he started to learn it by heart. Julian found some good stories and as usual he provided excellent casts, always with a star in the central part. Flora Robson, Margaret Lockwood, Rita Tushingham and more besides.

Gideon's Way was another of the earlier series. John Gregson played the lead in a string of John Creasey's Scotland Yard stories, again notable for good scripts and strong casts. George Cole turned up in one of them, playing an arsonist. I hadn't seen him since *Morning Departure*.

There were a lot of fads and fancies around at this time. The most popular was called deep foreground, which meant shooting past a pot of flowers or a lamp. In the dear old days before the war this was known as a jingleberry, the idea being to give depth to the picture, or as it is still used, to blot out a hot sky. In *The Avengers* it was regarded as essential to every set-up. Wait long enough and fashion comes round again.

Julian had brought in this most intriguing series. The original – wildly successful – videotaped television programme starring Patrick Macnee and Honor Blackman was now to be shot on film. Diana Rigg replaced Honor as Pat's sidekick. The stories took place in limbo, a constructed myth in a fantasy land, and yet they looked entirely real, if not realistic. It was the rule that Steed and Mrs Peel should never be seen with real-life characters, the ideal being, for instance, a shot of the Houses of Parliament with the two of them walking by, but no other person in the shot. The settings were odd: one was an enormous country house, owned by a Dickens fanatic, so the place was crowded with Dickensiana – so, for a Christmas party, all the actors were dressed as characters from Dickens. Another story was set in a huge modern comprehensive school during the holidays, so there were no children about. This we shot at an abandoned airfield in Norfolk.

The design of Diana Rigg's clothes was based in each episode on the theme and settings of the particular story. So in the school one she turned out in a dark blue frock with a very short skirt which looked like a gym-slip, black stockings and a pair of gold-rimmed granny specs. Needless to say, she looked stunning. Rising to the occasion I photographed this vision in full-length figure and in big close-up to show the specs. I got into some trouble for this. The first mini skirt to be shown on the world's screens! Shocking! The full-length shot was out and the close-up had to be retaken without the spectacles. Later on, doubts were expressed by higher authority that my stuff wasn't sexy enough. There are times when you don't know where you are.

Some of the scenes were quite jokey – one had Diana Rigg playing the tuba. I placed a proper tuba player at the side of the set where he could watch as Diana fingered the valves and he sounded the appropriate notes. Roughly.

My favourite episode was *The Girl From Auntie*. At the beginning of the story Mrs Peel is kidnapped at dawn as she leaves a fancy dress ball. She went as a bird, dressed in a white mesh body-stocking with a few tactically placed white feathers. Naturally the kidnapper keeps her in a large birdcage which he happens to have, he being an antique dealer on a big scale – busily negotiating the sale of the Eiffel Tower to an American collector, who wants it for an oil well. There is simply the tiresome problem of delivery to Texas.

Steed returns from a short holiday to find that Mrs Peel has disappeared. In her flat, in her place, there is another woman who announces herself as Mrs Peel. Steed knows she is an imposter but she is the best clue he has to tracing Mrs Peel. So, bewildered and yet frightened, she finds herself recruited into that part. It was a splendid part for Liz Fraser, who was funny and touching as needed.

Speaking as we were of muddled identities, there had been occasions of confusion around the studios and in the telephone and postal services during the last few years, because there were two Roy Bakers. One might well be enough. There was me, the director and there was the other one, the dubbing editor. I got letters and a few phone calls which were intended for him, not me. I passed them on. Then he decided to move house, which brought him into the same tax district as mine. My accountant was quite rattled, accusing me of concealing a second income, or at least, that's what the inspector had queried. It was annoying but it was soon explained and resolved. I suggested to my doppelgänger that a small change of name, perhaps inserting an initial, would avoid future confusion, but nothing was done. By this time I was again shooting *The Saint* and by accident Roger Moore took a hand.

The telephone on the studio stage was a magnet to him. If it rang when he was anywhere near it, he delighted in taking the call, politely taking messages, etc. I noticed him talking at length one day; once or twice he looked across the set at me. Then he came over and told me to expect a visitor, a lady. She was demanding to see me but she wouldn't give her name. Roger vaguely hinted that this might be a private matter; obviously it was none of his business. One of those eyebrows went up. I guessed there might be a leg-pull in here somewhere but I thought no more of it until later that afternoon when Roger appeared on the stage escorting an attractive lady. He guided her up to me with a benign smile. I had never seen her before. She looked at me and said, 'That's not him!' and turned on her heel.

This reminded me of a family joke beloved of one and all at 20th Century-Fox.

In the old days, when it was plain Fox Films, one Sol Wurzel was head of production. The Wurzels were a large family: the head of the carpentry shop was a Wurzel, another was head of transport – they were several more, all over the studio. The joke was at the expense of a new starlet on the lot who was anxious to advance her career in what was then and still is the usual way, stepping out with Mr Wurzel. After some time she began to worry. She was getting nowhere. At last she discovered why. She had been stepping out with the wrong Wurzel.

Among several more episodes of *The Saint* we did a two-parter, *The Fiction Makers*, which was shown as a feature film overseas but not in the UK. It had a brilliantly clever script by John Kruse and was a satire on the James Bond type of story. It was big in scope and ambitious beyond the budget and more especially the schedule. It was a two-hander with Sylvia Syms opposite Roger. Sylvia was perfect for her character: a world famous thriller writer. Sylvia is intelligent; apart from other qualities, she made you believe she could write. When she and Roger are on the screen the whole thing lights up. The supporting cast all did their best but in the face of a 20 day schedule for a film running one hour 42 minutes ... well, keeping up an average of more than five minutes a day for that length of time leaves no time at all to get everything right, really right, I mean. Like proper rehearsals. It is still a good film, but the ship was spoiled for a ha'porth of tar. It could have been better. But then, everything could, couldn't it?

The Baron starred Steve Forrest in the lead, who took one look at me and demanded to know the name of my tailor. He was a tall, square-jawed American gent who settled in happily with the Savile Row/Jermyn Street axis. The scripts were overseen and many were written by Terry Nation, who was famous for inventing the Daleks in the BBC's *Doctor Who*. *The Baron* was to be sponsored in the USA by a cigarette company. Therefore characters who smoked had to be carefully selected and they were allowed to light up only in moments of leisure, never when they were frightened or under any duress. Oh dear.

Stuart Damon, also from America, led the cast in *The Champions*, in which the heroes were endowed with superhuman physical prowess, overpowering all comers. This idea had been inspired by the sight of some prodigious feats at the Olympic Games, only more so.

If you remember the old parlour game of statues, you will see how the ghost of Kenneth Cope appeared in *Randall & Hopkirk (Deceased)*. When he was to materialise in a scene, the director called out 'Freeze!' and the actors all obediently froze, Kenneth jumped in on to his mark and the scene resumed. The frozen bit was then cut from the film. It was a jump cut, but it worked.

Thus five years rolled by and I had totted up 41 one hour episodes in seven different series. At this time, 1967, there were five different filmed television series in production. In one week I had availability enquiries from all five of them. A crowded week, that was.

HAMMER

QUATERMASS AND THE PIT

At the end of that same week Anthony Nelson Keys, a producer at Hammer Film Productions, asked me to direct *Quatermass and the Pit*.

Nigel Kneale had first written this as the third of his stories about Professor Quatermass, in six half-hour episodes for the BBC. It was enormously popular. He now boiled the script down from three hours to one-and-a-half. It was taut, exciting and an intriguing story with excellent narrative drive. It needed no work at all. All one had to do was cast it and shoot it. I met Tony Nelson Keys for preliminary talks at Bray Studios and all went well with him and with Anthony Hinds, the executive producer, but we were not going to shoot there. Hammer were moving their production work to Elstree. Our next meeting was at Hammer House in Wardour Street and this was another pleasant surprise: if you counted them all the entire operation was run by seven or eight people, including the charming telephone operator. Decisions were made swiftly and, well ... decisively – and they were adhered to. Some contrast with Pinewood and 20th.

I was delighted to be shooting a film again, working with a stimulating crew, all of them new to me, especially with such a promising script. Hammer had filmed the first two stories already and they had done well, despite the previous showings on TV. The luck continued when Elstree Studios blandly announced that they had no space for the picture. We had to go half a mile up the road to the MGM studio, which was better equipped, with a huge back lot, and no other picture shooting. Marvellous!

Arthur Grant, the lighting cameraman, was a treasure, with long experience of Hammer films, although this was a science-fiction story, not the usual horror. The art director was brilliant, Bernard Robinson, whose genius lay in conjuring up magnificent sets and then putting them up on un-magnificent budgets. The special effects played an important part in the film and Les Bowie, also a Hammer regular, rose to the occasion. We had a row at the beginning when Les wanted to run the pre-production conference because he thought the film was all special effects and nothing else. Having settled that, all went on smoothly. Bert Batt was my first assistant and he drove the shooting on at a good, steady hunting pace. He particularly gloried in managing the live effects on the sets and directing the crowds. He was a tremendous help.

Andrew Keir was certainly the best of the Quatermasses and was acknowledged as such by all and sundry. Thirty years later I was astounded to be told that he thought that I wanted Kenneth More for the part – quite untrue – and therefore paid no attention to him and was no help to him at all. I cannot imagine what got into him. I had no idea that he was unhappy while we were shooting. His performance was absolutely right in every detail and I was presenting him as the star of the picture. Perhaps I should have interfered more. James Donald and Barbara Shelley were outstanding. I had met Julian Glover previously on an episode of *The Avengers*. He turned in a tremendous character, forceful, autocratic but never over the top.

The confusion with the other Roy Baker was getting worse; he was now working at Hammer as a dubbing editor. I now made a rash and damaging decision. I decided to change my screen credit to Roy Ward Baker. I chose Ward because it was my mother's maiden name. I didn't stop to think that the reputation I had held in films five years ago would now go for nothing. Once again I underestimated the experience I had accumulated from 1946 to 1962, which undoubtedly had some value. At the press show of *Quatermass* one of the journalists, an old acquaintance, told me he was glad I had come in person because he had assumed from the titles that this Roy Ward Baker was a new director, who didn't want to conflict with me. Thirty years later I still find foreign critics who know me well as a Hammer director and are unaware of all the films I made prior to 1962.

Hammer was widely regarded by the UK public and the press as being a law unto itself, with its own audiences who rarely if ever read the film critics. *Quatermass* therefore received the usual cool reception here, but it was a big success elsewhere, especially in France and most continental countries – and in the United States. A group of French critics included it in their list of the ten best sci-fi films of all time.

Bette Davis was once again in London, to do a picture for Hammer at Elstree. She was due to star as a one-eyed harridan in *The Anniversary*. We had dinner soon after she arrived, but straight away she was busy on the film, and we had no further contact. After *Quatermass* I had returned to TV episodes, as before at Elstree. I heard some studio gossip that progress on Bette's picture was slow and troubled, but I took no notice. I had just finished editing my episode and I was surprised when producer Jimmy Sangster asked me to read the script of *The Anniversary*. He had abandoned shooting and wanted me to take over.

Jimmy was the producer and had written the script from the stage play by William McIlwraith, which had had a successful run in the West End. It was a good script. Jimmy had opened it out from the confines of the theatre in a few places where it was reasonable to do so, but otherwise had left it alone. He is a most likeable man of great good sense, with a quick mind which goes straight to the heart of things with admirable simplicity. And of course it was a vehicle for Bette.

I did not at all like the idea of taking over someone else's picture. I did like the idea of doing a film with Bette for all the obvious reasons, beside which we had been friends for 15 years. Today was Thursday and the suggestion was to start again the following Monday. Not much time to decide. I agreed with Jimmy and we talked about the practical aspects. I proposed that I should not use any of the material they had already shot and I didn't want to see it. There wasn't much of it anyway. The sets were all standing and fully dressed, so we walked round them. They were perfect in style and atmosphere, hitting the right note exactly. I made a rough check of the layout of the scenes and I suggested some alterations to fit in as I envisaged the staging of the scenes. The art director was Reece Pemberton, an eminent set designer in the theatre. He agreed and the necessary work could be done over the weekend. I didn't see any need for revisions in the script or in the cast, which was excellent. Several of the actors had been in the play.

Monday morning came and we all met together for the first time. I had spoken to Bette on the phone over the weekend and she was happy. The other actors were in a worrying position, and I had great sympathy for them. None of them had ever worked with me before. They had all got their characters keyed and were understandably worried that a new director might demand some fresh approach. Once an actor fixes a character it is difficult to revise it. They were all standing in a group on the set, looking slightly doubtful. Bette stepped forward and addressed me in the old Hollywood tradition: 'Good morning, Mr Baker.' Then she said with a sweet smile and one wide-open eye: 'Here we are. Please tell us what you want us to do.'

The essence of the story was that the mother was the central character who dominated her family ruthlessly. It had occurred to me that there was the possibility that the balance of the story had changed somewhat, possibly during the run of the play, so that the family had come to dominate the mother, rather than the other way round. The mother was the star part and it must be played to the full by Bette. It was also clear that whatever she did would be valueless unless the family played against her with complete commitment and energy. We would simply have no story and no film, which, by the way, was meant to be funny. Therefore they could each expect the fullest support from me and each character would get full coverage as it was properly required in each scene. One by one, during the next few days, I managed to allay some of the worst fears in the other actors and developed a guarded sort of trust between us.

Harry Waxman was the lighting cameraman and the shooting went smoothly. Since all the sets were up we were able to shoot through the script in continuity, which is a rare luxury. I was lucky to have Bert Batt again as first assistant, though Bert wasn't so happy. There was nothing for him to do. There were no crowds, no special effects, no fun at all for Bert. Still he did his best, which in his case is always excellent. In the end it was a popular film and no one had much to grumble about, but I'm not sure I got as much sparkle into it as I'd hoped.

Jimmy Sangster had written scripts based on two of his novels and the American ABC-TV wanted them for their *Movie of the Week* programme. They were Cold War spy stories: *private i* or, in the US *The Spy Killer*; and *Foreign Exchange*. The bright idea was that both had the same three leading characters. Several of the sets and locations also featured in both. Therefore we could shoot both films simultaneously. Believe it or not, it worked well. Robert Horton played the private detective and very well he did it. He was as good as gold and we got on famously. He was extremely careful of his appearance, always wearing beautifully cut suits, shirts and immaculately polished shoes. Rather different from the character as written.

In the first scene we discover our hero in his dingy office in a sleazy back street in Soho. He is unshaven and is using a pair of nail scissors to trim the fraying cuffs of his shirt. He is slovenly and lazy and it appears later that he only comes to life when his back is right against the wall, in imminent danger of his life. Then suddenly he is artful and deadly clever, scrambling out of the predicament, driven by sheer terror. He alternates wildly from being broke, most of the time, to being in the money, rarely. One of the virtues of such a vulnerable character is the suspense whenever he blunders into a dangerous situation. If one has a self-assured, confident hero the audience knows he will get out of anything; the only interest is in how he will escape. There can be no doubt that he will. With our character it's not only how he may give the villains the slip, but also if he will survive at all.

Quite a predicament for Jimmy and me, especially because we knew there was no way out of it. ABC-TV had chosen Robert, he was here, ready to shoot. Of course Robert worked willingly and well, being a genuine professional. He is an honest actor but if he had tried with all the will in the world to play it the other way, I believe the result would not have carried conviction. He would have been playing a part. ABC were well pleased with the resulting films, so there we are. Now and then I think wistfully of that other character. That's showbusiness and that is truly what it is.

Sebastian Cabot was a first rate British spymaster. We also had Jill St John: beautiful, with the proper kind of discreet but devastating sex appeal. She was professional, efficient and one of the most completely self-contained women I have ever met. I don't mean cold, not that at all, but utterly independent. She had many friends in high places. Certainly she always travelled first class. Any old hotel provided for her by the production company was never considered. She put up at Claridges and the company paid the bill. Where else, my dear?

One day she was being interviewed by an American journalist on the set and I was sitting close by.

Journalist: I believe you are a collector, of antiques?

Jill: Yes, that's so.

Journalist: Jewellery ... and Faberge?

Jill: I have some pieces, yes.

Journalist: You live in an apartment ... do you worry at all about thieves, break-ins?

Jill: Not at all. I keep everything at the bank.

Journalist: Oh ... don't you wish you had the things around you ... to enjoy?

Jill: I go down to the bank sometimes, to look.

Journalist: Don't you ever want to bring anything away?

Jill: No.

She was absolutely charming and a big asset to the enterprise.

HAMMER IN SPACE

The exploration of space began with Gagarin's orbit of the Earth in 1961 and there was intense activity every year after. Three Americans took a space craft in an orbit around behind the Moon in 1968 and a landing on the Moon looked imminent. In fact that took place in the following year. So the prospect seemed good for a story about the Moon being established as a colony of Earth. Michael Carreras found a story by Gavin Lyall, Frank Hardman and Martin Davison and wrote a script from it, which was called *Moon Zero Two*. The style was a skit on the old-time Western, with all the action taking place on the Moon. Ever since Georges Meliés there have been many stories staged in space or on the Moon, all done with the help of cartoons, puppets, miniatures and the like, but the first attempt to deal seriously with the realities was Stanley Kubrick's *2001*, written with Arthur C Clarke. The difficulties are immense, especially if you want to show people actually living and working on the Moon. Gravity is one-sixth of its value on Earth, there is no atmosphere and the night-time temperatures are sub-sub-zero. Therefore the only place to do it properly is on the Moon. Ha ha ha.

Stanley Kubrick was at the MGM studio. He was coming to the end of shooting *2001*. I went to see him and he spoke freely about the space problems. It was his habit to take a set of Polaroid pictures of every set-up. He showed me several large albums of these stills. He also gave me some good advice. He said he had tried everything and found that there is only one way to shoot an actor floating in space: he must be suspended from the roof of the studio and the camera must be placed immediately underneath him, pointing straight up. In that way the wire is behind the actor and can never be seen. He was right.

Back in 1968 everyone concerned with *Moon Zero Two* must be forgiven for any shortcomings in the film. I don't think any one of us fully realised the problems we faced until we were in it up to the neck. I'm sure I didn't. The special effects facilities available at that time were hopelessly inadequate for the demands of the action. Nowadays people can be shown floating weightlessly, making great 30 foot leaps: we thought of using acrobats jumping along a series of trampolines, but it wouldn't work. There was never enough space in the studio: we discussed the idea of using an old airship hangar, but it would have required several acres of black velvet to line it. There was no end to the harum-scarum ideas we mooted. One has only to consider the enormous effort that went into making Superman fly, which took about six months, with a huge crew setting up dozens of experiments. That sort of thing was far beyond our resources. We had difficulty with the simplest problems, for instance, flying Bernard Breslaw on a Kirby wire. It was physically risky and required an extra thick wire, which made it all the more difficult to lose the wire. Paul Beeson was the cameraman – and he is a master of photographic technique. He tried everything, experimenting all the time and with some success. He tried several different kinds of paint to disguise the wires. In case any one wants to know, the most effective was called 'Opaque', which was used for retouching black-and-white stills. Much much later, in 1997, *Quatermass and the Pit* was prepared in Hollywood for release on laserdisc and DVD and all the wires which can be seen in the original copy were carefully removed by Mr William Lustig and his blessed computers. The result is stunning.

When I read of the budgets of space adventure films today I realise that our budget would have been good for about two minutes screen time. It was truly hard and frustrating work and so much time was spent on solving the production problems that not enough attention was paid to the characters or the story. We turned out a reasonably entertaining picture, but it didn't realise our ambitions for it and never could have done, under the circumstances of those days. In any case people were now watching the real thing on their television screens.

HAMMER ON EARTH

Moon Zero Two was the third of the pictures I directed for Hammer but none of them were in the Hammer horror tradition. I was now to make three more which were. I was moving into a style which was new to me. It was a special style, which many people have found hard to define and many imitators have failed to capture, especially when they mount it on a much larger scale.

The first of these was *The Vampire Lovers*. It was based on *Carmilla*, a story by Sheridan Le Fanu. I had a vague memory of reading it when I was in my teens. The producers, Harry Fine and Michael Style, were fired with enthusiasm for the script which Tudor Gates had written, the splendid settings and a great part for the woman who was to play Carmilla. It gradually became apparent that they were even more excited by the possibilities generated by having female vampires and claimed they had uncovered an underlying theme in the original story, which Le Fanu had either discreetly suppressed or perhaps didn't even realise was there. By tradition, when a vampire bites someone, the victim automatically becomes a vampire too. When Carmilla bites a female victim she not only becomes a vampire – but also a lesbian. This one was full of traps for the unwary.

Harry Fine had been involved with Joseph Strick over the filming of *Ulysses* and was associated with David Frost when he first became involved in films in the mid-sixties. I knew nothing of Michael Style's background. He always carried a briefcase in which he kept several copies of a New York magazine. He seemed to be keen to show them to me. It was called *Screw*. It was in tabloid newspaper form and was entirely devoted to physical sex in all its forms, including full page photographs of full frontal nudes, men and women together, still fairly unusual in those days. Michael told me that the only photograph that was not allowed was of an erect penis.

For some reason I thought of George Stone, a corpulent gent in his sixties and a considerable joker, who ran the Moulin d'Or, the excellent restaurant in Romilly

Street, in Soho. He was crossing the street one day and was accosted by a man offering to show him blue films. George dismissed him, saying: 'No thanks, I don't need to see 'em because I appear in 'em, usually in the star part!' One can only treat this sort of thing as a joke.

Until I made *The Anniversary* for Hammer I'd had no association with them and as far as I can remember I had never seen any of their pictures, so I thought I'd better look up some of the earlier versions which Hammer had made of the Dracula story. Never mind the amazingly low budgets – which are not the audience's business anyway – they were lavishly presented, glamorous thrillers in the *grand guignol* style, with handsome heroes and lots of gorgeous girls floating about in diaphanous white nightgowns. All this plus Peter Cushing and Christopher Lee, two stars who built a solid relationship with the world public.

But this film was obviously intended by the producers to be a sensational exploitation picture. Strictly speaking, this was not generally the Hammer style. Looking at my previous record, this was not my style either. Still, all was not lost. First of all I had an excellent cast, with Ingrid Pitt perfect as Carmilla, and Peter Cushing, Madeline Smith, Kate O'Mara and George Cole all giving straightforward, honest performances. But they would, wouldn't they? They all followed my line, which was to play the thing simply and literally according to script, without camping it up or deriding the characters. If we had gone over the top, the result would have been merely risible and might even have been offensive to some.

When I was talking over costumes with Laura Nightingale, the resourceful Mistress of the Robes, I suddenly remembered the girls in the long white nightgowns in the previous *Dracula* pictures. It could clearly be seen through the nighties that they were wearing white knickers, modern bikini style. I mentioned this to Laura as being wrong historically, apart from looking ridiculous. In those times such a garment was not invented. The solution was simple: do without them. So they did and the dresses looked much better. No one took any notice and I doubt the audiences did either.

I decided that the style should be generally realistic but should include magic and suggestions of the supernatural. Elements of fantasy. Moray Grant was the lighting cameraman and he was most enthusiastic. One of the effects he cooked up was in a scene when the hero Carl (Jon Finch) throws a dagger at Carmilla (Ingrid Pitt). As it passes through her she becomes transparent and disappears. The dagger smashes into a vase of flowers which was on a table behind her. This effect could be done optically in the laboratory but we did it by a bolder procedure, to see if we could make it work. We set up a three-quarter length shot on Carmilla which we filmed down to the point just before the dagger hits her. The film was marked with a punch and, in the dark room, wound back a few feet. We then double-exposed this piece of film in the same set-up but without Carmilla; she would then be transparent. Then the dagger was thrown at the flowers. Intercut with Carl throwing the dagger the effect certainly works in the film. There were some other good atmosphere shots with Carmilla gliding through a graveyard in clouds of dry ice, which look quite unreal. By the way, I am aware that a few snippets of extra nudity were smuggled into the film after I had finished it but no great harm was done.

Also by the way, mention should be made of a scene in which a pedlar selling ribbons and gew-gaws comes to Carmilla's castle. It was parallel to the one with the tally man in *Jacqueline* and in the same way it was entirely cut from the film. Again, no reason was given. It was superbly played by Lindsay Kemp, a master of mime, who later presented his own shows with success. Pity, that.

When the picture was shown, the upshot was surprising to a lot of people: we got good notices. I had a good idea what the producers thought. Not, I fear, what they had been hoping for. They had been nagging me all through the shooting. I took no notice. If they wanted porn, they'd got the wrong cast and director. You don't get professionals with established reputations in that stuff. It is true that Hammer had often sailed close to the wind but they never actually capsized. A large part of their worldwide popularity was based on that discretion, though some of that may occasionally have been forced on them by censorship, sometimes official but more often by American distributors.

My next effort, *Scars of Dracula*, was my only true Hammer horror film. The script was brutal and cruel. I determined that if that was what they wanted, they should have it. Christopher Lee had made Count Dracula into a character of his own; the best there was, no doubt of that. During the last two or three of these pictures Dracula's presence in the stories had gradually waned, becoming a coat hanger, so Christopher was not displeased to see that this new script was clearly Dracula's story. Dennis Waterman played a strait-laced, serious, rather dull fellow whose younger brother was a riotous, hard drinking girl chaser, played by Christopher Matthews. Jenny Hanley had only to look beautiful, which she did anyway. Patrick Troughton as Dracula's servant, Klove, was outstanding. His was a genuine performance: no going through the motions for him.

Again I was looking for opportunities to bring in elements of magic and the supernatural. I suppose I was trying to inject a little charm into the general gloom. One arose when Christopher Lee had to pick up a girl, Anouska Hempel no less, and carry her from one room to another. So, with Anouska in his arms, Christopher gently asked me, 'Now, how do I open the door?' Quick as a flash I said, 'Oh, Dracula doesn't open doors. They open for him.' Thus with one penetrating glare from Count Dracula the door swung wide, he swept through, and the door closed behind him – operated by a prop man with a drawing pin and a piece of string. This fleeting moment has been criticised as out of key. On the screen it looks logical, but to a horror purist the element of magic is anathema. It seems they prefer the blood and gore straight, realistic.

The other magical effect was more difficult. After reading the script I did what one should always do. I went back to the source; I read the original book. In it I discovered something that had never been done before. Jonathan Harker looks out of the window of his bedroom, high up in the tower of Dracula's castle. Looking down, he sees an astonishing sight: Dracula is climbing the wall, stuck to it like some monstrous fly. Terrific – but how to do it? I talked it over with Scott MacGregor, the art director. He had succeeded Bernard Robinson when Bernard fell ill and, not long after, died. This was my fifth picture with Scott. He was keen to realise the idea but it would need a specially built set, which was certainly not in the budget. There was a lot of humming and ha'ing in the production department but eventually they managed it.

Another trick that Moray and I worked in this picture was when Dracula has to draw a red hot sword from a blazing fireplace and lay it across Klove's bare back. We used front projection, which had only recently come into use. Putting strips of the special reflective material on the blade of the sword, Moray then shone a faint red light on the whole scene, which was indiscernible everywhere except on the sword. The beauty of it was that Dracula could draw the sword from the fire and brandish it wherever he wished. There was no restriction on his movement. Wherever the sword was, it looked red hot. It is a horribly effective moment. That should satisfy the purists if anything could, but how do they explain it? Dracula draws the red hot sword from a blazing fire: surely the hilt would be too hot to handle? So there must be an element of magic. And that element encourages the audience to use its imagination.

Nowadays the audience is expected to be absolutely passive; they are given no encouragement to involve themselves emotionally with the film. Everything, sex, violence and all, is thrown at them in explicit detail. So they sit back, watching the thing from a distance. Perhaps they are flattered by the lengths to which filmmakers go in titillating their eyeballs. They don't seem to protest about the sheer vulgarity of it all; they remain uninvolved. What real pleasure they get out of it, I do not know. I believe that this attitude may be simply a bad habit which developed from watching television. The audience here usually consists of two or three people: doing homework, glancing occasionally at the sports page, or knitting. And then the phone rings. They are rarely involved in what is on the screen; apart from the commercial interruptions, which are often used for visits to the loo. This not a criticism of the programmes; this is the way things are and people develop a detached attitude.

FESTIVALS

Since those days I have seen a lot more of these so-called fantasy films when asked to attend festivals at Brussels, Sitges and Oporto. Brussels was excellently well run. I was president of the jury and I didn't agree with all of the votes, but the majority quite rightly awarded the prizes and it all ran smoothly. There were no absolutely disgusting films in the programmes, neither in the competition section nor those *hors concours*. I was flattered to have two of my own films shown. The welcome they gave me was superb and thoughtfully arranged. Altogether a most enjoyable event.

So when I was asked to be on the jury at Sitges I accepted straight away. This is the longest established fantasy festival of them all. My high hopes were soon dented. The welcome I got was unenthusiastic: I was over 25 and dressed like an ordinary Englishman, which was nobody's idea of a film director. Also I walked out of two films, one being a sequel, as if one were necessary, to *The Texas Chain Saw Massacre*. I'm glad I never saw the first one. My early departures caused some raising of eyebrows, shrugging of shoulders and sympathetic murmurs about 'Anglo-Saxon, one understands...' I probably wouldn't care for bull fights either, but I've never been to one so I cannot comment. I did see enough of these films to form an opinion of them and I adhere to my old motto: if you don't like the thing, don't buy it. It only encourages them. The Oporto Festival was shabby. The hotel was iffy. We were given luncheon and dinner vouchers, valid in two not very nice cafés, for two dishes and a glass of wine. Once we arrived no one took any notice of us at all. The idea appeared to us to be: invite a number of 'names' to impress the sponsors of the festival, after which they can be ignored. I was not on the jury so there was nothing to detain me. So I left.

In between these films I had been keeping my hand in with the TV episode industry and there is little to add to that, though *The Persuaders!* prompts some memories. Tony Curtis was remarkable. He mostly did his own stunts. Once he had to climb a high building. While we were still setting up two cameras to cover the scene, I noticed him talking quietly to one of the stunt men who was going to do the climb. Tony sauntered off as if to inspect the thing from the ground and I suddenly realised what was happening – he was going to do the stunt himself, without telling me. I bawled out 'Turn 'em over!' just in time. Up he went, right to the top and disappeared on to the roof. Crazy. I thank my stars the cameras were quick on the uptake.

Roger Moore was his usual good-humoured self, playing well with Tony Curtis, but the Anglo-American banter was not up to standard, callow and lacking the necessary wit. One eminent actress in one of my episodes was Dame Gladys Cooper. My copy of *Who's Who in the Theatre,* 13th edition, gives her *début* as 1905 and continues for two full pages – which takes us only as far as 1950. We are now in 1970. She had to play a refugee Russian Princess, which presented no difficulty at all.

Also in this episode, *The Ozerov Inheritance,* was a real gem of a performance by a new actress called Georgina Simpson. She was young and had little experience at this time but she carried herself with complete assurance. One of her scenes was quite long. She had nearly all the dialogue, in which she had to explain a complicated plot. Curtis had only one or two short lines to say off-camera, so he was bored and started playing the fool, but if he intended to put Georgina off her stroke he didn't succeed. She ignored him completely and played it brilliantly. There was no need for me to intervene. I was happy to find a couple more parts for her in other shows. Then she married Anthony Andrews, started a family and then found herself in charge of the eponymous shop in Piccadilly. Quite a capable lady.

The Gold Napoleon is worth a note because the word was that it was very well received by HQ, a rare comment. Alfred Marks was excellent in this and Susan George was very effective too: she teased me when she said, 'You don't remember me, do you?' Frankly, I didn't. 'It's all right,' she said cheerfully, 'I was only 12 at the time.' She had played a naughty schoolgirl in an episode of *The Human Jungle*.

In the world of volume production for television, people sometimes wonder where all the scripts come from. Well, an idea for a story may come from anywhere at any time. The cute people are the ones who recognise one when it appears. For instance, there was a group of us old lags at lunch in the restaurant at Elstree, discussing the insuperable difficulty of finding any developments in the stock horror yarns. *Frankenstein* had been fully explored in half a dozen Hammer variations, apart from the masterly original; *The Ghoul* and *The Mummy* had run out of steam after only two or three outings; *Dracula* had another half-dozen with Hammer, apart from several vampire variations; *Doctor Jekyll and Mr Hyde* underwent two or three permutations as well as the earlier motion pictures with Fredric March, Spencer Tracy, et al. Suddenly Brian Clemens sat up and quietly said: 'I've got it. Dr Jekyll drinks the magic potion and ... he turns into a woman!'

This set the table in a roar and in great good humour we all went about our business. Not so long afterward Brian – never one to fumble a catch – wrote a script, which he called *Dr Jekyll & Sister Hyde*. This was not just another episode which could be fitted into any one of the current television offerings; this was a film. Hammer took it up and Brian produced it with his partner Albert Fennell. When I was given the script it cheered me up no end: once again I had got a good one. It was ambitious, too. It demanded atmosphere and good performances. There were hints of the female characteristics in the male and vice versa and other subtleties to explore. Or to explore with subtlety.

I have been quizzed many times now at film festivals and in a lot of interviews about the undertones of these films, the overtones, the resonances, etcetera. I had to go to the dictionary for 'plangent'. Do you equate vampires with sex? and so on. Sometimes I have brushed these questions aside with a facetious remark, or simply changed the subject. I have no wish to offend the interviewer. The stumbling block here is my absolute conviction that these aspects of any story are only effective if they are not delved into and analysed in public by the authors. Sure, the audience and the critics are free to probe and parse a film and the motives of the authors of it, but the writer and the director will be wise to avoid such traps. Some do get a lot of publicity by sounding off in this way, but they always sound high falutin' and to some of us, downright silly. *Jejune*, one might say. *Of course* we know what the deeper emotions in a story are, but heaven help you if you discuss it – except possibly with the writer and then only with discretion. Obviously we know instinctively when the deeper emotions are *not* in evidence and we take steps bring them out. Also, one must be careful with the actors, for fear one of them may be a devotee of the Method: then you will be on a sleighride! Experienced actors don't need to be hit over the head with a baseball bat and neither should the audience.

I have sometimes noticed at the theatre that the programme offers a page long essay, written by the playwright, explaining what the piece is about. Why? Either he knows in his heart that what he is trying to say just isn't on the stage, or, he is patronisingly underestimating the intelligence of the audience. The principle in the cinema is, you make a film, pushing your abilities to the limit and one day it is finished. It is released to an audience. There is nothing more you can do, no programme to explain the subtleties. The audience's reaction to the piece is governed by what is on the screen, nothing else. Not quite true, that; the critics often have considerable influence.

HAMMER GLAMMER

Back to business. Casting started with Ralph Bates as Doctor Jekyll and couldn't be bettered. It was not so easy to find Sister Hyde and we were not making progress at all, until Hammer's Sir James Carreras rang up from Wardour Street announcing that he had got the perfect girl: Martine Beswick.

She had appeared in one or two Hammer pictures in the sixties, but had been living in Hollywood recently, so neither of us had ever met her. We didn't know what to expect. When she appeared it was plain to see how good she would be in the part. With some attention to their hair and slight adjustment of the heels of their shoes she and Ralph looked like identical twins. It was miraculous and was the key element in making the plot believable.

The producers decided to schedule all the atmospheric scenes in the first weeks of the shooting, leaving the story until later. Presumably they were worried in case we went over schedule and cuts were demanded by HQ. It was a sensible idea but it didn't help me in keying the characters, which obviously one wants to do early in the proceedings. Part of this atmosphere was provided by a blind beggar, played by Lindsay Kemp; this time he wasn't cut out.

The all-important first transformation from Doctor Jekyll into Sister Hyde called for some sleight of hand. The script simply called for a series of dissolves. I have been asked about this scene by people who cannot figure it out from what they see on the screen. They refuse to accept that it was done in one shot, but it was. This is how I devised it:

The camera is on Doctor Jekyll as he staggers out of the laboratory into the drawing room. The potion is taking effect. He weaves toward an armchair. In front of the armchair is a cheval mirror. Doctor Jekyll is reflected in the mirror as he collapses into the armchair. The camera moves closer and crabs to his left and on to his back as he rests his head on his knees – we can no longer see him in the mirror.

Out of picture, another identical armchair is now slid into place beside him. Sister Hyde sits in this chair with her head on her knees in the same posture as Doctor Jekyll. She wears a dressing-gown identical to his. She can see him reflected in the mirror, still out of picture. This takes only a few seconds.

Doctor Jekyll begins to recover from the impact of the potion. He raises his head from his knees. The camera eases back to accommodate this movement and over his shoulder we see him – apparently it is him – reflected again in the mirror.

Sister Hyde has to imitate exactly all Jekyll's reactions as he stares at his reflection, because it is she who is now reflected in the mirror.

He rises to his feet, appalled. Obviously, she rises with him. He moves closer to the mirror. So does she. The camera tracks in to a closer shot of Sister Hyde. She stares back at herself in the mirror and pulls open her dressing gown to reveal her breasts.

That is how it was done, all in one shot. Then the scene continues with her as we cut to her standing in Jekyll's place as she steps closer still to the mirror.

The picture was extremely well edited by James Needs and was well received. It has grown in popularity since then, especially abroad.

I then slid back into the fun factory with a few more TV episodes, notably *Jason King* with Peter Wyngarde in the lead. One of the stories, *Wanna Buy a Television Series?* had some good in-jokes, too. Then my agent, the redoubtable Michael Whitehall, introduced me to Milton Subotsky.

HOW TO WIN A GRAND PRIX

Milton, in his quiet and unobtrusive way, had made about 30 pictures since he came to England from New York. A dedicated Anglophile, he took British citizenship. He had made a number of films of the magazine type, taking four or five short stories and stringing them together, usually enclosed in a suitable envelope. He persuaded strings of star names to appear in them and they were successful. *Asylum* was another one of that style. He had selected five short stories written by Robert Bloch. He sent this plan to Bloch, together with a suggested envelope. Not surprisingly, Bloch wrote a cracking good script.

All the characters in these stories were lunatics except one and it was vital that their obsessions and fantasies should be absolutely genuine, NOT people putting on an act. Milton assembled a marvellous cast which was simply a list of first class actors who all responded beautifully. I was in my element and thankful to have such a group around me.

Before we began shooting there was one sad incident. I had asked Arthur Grant to photograph the film. He read the script and was as enthusiastic as I was, but only ten days before the start he came to me, full of apologies. He was ill, and he felt it would be irresponsible to continue. He said he knew that he couldn't do the job. I didn't ask any questions. I never knew what he was suffering, but only a few months later, he died. A sad loss to us all. He was so good-natured, unpretentious and good at his job. He was an ace at photographing dramatic night sequences: his motto was 'Never mind how dark it's supposed to be – the audience has still got to see what's going on!' And yet it still looked like night.

Denys Coop was dubious about taking over at short notice but I managed to persuade him. He was a real top-rater. He had high standards and you wouldn't find him photographing any old rubbish. We worked well together and I was glad to have him on my next two pictures. After that he became one of the principal members of the team that made *Superman* fly and you couldn't see the wires because there weren't any.

Asylum is one of my favourite films. The shoot was smooth as silk, Tony Waye being the first assistant; he later spent a lot of time as a line producer on the James Bond films. There is no point in describing the stories or in picking out individual performances: they were all excellent, although I must just mention Herbert Lom's piece, which was utterly convincing. It was all shot in one day too, not that that's important. And the joint efforts of Charlotte Rampling and Britt Ekland were really smart. I like the picture because it all fits together so neatly, with terrific pace, too. During the following year, 1973, I was invited to Paris to collect a prize for it.

This was the Grand Prix for Best Picture awarded at the Paris Convention du Cinema Fantastique. *Asylum* had been shown among other pictures during the run of the festival, but it was *hors concours*, not entered in the competition. The jury rejected all the films they were shown in the *concours* and awarded the prize to us! Very gratifying, to be awarded first prize when you haven't even been in the race.

Milton and I had now established a solid working relationship and I directed two more pictures for him. The first was from a modern novel called *Fengriffin*, a serviceable ghost story set in 1785. The hinge of the plot was revealed in a flashback to the early 1700s, with the lord of the manor exercising his *droit de seigneur* on a village maiden who has just got married to his gamekeeper. Two generations later his descendant marries and on the wedding night the bride sees the ghost of the cuckolded gamekeeper and collapses hysterically. Or was it the gamekeeper's grandson in person? At the end of the story the bride gives birth to a son, who bears the same hereditary birthmark as the gamekeeper's grandson. This was another instance of magic with no explanation.

It was a pity nevertheless that the story hadn't more bite, because everything else about the film was good. Tony Curtis was the art director on all three of these pictures, doing a marvellous job, cobbling together bits of set from all over the place. This one certainly looked beautiful, with Denys lighting as well. The centre of the piece was the leading lady and Stephanie Beacham filled the bill perfectly.

It is true, *Fengriffin* is not much of a title for a film, so Milton's partner, one Max J Rosenberg, barged in. He was the exact opposite to Milton in every way and it is just as well he stayed out of the way, doing deals in New York. The title he chose was ~~*And Now the Screaming Starts!* Come to think of it, *Fengriffin* is a perfectly acceptable title and a lot better than the one wished on us.

The third picture was *The Vault of Horror*, another of Milton's magazine scripts, based on the famous American EC comics. It had another star-studded cast, who were all amiable and did their stuff. I had never met Curt Jurgens before; the charm just poured out of him and the suavity of manner was incredible. But the stories weren't strong enough and the result was not up to the standard of the previous ones. It is difficult to capture the style of strip cartoons in moving pictures. It was done later with *Dick Tracy*, which was meticulously copied from the original cartoons regardless of expense, but the actors wallowed in a sea of self-indulgence and finally sank. *Superman* and *Batman* brought off the style brilliantly.

Some years later I directed one more picture for Milton, *The Monster Club*. Another magazine film, with Vincent Price, John Carradine and another distinguished cast, which again included Britt Ekland, a much underrated actress. Vincent Price and I exchanged some reminiscences of Hollywood in the fifties. Price was disdainful about Zanuck: 'A common little man' he said.

Everything was going for us but there was a fatal flaw in the project. The envelope was The Monster Club where Price and Carradine introduced the stories. Also in between them there was a cabaret of rock bands. The flaw was the terribly short duration of the bands' popularity, compared to the time it takes to complete a film. Anyway, all the money in the world wouldn't have got us the Beatles or the Rolling Stones. Milton broke all records in delivering the picture, doing all the post-production work in about four weeks.

Milton Subotsky was one of the nicest people I ever worked with. Shy, honest, modest – not the popular image of a film producer. I should have underlined the word 'popular'. Of course all producers are shy, honest, etc. Milton was no good at publicising himself, never put himself about. Always anxious to give the credit for a success to any one but himself. He was an innovator. He filmed Harold Pinter's *The Birthday Party* directed by William Friedkin. He was first to revive the Sword and Sorcery style – and first into insects, with a plague of bees! After *Dead of Night*, which had no follow-ups because it was so good, he revived the magazine format with macabre stories. His productions were in the same field as Hammer but were always somehow different. An admirable man. He loved the stories and he loved film; to him, it wasn't just a business.

FOREIGN PARTS

More than ten years had passed since my last foreign location. Now came another period of globetrotting. The first trip was the farthest and decidedly the farthest-fetched.

Michael Carreras had taken over Hammer when his father Sir James finally retired. Hammer had become a world famous brand name but the stock of stories and scripts had dried up; the public was looking for something fresh and so was he. Simply to continue on the old lines would be useless. Just about this time, his eye lighted on the appearance of the kung fu pictures. Why not make a picture combining the best aspects of the two? So *The Legend of the 7 Golden Vampires* was born. Screenplay by Don Houghton, who was also the producer. I understood that he was an Australian, now living in England. His wife was Chinese, an actress named Pik Sen. A co-production deal was set up with Sir Run Run Shaw and the film was to be made in the Shaw Studios at Hong Kong.

This was another classic example of inadequate liaison, reconnaissance and planning. The advance party set off a couple of weeks ahead of the shooting date: Jean Walter, production secretary; Christopher Carreras, production supervisor; Don Houghton and I. As soon as we arrived Houghton withdrew to an office somewhere to re-write or complete the script, which was in a fairly rough state. So I walked around the vast studios with Christopher. Now, we had come to shoot the picture in the usual way: direct recorded synch sound in English. We found the stages were enormous tin sheds with no sound proofing at all. We noticed a number of stray dogs bounding about, barking their heads off. Kai Tak airport was not far away. The answer was simple: the usual local method was to shoot everything silent, because the release of their films in the enormous territory of the Far East was to audiences who spoke several different languages. So the actors spoke their lines in their own way, which could then be roughly dubbed into any speech suitable to any market. These divergent approaches led to friction which was never satisfactorily solved.

The standing sets in these studios had to be seen to be believed. They were magnificent, the best that you would expect from Chinese design. They had been standing for years and the dust underfoot was four inches thick. Unfortunately very little use was made in our script of these facilities; in fact I can't remember any. So we had to build sets. The art director was Johnson Tsao, a charming man who spoke English well and delivered some splendid settings. He was a great man to work with and a bonus in the whole operation. What he could not supply and neither could anyone else, was locations. The script called for a caravan crossing a desert. Hong Kong is barely three times the size of the Isle of Wight, which has a population of 125,000. HK had a population, then, 25 years ago, of four million people and rising daily. The only suitable open space left was a spot on a hill right by the border of China proper. It was a few hundred yards square. The carts for the caravan were provided from stock, but the only horses available came from the Hong Kong racecourse. They did not take to being put in shafts at all.

The sad part of this adventure was that we were unable to take advantage of the opportunities that were at hand, which were considerable. The writer and the director should have been sent out there at least two months ahead of production, to tailor the script to the local capabilities. We had no lighting cameraman, because the local method was for the gaffer to light the set-up and then offer it to the director for approval. Toward the end of the shoot we got John Wilcox out from England, which helped. There were innumerable problems of communication between the British crew and the Chinese. If the camera operator wants the dolly to go forward a half an inch, it is useless to say to a Chinese grip, 'Take me in a gnat's.' Matters are only made worse if you shout at him.

The sound recordist, Les Hammond, worked under the most appalling difficulties, but he managed his relationships with the crew well. He and his two assistants kept themselves strictly to themselves, both on duty and off, with discretion and dignity. I admired them greatly. I felt that the heaviest influence on the production was Chinese, as it inevitably would be, but my responsibility as I saw it was to make a Hammer picture for distribution in the English-speaking markets. The sound recording team were the key to that. There was continuing pressure to abandon direct sound and post-synch the dialogue. What? All of it? Back in London? The effect on the performances would have been disastrous. Some of them were shaky enough anyway. One or two of the actors were unable to take the job seriously; to them, it was a paid holiday in Hong Kong. This attitude was shared by one or two of the English crew as well. Whoopee! Thanks be for Peter Cushing, quiet and reserved as usual, a rock.

On the way home I completed my circumnavigation of the globe by travelling back to England by Los Angeles, where I took up a long-standing invitation to stay with Samuel Goldwyn Jnr. This was the holiday of a lifetime. He quickly realised that I was shell-shocked after the Hong Kong farrago and did everything he could to brace me up. He had his own troubles at the time, because his father had been ill for a long time and died, aged 94, at the end of January.

Among local events, *The Exorcist*, directed by William Friedkin, burst on the screen. It was such a hit that you had to queue to get a ticket, which gave you some priority in queueing again on the following day for a seat. I hardly ever go to the cinema and Sam doesn't approve such behaviour, so he dragooned me into seeing it. Sam hadn't seen the picture yet so I refused to tell him what I thought of it until after he had. I left for England before he did see it, so I never did speak my piece. Well, now I will. I thought it was no more than a 13 million dollar Hammer picture. Repeating what I said before – it is worth another airing – the big bucks have taken over the horror department and not all of them have been as effective as the earlier Hammer films. It didn't surprise me and I am not by any means the only one who could have offered a few cautionary words. No one wants unpalatable advice – or any advice. The little bucks pictures have gone ever lower into the depths of pornography and sleaze, so nowadays there is nothing comparable to the original Hammer glammer style.

The Legend of the 7 Golden Vampires opened at the Warner, Leicester Square to an excellent notice in *Time Out* and lukewarm or dismissive reviews elsewhere.

THE OTHER SIDE OF THE COIN

THE WHEEL TURNS

The greater part of this book is aimed at people who want to spend their working lives in films or television and '...of course, what I really want to do, is to direct.' I have dwelt at length on the superficial joys of such an occupation: the association with interesting, eminent people, creative people, the beautiful people, the travel, the fame, the press cuttings, the money – sometimes – all this is dazzling enough. Most important of all is the deep satisfaction which comes on the rare occasions when you know you have made a good film.

Feeling good? Right. This is just the moment to describe another facet of this scintillating diamond. It is an essential element of this profession and no one can avoid it. It comes to everyone sometime. A precious few can afford it, but even then it is still painful. Even if you don't have to worry about money, being out of work for long periods – sometimes years – is a debilitating experience. After *The Legend of the 7 Golden Vampires* my sojourn in the desert lasted four years. Not that I was idle during all that time. I wrote scripts, treatments, outlines for television series and ideas-on-the-back-of-a-postcard and bombarded everyone I knew with them. I found no takers. Not all the ideas were good, but one or two were. However good the idea, the timing has to be right, it has to come up at exactly the right moment. Mine didn't.

One of my neighbours ran a business designing and printing all kinds of art work for advertising agents. He had heard about audio-visual presentations, which were just coming into use. He'd had one made, to publicise his own company, so he asked me if I'd care to look at it. It wasn't good. I made some suggestions. Before I knew it I was fully employed in this business. So it is not true to say that I had four years with no money. During that time I had two years with a car and a tiny wage and in the end I was left to redeem a debt to the bank of £4000. So I did all that work for nothing. I must have been mad. It shows the debilitating effect of being long-term unemployed.

This lecturette may be depressing and a bore, casting doubt on the popular view of the glamorous life of a film director, but it must be emphasised that, while work-ing as a freelance has many advantages it's not beer and skittles all the time. The best one can do is to live well within one's income. Well within. Let me repeat, these were still the days of low pay and high income tax, so life may be a bit easier to manage nowadays. Nevertheless, these admonitions still apply. What a freelance needs is a private income and a big one at that; one that will support family, housing and edu-cation at minimum. If you want food and a decent bottle as well ... Ho ho ho.

Having said all that, I swear I wouldn't have, couldn't have, done anything else, not for all the tea in China. I have had some good luck and I have had some hor-ribly bad luck. Except I don't believe in luck. Some of it was due to talent and some to mismanagement. But – you may depend upon it – the wheel turns. So it did. There are still some good things to come.

BACK TO WORK...

Robert S Baker was the one who broke the spell. He invited me to see him at Pinewood where he was making a TV series: *The Return of the Saint*, starring Ian Ogilvy. He said, 'You've been out for a long time, haven't you.' I admit, I flinched a bit at the choice of phrase, but he was right, it was true. 'And you want to get back in again?' A script was handed over; two of them in fact. One by John Kruse and the other by Leon Griffiths, so that was all right and I plunged in with gusto.

Then Christopher Neame got in touch. Long ago he had first appeared as second assistant on one of my pictures; later on, as production manager; now, as associate producer on a series called *Danger UXB*. This was perfect casting for me, being about a bomb disposal unit during the war. The leads included Anthony Andrews, Maurice Roëves and Judy Geeson. John Hawkesworth was the producer.

Now, at long last, TV series production had quitted the film studios. They were no longer necessary, not even as bases. The technique was still strictly according to motion pictures but otherwise everything was done on location. This production was based at a disused school on the far side of Clapham Common. It was ideal because it afforded all the interior sets that were needed, plus offices and dressing rooms and of course the playground was the car park. Most of the actors appeared in all the episodes and they were well tuned in and looked like soldiers. At the end of shooting of my episode John had only one more script without a director, toward the end of the schedule. The script wasn't finished yet but he gave me the outline, which was interesting, dealing with the beastly butterfly bombs.

But in a few days Chris was on the phone again. The director shooting the cur-rent episode had to be replaced at once. The first two days' rushes were unusable. Please will I take over, as soon as possible. I thought, I shall get a reputation for this sort of thing. I drove over to Clapham and looked at the rushes. They were quite extraordinary. The set-ups all related to one scene but they were completely unrelated to each other. There was no way of cutting them together. It was most odd. All I heard was that this unfortunate chap had never directed before, he was a poet and did quite a lot on Radio Three. All this may have been a leg-pull. Anyway I mugged up the script and was on location the following morning early, before the unit arrived. Morale had sunk low during the last three days and I wanted to be ready. The weather was good. The site was a vast section of railway lines, six or more parallel tracks on a long curve, with a signal box at one side. It was a good choice. It fitted the action well.

I walked around a bit, settling the scenes in my mind. I chose a vantage point on the railway embankment, planted my shooting stick firmly, sat down and started the *Times* crossword. As the unit vehicles arrived I placed them where they would be out of sight of the action. Then there were the Army vehicles belonging to the bomb disposal squad, including a small mobile canteen. I placed them in the right relationships for the action. Then the crew began to arrive. I ordered a 30 foot camera track to be laid beside the railway tracks, starting from the canteen and ending by one of the Army wagons. There was some tentative doubt expressed about these high-handed methods: suppose the track is in the wrong place? Couldn't we have a rehearsal? etc. The answer was that we were already three days behind schedule and had it all to do. I directed a zoom lens to be put on the camera and by the time the actors were made up and dressed they walked straight on to a ready-made set-up and I had done half the crossword. Two or three rehearsals and first shot in the can by nine o'clock. Directors should not indulge too often in this sort of behaviour, because if it doesn't come off you'll look rather silly. Some crews I have worked with recently are apparently not used to directors who know what they want and are only too anxious to put in their two cents worth. This time it had the desired effect and I enjoyed it as well.

Jeremy Paul had written both these scripts and was half way through the butterfly one. He suddenly got an offer he couldn't resist – to go to Hollywood, I think. We had the story outline but John Hawkesworth and I were left to complete the job. No credit, no money, of course. It was not the first time this had happened to me, nor would it be the last. There is no doubt that some writers are treated badly. Their scripts are accepted and when they see them on the screen all sorts of changes appear: dialogue cut, dialogue altered, new scenes interposed, endings rewritten. It must be disheartening. They may feel it's not worth the effort to supply a fully finished script. Whatever sympathy one may have with the writer's problems there is no justification for leaving other people with a job unfinished. It is certainly true that in the transition of a script from the typewritten page to the moving picture, some modification will be required. It is in the nature of the beast; no one is interfering for the sake of it. In films, I have worked with three writers whose scripts needed the absolute minimum of alteration: Eric Ambler, Howard Clewes and Nigel Kneale, and any necessary changes were done by the writer. All the others had varying degrees of change, not always in collaboration with the writer. Television series episodes were generally much better worked out;

they have to be, but even in the case of *The Saint*, where all the scripts were scrupulously finished, there were minor changes of dialogue during the shooting. But in the last few years I have had three or four television scripts which had to be rewritten throughout, with no reference to the writer. Certainly the lack of discipline now would horrify men like Bob Baker or Julian Wintle.

This series had its lighter moments. Our art director drove a small station wagon, which carried Northern Ireland registration plates. It was usually full of prop bits and pieces used here and there during the shoot. His wife rang up one morning in great excitement: she had somehow got two tickets for *Evita* for the afternoon performance that very day. Could he possibly skive off work to come with her? Off he went after lunch, drove to the theatre – which was in Soho – parked the car round the corner and very much enjoyed the show. When they came out they found the street cordoned off, alive with policemen and bomb disposal experts, all eyeing the car with caution. Inside it they could see suspicious-looking canisters and a large aerial bomb. Explanations were demanded...

THE IMMORTAL SHERLOCK

Sheldon Reynolds, an American producer, decided to set up a series of half-hours called *Sherlock Holmes and Doctor Watson* in partnership with the State Television of Poland. They have a huge TV centre in Warsaw. A large section of Baker Street was built on the back lot for the series. It was even bigger than the one Billy Wilder had at Pinewood.

Poland lost its independence in 1795 but it was restored in 1918; only 21 years later in 1939 it was carved up again between the Germans and the Russians, so the Poles hadn't enjoyed their republic for long. We are now in 1979 and the Russian hegemony still ruled. It was a strange atmosphere; never much traffic on the streets and the cars were identical, few in number and all the same colour too. The tram system was splendid. The Hotel Victoria Intercontinental, being foreign built, was lavishly appointed. The restaurant was vast, with first class linen, plate, china and glass and a menu as thick as a phone book, but the only dish available seemed to be a pork chop. It really was a city where queues would suddenly materialise at a shop where apples or grapes were rumoured to be available.

Dinner at the Sheldon's house was another number altogether. The authorities had installed them in a large house in Millionaires Row, Warsaw. It was fully staffed, with servants all over the place. Mrs Sheldon was in full command, as to the manner born, being a lineal descendant of the Empress Maria Theresa or some such. She was grand, charming and beautiful and she was very nice to me. She had a sense of humour too. She showed me round the house, including her bedroom, where a previous tenant had installed a huge mirror on the ceiling over the bed.

The crew was mainly Polish, hard working, and cheerful in spite of their miserable existence. The first assistant, the associate producer and the sound recordist were Italian and efficient. The recordist was one of the top notch men in Italy. In particular he was most interesting because he believed – rightly – that the key to good sound recording lies in where you place the microphone; so he was his own boom swinger. He prowled around the set with a long fishing rod with a tiny microphone on the end, insinuating himself into the most unlikely nooks and crannies. His headphones were two small buttons which he stuck in his ears. Unobtrusive is the word for him; you never noticed him at all. He had only one assistant, who sat meekly at the desk, operating the Nagra.

Shooting was in English, though distribution was to be east of the Iron Curtain. Geoffrey Whitehead was Sherlock Holmes. He played the gamekeeper in ~~And Now the Screaming Starts! Watson was played by Donald Pickering. Each story had some distinguished visiting actors, including Bernard Bresslaw, who took the opportunity of a day off work to go to the city of Breslau, as the Germans used to call it, now known to the Poles as Wroclaw. There he traced a lot of his ancestors. He never did tell me if the news was good or bad. Bearing in mind the Holocaust, it may have been tragic.

It was an interesting experience and different, but I have never got used to the half-hour format. The characterisation, atmosphere and plotting are sketchy at best. It seemed that Sheldon had previously made the same series in Paris and was now recycling the stories. Shelly was absent quite a lot of the time, touring around the capitals of Europe. This was the moment for the associate producer, a lady named Laura, to seize the levers of power. I thought she was tiresome.

I made five episodes which were all apparently satisfactory, though I can't regard them as among my finest work; then returned to London. Soon after shooting was completed, I read in a newspaper that the head of Polish TV, who had sanctioned the enterprise, was arrested on alleged charges of corruption. He was supposedly found in possession of two country houses, three American cars and four each of heaven alone knew what else. I think Shelly was on one of his trips at the time, so, instead of him, Mrs Reynolds was arrested but she, being the formidable and noble lady that she is, was having none of that. She was soon released. Can you imagine such a thing? She wouldn't stand for any nonsense, that one. A little of that attitude would have helped me when I was arrested in Brussels all those years ago.

MINDER

The Sweeney was a long-running, immensely popular series made by Thames Television, starring John Thaw and Dennis Waterman. Inevitably it came to its end and the search was on for a replacement, a new series with the same pace and excitement. As usual the searchers were after something which would pull in an enormous audience as The Sweeney did, but not a carbon copy of it. They wanted something the same, only different. Something different, only the same.

These requirements are impossible to fulfil. What is possible is to find a format which will fit into the style of the vacant slot, with a core idea which will generate dozens of stories centred on the adventures of two or three characters. However this is only the beginning. When this nugget is discovered it must be handled with care. If the new show is successful it will develop characteristics of its own and it is useless to grumble if it doesn't match exactly with its predecessor, or if it doesn't even follow precisely the preconditions of its own original brief. It can be guided, but it is unwise to force it to comply strictly with the original concept. One of the great gifts of television in the UK is that a series may continue even if the first couple of showings are not instant hits. Unlike in America, where a series of 13 shows can be junked after only two episodes have been shown, if it doesn't instantly catch on with the public.

Leon Griffiths was the man who came up with the goods. *Minder*, with Arthur Daley and Terry McCann – the two characters so brilliantly brought to life by Dennis Waterman and George Cole. The saga of the shifty second-hand car salesman and his poor but honest henchman originally ran from 1979 to 1988. The producers were Lloyd Shirley and George Taylor. The crew were highly experienced in series production, led by two first-rate cameramen, Dusty Miller and Roy Pointer, who photographed alternate episodes. Roy is full of jokes and yet strangely self-effacing; it may be he is shy. It took a lot of probing to discover that he was a rear-gunner in bombers during the War, a 'tail-end Charlie'. Dusty is another pro who goes quietly about his business, never wasting time on irrelevancies. I directed twelve episodes, plus one double episode. I was fortunate in having five scripts by Leon. There were several good writers contributing, notably Tony Hoare and Andrew Payne, who wrote all the others that I directed – except one, which was a dud. It was fascinating to follow the development of the programme over those years.

The first one I directed was very early on – the third episode, by Leon. It appealed to me, because of the plain common sense of the story. A petty sneak-thief, Scotch Harry, steals a briefcase. Harry turns to Arthur for help, asking him to change a hundred dollar bill. Arthur smells money and he and Terry go to Scotch Harry's squalid attic, a perfect location which smelled worse than the money. Harry proudly shows them the briefcase, which is full of hundred dollar bills. Harry is surprised and dismayed when Arthur takes one horrified look and says, 'You've got to find the man and hand it back! That sort of money – people get killed for that.' But he agrees to help – for a fee – and makes a hurried exit. Terry chases after him and they get jammed in a narrow staircase. Arthur orders him to stay with Scotch Harry and the money. Terry realises that he will always be left to do the dirty and dangerous work and accept whatever share of the booty Arthur gives him. Furthermore, Terry will be expected to extricate Arthur from difficult situations involving any real villains he may have upset and of course the fuzz. After we had shot the scene, Dennis told me that this short scene had given him the key to the relationship with

Arthur. Some years later Leon wrote another story for Scotch Harry, which I also directed. The part was played by Phil McCall, who fitted it to a T.

It was amusing to watch how the series developed into a Terry and Arthur double act, as did Morse and Lewis, Poirot and Hastings and many others: audiences enjoy watching two characters playing off one another. Some writers and producers deplore the use of such a shorthand description: 'We're not doing Morecambe and Wise, you know'. They are right of course; shorthand is another of those aspects of our work that should remain undiscussed. Once it is mentioned it is vulgar – as long as everyone concerned has got the drift. It's all in the sublime cause of avoiding self-consciousness. Know what I mean?

Another of Leon's scripts, *Aces High – And Sometimes Very Low*, was about a professional poker player, which was exciting to do because the games were presented in such a way that the audience could follow the action without knowing anything about the rules of poker. This one was superbly edited by Roger Wilson. The gambler was brilliantly played by Anthony Valentine. Leon did another script with the same character, later on.

There were three other running characters, all stemming from the original concept. Glynn Edwards gave us Dave, the proprietor and barman of the Winchester Club, who was rightly popular with the viewers. There were two plain-clothes detectives. Peter Childs was DC Rycott, who always thought he knew what Arthur was up to, was always wrong and too thick to nab him anyway. Patrick Malahide was DC Chisholm, manic and forever tripping over his own self-importance. All three played with a delightfully deadpan sense of humour. Very skilful stuff.

The first showings were not by any means widely popular, but they developed a cult following which arose out of word-of-mouth publicity, which is by far and away the best kind of advertising. It costs nothing, because it can't be bought and is influential because it is usually trustworthy, being based on people of like tastes talking to each other.

The great Theo Cowan had many wise words to say about public relations. He once said to me, 'The honest truth about advertising any film is, that the best we can do is to make sure they know it's on.' While quoting Theo I must include another instance of his wisdom. When *Fiddler on the Roof* was about to open in London the backers were worried that there seemed to be no way of publicising the show and nobody had even heard of Topol. Theo said, 'Don't try. Topol is great, so let the critics and the audiences discover him for themselves'. And so it turned out.

THE FLAME TREES OF THIKA

Interspersed with the diverting experiences of Arthur and Terry, which were based at such definitely unglamourous depots as Hammersmith, Putney and Wood Lane, I was again flying off abroad, first of all to Kenya.

Elspeth Huxley was a writer of stature, author of three dozen books, on politics, biography, some crime novels and three works of fictionalised autobiography: *The Flame Trees of Thika*, *The Mottled Lizard* and *Love Among the Daughters*. John Hawkesworth was keen to film *The Flame Trees*. Since it was a long story, he decided to present it on television in seven one-hour parts. Thames Television backed it and Christopher Neame was co-producer with John, who was also writing the script with Elspeth Huxley.

Elspeth was never quite clear about the ratio of fact to fiction in the book. She was deeply concerned that there should be nothing derogatory about her parents, which is quite as it should be. She shouldn't have worried, because there was nothing seriously derogatory to say, but her influence induced a general blandness in the script and in the relationship of her father and mother. They were trying to establish a coffee estate on land that had never been farmed, in the East African Protectorate, or British East Africa, in 1912. Her mother did some research in England before they left, but they were greenhorns who had no idea how tough it was going to be.

Elspeth's father, Josceline Grant, came of good family, a long line of proper Highlanders from Inverness. He served in the Royal Scots in the second Boer War. A comfortable inheritance was his undoing, being sufficient to allow him to avoid taking up a career – he was intended for the Diplomatic – or buying a house or land. Unfortunately a large part of this money disappeared down a diamond mine in Africa which produced no diamonds; some more was lost in motor manufacture, in a car which would only go downhill. In Elspeth's words, 'He was a gentle, humourous, dreamy, impractical and most unaggressive man, with a faith in human nature carried almost to the length of gullibility ... shy and, at heart, diffident.'

Her mother, Nellie, was the youngest child of Lord Richard de Aquila Grosvenor, who was the younger brother of the first Duke of Westminster. Lord Richard served 25 years as a Liberal MP until he resigned when Gladstone split his government over Home Rule. He received a peerage, choosing as his title Baron Stalbridge. He inherited an estate in Dorset of 10,000 acres, which included the town of Shaftesbury. Nellie's background was therefore aristocratic and wealthy. She was an Hon. But in her late teens her father crashed spectacularly through no fault of his own.

While still an undergraduate at Cambridge, he had underwritten a note of £100,000 for a friend, who was supposed to destroy it as soon as he had paid off his debts. He didn't fulfil either obligation and 30 years later the note was suddenly called in. Everything had to go and they finished up in a small house in Sussex Square, 'on the wrong side of the park.' Bayswater and perilously close to Paddington. So Nellie had some experience of disaster as well as the grand country house life. She had brains and did well enough at Cheltenham Ladies College to have passed easily into an Oxford College, but it was decreed that she return home 'to be the daughter of the house'. Despite the straitened family economy she 'came out' in proper style, living for the season at her Aunt Katie Westminster's house in

Grosvenor Square. She was presented to Queen Alexandra by another relative, the Countess of Shaftesbury, who was a Lady in Waiting, which gave Nellie the entrée, a precedence over the other débutantes.

John Hawkesworth had never considered any one other than Hayley Mills for the part. Hayley had stunned everybody with her performance in *Tiger Bay* at the age of 12. The film had also established John as a writer and producer. Hayley was whisked off to Hollywood to play Pollyanna for Disney. Before she was out of her teens she was an international star with a large, devoted following. All this was based on the character of Pollyanna and most, if not all, of her formative experience was with Disney. In our first discussion of the script Hayley announced, 'I am not going to play this part with an upper class English accent.' Imagine my shock/horror. Not much later she declared, 'I am a rich woman and I can do as I like.'

Nellie was certainly not a half-barmy English eccentric but she was a 'character' if ever there was one. Nellie was a wonderful part to play: always optimistic but never fatuous, shy but self-assured, intelligent, educated, tough in adversity and with a considerable sense of humour. She adored Jos, who was, frankly a bit of a ne'er-do-well. She was the backbone and moving spirit of that little family; indeed their only child, Elspeth, came out of it very well indeed.

David Robb was good casting, looking and sounding exactly right for Jos Grant. He was well prepared; he had improved his riding at an Army school of equitation. Unfortunately we got at cross purposes on the first day of shooting. The scene was Nellie, Jos and Elspeth riding in open country to see the 500 acres of barren land that Jos had bought for £4.00 an acre. David had trouble with his mount. The lady who had provided the animals called out, 'If you abuse that animal, he'll do nothing for you!' All he had to do was walk gently toward camera and stop. I got the impression that David wanted to make a dashing entrance, rushing up to camera, swerving to a halt and rearing up. Doing an Errol Flynn. David was riding a mule.

It was a nice animal but – of course – it reacted in a mulish way. Jos was riding a mule because the Grants were so short of cash, it was all he could afford. Also it would be needed to work on the farm. One way and another it was a bad start to a long schedule and I wasn't grateful. It was unnecessary and boded ill for any more work with animals. If you are shooting anywhere near the studios in one of several European countries, you can usually call on a stable where there are animals – not only horses – which have been trained to work for films. For *The Singer Not the Song* I brought a special horse and its trainer, the famous Jack Munt, to Spain for Dirk Bogarde. It pays to be cautious: Roy Kinnear died after falling off a horse in Spain. Some of the trainers in Hollywood produce marvellous results, taking months and even years of schooling to achieve them. This is a help, but I have found that there still are limits to what can be expected. There were no such beasts available around Nairobi any more than there were around Hong Kong. There is another factor: you cannot expect private owners to allow you to borrow their animals to be knocked about by some stranger.

One way to handle the action is to place wranglers behind bushes, or whatever, put fodder down and so on, so laying a trail which the animal is most likely to follow naturally. I've had some success that way with dogs, for instance. By the way, if you are photographing a pack of hounds, it is essential to lay a scent for them. Then they will keep their noses to the ground and look as if they are hunting; without it they will prance along with their heads in the air. This may not matter to the general audience, but it is worth remembering that there will surely be some people in the audience who have more experience in real life than you have, of many of the things you are showing them. Hunting is only one example.

So by the end of the first day of shooting I discovered I had a rebellious cast, for the first time in my life. I was really shocked. It had simply never happened to me before. It took me a few days to get a grip. I knew I had to resign myself to a hostile atmosphere because there was no way of curing it, especially when more members of the cast arrived from England and were soon in some mysterious way infected by the virus. The only part that seriously annoyed me was that I never got on 'best friends' terms with Holly Aird, who played Elspeth, aged 12. I could not see any reason for this and I still can't. To find Holly we had interviewed over 200 little girls. We were looking for some one who was neither Shirley Temple nor Lolita. We then had readings with about 30 and finally produced a short list of six. These we gave a full scale test on video. Holly stood out clearly as the one and I told Christopher so, before we had viewed the tests. How right we were. She came over as a genuine little girl. She was never a pert little madam or a precocious bimbo. And she looked and sounded truly in period 1912. She was behaving so unselfconsciously and naturally I was anxious not to over direct her. I repeat, the old axiom is true: 'If it ain't broke, don't fix it.'

Some confusion and distrust was caused by my method of shooting, from which the inexperienced may derive the impression that the director doesn't know what he is doing. The story was broken down into seven one-hour episodes but we were not going through it part by part. We were shooting as for a motion picture, which would run six and a quarter hours. As is normal with film schedules, any one day's work might include scenes from two or even three sections of the story, sometimes in the same set, but not invariably. Also, I was not prepared to indulge in protracted master scenes, of which the greater part would end up in the cutting room trims. Not 'on the cutting room floor' as the cant phrase has it. No editor would do such a thing. A few of the actors were unable to follow the drift through lack of experience, or experience of an old-fashioned kind. Nobody expects them to understand the intricacies of film technique; if they do, well and good; but if they don't, they should leave it to the director and be thankful; the responsibility is not theirs. If an actor finds that this method of production, known as cutting in the camera, is upsetting, he should make it his business to find out how it is done and why it is done. It might be good for his nerves and he might be less of a pest to people who do know what they are doing.

David Robb unburdened himself to the *TV Times* in November 1986: 'There was a breakdown of communication between the director and myself. We didn't like each other and that's not good news when you're thousands of miles from home.' Once we got the Errol Flynn idea out of the way, I had no cause to dislike him. There were at least two occasions when I tried to encourage him by telling him what I still believe to be true, that he was giving the best acting performance of all of them, in a part that was not easy to play. This would be a very successful television serial. He would be on the screen in the same slot for seven successive weeks with a vast audience. What more did he want? Too bad he didn't like me. What has 'liking' got to do with shooting a film? We have all seen the self-indulgence that ensues when everyone falls in love with everyone else, to the detriment of the production. Mutual professional respect is what we want and he had mine. He also said he had run up a bill of £800 for telephone calls. He was homesick, that's all. So were one or two of the others. One had left behind a pregnant wife. He was very cross indeed when the schedule had to be altered and he couldn't get back home in time for the birth. As they used to say in Hollywood, 'That's mo'om pitchers, son'.

Christopher Neame stayed in Kenya all the time. The executive producer Verity Lambert and John Hawkesworth were based in London. They came to Kenya for a few days on two occasions I think and spent a lot of time with the actors, who probably had more to say than I had. I have never carried my problems to the producer of any of my pictures, believing that the responsibility of solving them and the ability to do so lay with me. Anyway Verity and John told me they were very happy with the rushes. There wasn't really much more to say. John even went so far as to tell me not to worry too much about progress, a day or two over schedule wouldn't hurt. Little did he know that we were all mad keen to be home for Christmas!

Fortunately there were several other members of the cast who behaved normally, John Nettleton pre-eminently so. He has brought normality to a fine art. He is a really nice man. He too looked and sounded exactly right in his character. Well, yes, minister, he always does. He had a part which appeared two or three times at intervals during the schedule, so he was shuttled back and forth between England and Kenya. He was a real friend. On every journey he made personal contact with my home base in London. He went to a lot of trouble collecting letters and parcels and conveying personal messages. I am truly grateful to him.

Thanks be, the other side of the camera was all right. The cameraman, Ian Wilson, was a miracle worker. The only rushes we had were inevitably two or three days late and they did not look very good on the video of those days. Looking at the rushes, all one could do was to check the action. Ian gave up after the first showing and photographed the whole piece without seeing a foot of film. Peter Sinclair the operator was really good. We used the steadycam once or twice, which was then a new piece of equipment and very heavy. Not an easy thing to handle in the equatorial sun, if you are walking backwards, ahead of two people riding slowly down a sloping field, while they play a dialogue scene. Especially if the lady fluffs too often. After six takes Peter was exhausted.

The first assistant was Gino Marotta, a man of long and varied experience. He was an absolute genius with the background action. The people were all locals who had no experience of films, spoke little English and Gino had even less Swahili. Somehow by magic he communicated with them and it all worked perfectly. It was remarkable. He again exercised these miraculous powers to great effect on *Ghandi*.

Costume dramas bring with them all sorts of difficulties but they were all handled beautifully by my dress designer, Margaret Quigley. We had first worked together on *Minder*, which obviously didn't offer much scope for the wardrobe department. Margaret really took off on *Flame Trees*. Her research was imaginative and detailed down to the last button and bow and especially the underdress. If the ladies are not properly corseted their dresses will just look wrong. They don't feel right to the wearer either. The same rules apply to the men's outfits. It may have been uncomfortable in tropical climes in 1980 but we were all living in 1912. Margaret was very strict about these matters. So many of the present day costume dramas neglect this necessity with the result that the characters don't look right and they don't move properly. Too many people just don't care; they believe the audience doesn't know the difference anyway. Quite true, they don't know the difference, but when a film comes along which gets it right, they do know they are watching something authentic. The people will be behaving according to their age and station in the culture of their time and place, and there is more satisfaction in that. I would offer *A Night to Remember* as an example.

Margaret was a gem and a great support to me. Naturally she was privy to the wardrobe and make-up gossip and knew what was cooking in every pot, but she never let on to me, not a word. She knew and I knew that she knew and she knew that I knew she knew, about the tiresome waste of effort I was obliged to make, coping with the obstinacy and sheer mischief of some of the cast. She later gave up dress design, studied art for some years and is now a considerable painter.

Most of the locations were fairly close to Nairobi, but we went up country for a week or so, to the White Highlands, as they used to be called. Crossing the equator we established a camp on David and Delia Craig's ranch at Lewa Downs. Their hospitality was a new record in generosity and kindness; they were marvellous. They insisted that I stay in their house in the best bedroom and bathroom and that was a real privilege. David worked 18 hours a day on our behalf, in particular providing a huge covered wagon, drawn by three span of oxen. That was a sight to see; indeed nobody had seen such a sight for many years in Kenya. Neither had the animals. A point of interest for anyone intending to shoot such a scene: once you get the thing going and it passes through the shot, you can't turn it round or even back it up for another take, like you can with a car. You have to outspan the animals and drive them back to the starting point. You then turn the wagon round manually and tow it back to the oxen by tractor; then you inspan the animals again and at last you are ready for take two. David was absolutely brilliant at this manoeuvre. I had always rather regretted that, while I was in Hollywood, I never got the chance to direct a western. My opportunity had come at last.

Mike Fox was the appropriately named second unit cameraman who filmed some wonderful coverage of animals, especially a leopardess and plenty of elephants. We had a scene in which Elspeth goes walkabout in the bush with only the headman as escort. They hear the approach of a herd of elephant. All they can do is hide in the undergrowth and pray that they are downwind of the animals. Sighs of relief when the herd passes harmlessly by. The headman got a reprimand and Elspeth got a smack from her father for that little escapade. All done without an elephant within miles, thanks to Mike Fox. I could have done with him when I was in the Congo, but he wasn't born then.

There was another star in the film: the landscape. It sounds obvious and it has been obvious to many directors ever since the cinema began, but still to this day there are directors who will cheerfully shoot a scene of, say, two people on a balcony which overlooks a magnificent view – and they don't show you the view. I stuck to this principle all through: why come all the way to Kenya if you're not going to show it to the audience? A large section of the television audience simply adores 'lovely views'. Every single scene must be played against the landscape unless it is truly impossible to do so. Also, put the actors' backs to the sun and their faces to the wind, wherever possible. This was a big factor in the success of the picture.

All things come to an end and we did get home by Christmas. After the usual post-production work the seven episodes were ready for transmission. I was not surprised when the top brass at Thames Television expressed their delight with the programme. So did the critics, though I thought it curious that not one of them mentioned my name.

Thames gave a splendid launch party at the zoo and showed the first two episodes, which went down very well. There was a lot of excitement in the audience. I don't remember what Sharon Maughan, Ben Cross, Nicholas Jones, David Robb or Holly Aird had to say or even if they were present, but Hayley came dashing up to me and said, 'I take it all back'. I was delighted to hear it, but I remembered Evelyn Waugh's description of 'the saddest words in the English language: "Too late".'

THE OBLIGATORY HARD LUCK STORY

'It's always depressing when you see friends working so hard on a project which you know will never be made.' So said Johnny Goodman. We were chatting about story ideas and the remark has stuck in my mind. We first met when he was production manager on *The Saint*. Later he became production controller at Euston Films, progressing to executive rank with HTV and Carlton, so he spoke with all the inside experience of the production side, of what would be likely to be made and what would not, however regrettable some of those decisions may turn out to be. I know the feeling well, from the other side of the fence. Nevertheless, once you fall in love with a subject you plough on regardless, deliberately suppressing any niggling doubts you may have. So much time spent on writing a treatment, or more often a full script and nothing at the end of it. Well, not 'nothing' exactly – the work is never entirely wasted. There is a benefit to experience and occasionally one gets some idea of what not to do next time.

Ever since 1936 I had carried with me the deep impression *Tudor Rose* had made on me, as I described earlier in this book. When I arrived in Hollywood I sought out Robert Stevenson, who had been ensconced in the Disney studio for some time. We talked about the film and he agreed that the subject could done again, if the right girl came along. Some more years elapsed before I started to read up the background. I found most of the books confusing. There are so many important characters in the story, all pursuing different ways to the same end. Too often the authors follow the life of Mr X for some time, ignoring the lives of Messrs Y and Z. Then in the next chapter they jump back in time to deal with Y and Z, covering the same ground from a different point of view. Especially in an historical story there must be a more straightforward way, otherwise the inexorable narrative drive of events is lost. That is where the heart of the drama lies.

Using *The Handbook of Dates* by CR Cheney I set down the actions of all the people in strict chronological order, sometimes day by day, from the death of Henry VIII through the reign of Edward VI to the execution of Lady Jane Grey. Apart from enabling me to follow the developments clearly, it revealed much more of the intrigue, political manoeuvring and plotting that was going on, just as it was happening. All the material events and almost all of the conversations, statements and letters are in the records, offering almost verbatim dialogue. I modified the speeches where some of the usages would be unintelligible or misleading to a modern audience, but otherwise left them in the original. I was deeply involved and thoroughly enjoying myself.

All this was done at intervals over several more years, until *The Flame Trees of Thika* came along and with it, Holly Aird. I was convinced that she would play Lady Jane beautifully. Soon after the launch party of that film, I noticed quite by chance that the Museum of London was putting on a season of London-made films and *Tudor Rose* was one of them. I went, of course. The copy had been badly cut about but the spirit of the thing was still there. As the audience filed out at the end I noticed two men who didn't seem to belong to the rest of the people; they seemed to be there for a purpose, as I was. Were they film people? I didn't recognise either of them. I wondered if they were on the same track as I was. I chose to ignore them; there was nothing I could do anyway.

I pressed on with my script, which I called *Jane the Quene*, again at intervals interrupted by other work. Incidentally, I never mentioned this to Holly and she

Left: Roger Moore (*The Saint,* Bamore/ITC)

Left: Margaret Lockwood (*The Human Jungle,* Independent Artists/ABC)

Right: Sharing a joke with Patrick Macnee (*The Avengers,* Telemen/ABC)

Right: Liz Fraser, Patrick Macnee and Diana Rigg (*The Avengers,* Telemen/ABC)

Right: Barbara Shelley, RWB, James Donald and Andrew Keir (*Quatermass and the Pit,* Hammer/ Associated British Pathe)

Left: Andrew Keir celebrates his birthday with Barbara Shelley (*Quatermass and the Pit*, Hammer/Associated British Pathe)

Below: Bette Davis and crew celebrate the fourth of July (*The Anniversary*, Hammer/ Associated British Pathe)

Right: Ingrid Pitt, Madeline Smith, Kate O'Mara, Pippa Steel and Kirsten Betts (*The Vampire Lovers,* Hammer/ MGM-EMI)

Right: Christopher Lee and Patrick Troughton (*Scars of Dracula,* Hammer/Anglo-EMI)

Right: Ralph Bates and Martine Beswick (*Dr Jekyll & Sister Hyde,* Hammer/ Anglo-EMI)

Left: Britt Ekland, Milton Subotsky and Charlotte Rampling (*Asylum,* Amicus)

Left: Receiving the Grand Prix at the Convention Française du Cinema Fantastique

Left: Terry-Thomas, Tom Baker, Daniel Massey, Michael Craig, Curt Jurgens and (at rear) Denys Coop (*The Vault of Horror,* Amicus)

Right: Peter Cushing and Shih Szu (*The Legend of the 7 Golden Vampires,* Hammer/ Warner Bros)

Right: Anthony Andrews and Maurice Röeves (*Danger UXB,* Euston/Thames)

Right: Peter Bowles (*The Irish RM,* Ulster/ Channel 4)

Above: Dennis Waterman and George Cole (*Minder,* Euston/Thames)

Left: Recording the audio narration for a Hammer DVD: Francis Matthews, Barbara Shelley and Christopher Lee

Below: A round of applause for the reader, with thanks! (Peter Everard-Smith)

knows nothing of it. There was no point in doing so until I had some firm basis for a production. After another two years she was now the right age and the script was complete, so I started to offer it to producers but soon came up against the news that somebody else was presenting the same subject and had already sold the idea to Paramount. Their idea, as it later turned out, was a story of two teenagers with ideals who try to change the world for the better but are brought down and executed by their elders. (cf, page 19).

So this one *would* be made, but not by me. Reading my script again, it is too long and too complicated, but it is good. It is truly a tragic story and very moving. Perhaps I shall prune it one day, just for my own amusement. It was undoubtedly the biggest disappointment I ever had. Thank you for allowing me to rest my head on your shoulder.

THE IRISH RM

After a couple of episodes of *Minder* I showed up for another of John Hawkesworth's ventures. This was Anglo-American, with Sam Waterston playing a pastiche of Sherlock Holmes and Doctor Thorndike, pre-1910. Then the redoubtable Michael Whitehall presented me to James Mitchell, who was shooting a series of six episodes of *Some Experiences of an Irish RM* by E Œ Somerville and Martin Ross.

This was really intriguing. So many people had tried to film this famous book. The first stories were published in book form in 1899, a second volume in 1908 and a final volume in 1915; I believe they have never been out of print. The original books have excellent sketches of the characters, done by Somerville. They are immensely popular, not only in Ireland and the UK but all over the world. Since the 1950s there were two or three serious attempts to set it up but they had all failed: the main objection being that there is so much fox hunting in them.

I directed three of the second series. The following year another series of six was set up and I directed all of them. It was one of the most enjoyable times of my life. First of all, James Mitchell. Some time about 1980 he realised, as an executive producer, that England is not the only place where films can be made – nor is Hollywood for that matter. He doesn't have a parochial outlook; he is a true European, being multi-lingual in French and German. Just at this time, the Irish Government decided to encourage the arts, including film, by tax accomodations. James went to Dublin to make pictures and has been there ever since, making film after film. The films are all made in Ireland, in collaboration with Radio Telefis Eireann, Ulster Television and groups all over Europe. He has itchy feet, spending most of his time flying around the continent. The most endearing point about him is his taste, which is only for the finest.

The other endearing point about him is his wife, Jane, a daughter of the Irish landed gentry, bright as a beautiful dawn and devastatingly attractive. Always perfectly turned out, she has a wicked sense of humour and is an incorrigible flirt. She likes you to think she is naughty, but she isn't. She is jolly and passionate and a delight to be with. She is a stickler and appreciates good manners. The luncheons she gave when they were staying at Luggala will never be forgotten. Quick-witted and well read, she was once a publisher's reader and I suspect has some influence on the activities of James' companies, although she would never acknowledge it. James lives in Dublin, though not a lot. Jane lives in Paris and so they meet there and in London and Madrid, or Frankfurt; they may ski for a week in France or go to Israel. Jane has lately taken to visiting Cairo, to look after lepers.

There are 34 stories in the Irish RM books, but many of them are merely anecdotes and sketches, not giving enough material for an hour-long story. As regards the second and third series, ten of the shows were achieved by clever dovetailing of two or three of the original works into a single story. All hail to Rosemary Anne Sisson, Alfred Shaughnessy and Bill Craig, all writers of high repute and long experience. The other two episodes were original stories by Hugh Leonard which fitted in perfectly with the style of the books. All of which goes to show what can be done by first class writers. They started with a world famous book which has wonderful style, dozens of great characters and splendid settings, but filming it is another matter. Filming it entails close inspection of the material, which was revealed to be thinner than could be desired. They found ways around that problem but on top of that they brought a sympathetic understanding of the spirit of the thing. I have met a number of people who saw the programme or some of it, many of whom had read the book and loved it; no one complained of distortion or abuse of the original tales and many were delighted with the life-like presentation of the well known characters.

When a writer transfers a book to the screen he is usually criticised for being unfaithful to the original. The first handicap he meets is the strong impression the book has made on its readers, which varies widely from person to person. Then the work must be visualised; also it must be condensed, etc., etc. Then the screenwriter's own selections and emphases will have their effect. Tricky stuff.

We were based at Rathcool, in Wicklow, about 30 minutes drive south of Dublin, in an appropriately run down large country house – so the locations were all around us. As usual I pointed the camera at the landscape with the actors in front of it. We did some effective work in bitter cold and pouring rain; there's nothing like genuine rain, on film. Nothing like a genuine fox hunt, either. The Kildare pack came out for us, splendidly turned out and mounted and hounds are really hunting, with noses well down to the scent. They drew a real fox too. He got away.

Jack Conroy was the cameraman, a grand man, a real contributor and a great leader of the crew. At this time, 1983, the Irish film world was in the dumps. Bray studios at Enniskerry was about to close. Everyone was determined to show that they could deliver a film as well as anyone and they proved it. They certainly worked hard and long hours, without a single moan. We all got on well and they were especially nice to me.

The actors were all around us too, breathing real life into those famous characters: Flurry Knox, Slipper, Mrs Cadogan, Sally Knox and Peter, all in the safe hands of the cream of Ireland's actors and actresses. I managed to persuade Noel Purcell to emerge from retirement to play a special part in one of the stories. I sought him out mainly because I hadn't seen him since he was such a help to me in *Jacqueline*, which was now 30 years ago. He was now well on in years but I knew the part would suit him because the character never stirred from a comfortable armchair. He did it beautifully and everyone was glad to see him again: he was an immensely popular figure in Dublin. We had a few visitors from England, among them Dinsdale Landen and John Wells. This was one of John's first appearances on film, I think.

The main burden of the opera was carried by Peter Bowles, as the RM. Not an easy task: it is another case in which the central character can so easily become a stooge to all the others. The humour of it comes from the wiles of the locals, who are all working to a different set of rules from the RM, if they have any rules at all. All this was adroitly managed by P Bowles. His final triumph comes in the last episode of the series, when he turns the tables on them all.

Peter is a special actor, definitely special. He tells the story of his first encounter in the profession, when he was searching around for jobs. Some agent took one look at him and said with a shrug, 'Well, I suppose you could play Italian waiters, that sort of thing'. This may have given him the idea, rightly or wrongly, that to get anywhere in the profession he would have to work very hard indeed and that he did. Lately he has delivered some outstanding performances in the West End theatre. All this hard graft has resulted in a profound knowledge of the theory and practice of acting. His technical knowledge is complete, but it can sometimes complicate matters. He can take a short speech of only a couple of sentences and purvey four or five different shades of meaning and emotion in it. I used to pull his leg by asking if we might have just two out of the five possibilities on offer. 'Of course,' he would say, 'just tell me: which two do you prefer?' We developed a great mutual confidence. I think he may have been pleased that at least I had noticed that there were five.

One incident must be mentioned as a final tribute to the devotion to duty of the Irish cast and crew. One of the actors, Don Foley, appeared as Walkin' Aisy. He played his main scenes well and then had to wait a week or so for a final day's work. By this time I had discovered that he should have been in hospital. When he turned up for the final scene he was clearly unwell. He had postponed the hospital appointment. He insisted on going ahead. More than that, he heard me fumbling around, trying to remember a snatch of Mozart which I wanted for another character to hum. Don supplied words and music, singing lustily. He then went straight to hospital to be treated for tuberculosis. Indomitable, that man.

Meanwhile, back in England...

THE MASKS OF DEATH

Sherlock Holmes had manifested himself once more. The producer, Kevin Francis, had conjured him up and this was to be a film by Holmes buffs, for Holmes buffs. Based on a story by John Elder (the pen-name of Hammer's Anthony Hinds), the script by NJ Crisp was packed with in-jokes. It also had a number of twists on the traditional style: Holmes is no longer infallible and makes several mistakes, which he admits; Irene Adler re-appears, in the person of Anne Baxter, but this time she is a goodie.

Over recent years there had been several versions of the Sherlock saga, plus pastiches, new stories, etcetera, etcetera, some very fanciful indeed. Peter Cushing, Sir John Mills and I met for a discussion of the relationship between Holmes and Watson. Not surprisingly, we were all of one mind: we had re-read the books and our opinions were based on what we had read:

They were both bachelors of a certain social status. They were both looking for a modest and comfortable set of rooms in a respectable area not too far from the centre of London. They each had a small income which wouldn't run to a suitable place, but if they shared the expenses they would be able to rent such a set, together with a housekeeper. They scrupulously respected each other's territory, using the sitting room as common ground. It was an exclusively male existence and they became fast friends. In the course of the adventures they came to depend on each other. Contrary to the speculations of some latter-day commentators, they never evinced the slightest interest in homosexuality. The period of *The Adventures* runs from 1881 to 1903; the present story *The Masks of Death* is set in 1913, with Holmes being dragged out of retirement.

Peter was one of the best of many actors who had played Sherlock Holmes. This was his seventeenth and final bow in the part; he knew the man and understood him perfectly. Johnnie had never played Watson and to my mind, his was the best version ever. It is the devil of a character to convey as a real person. He is usually presented as a thick-headed stooge to the great man, which of course makes one wonder how Holmes puts up with him – that can't be right. Holmes is the eccentric, imaginative figure, while Watson is down to earth, methodical, practical: after all, he is a doctor of medicine. The two men are complete opposites but in their different ways they are equals, or at any rate of equal value to each other. They respect each other. I guarantee that this picture is worth a look just to see this performance. I don't mean to belittle any of the other actors, who are all fine: Anne Baxter, Anton Diffring, Gordon Jackson and Ray Milland, all in great form.

The crew was largely a collection of old friends. Anthony Mendleson, the brilliant and much regretted costume designer, who supervised the dozens of uniforms, badges and medal ribbons on *The One That Got Away* and three stalwarts from Hammer: Roy Ashton, Chris Barnes and guess who as sound editor – the other Roy Baker. Ray Sturgess was the camera operator. We had worked together several times before but this time he was presented with some special problems. The ruling was that we must use camera equipment from the Pinewood camera department, which hadn't been used for years. Pinewood had been a wall-to-wall studio for ages. Therefore all the visiting crews brought their own gear with them. Anyway the Pinewood stuff was cleaned up and tested but it was old-fashioned, which didn't make life easy for Ray. It was due to his efforts that everything worked out well. Brendan Stafford was the lighting cameraman who, like Holmes, had to be dragged protesting out of retirement to do the film. He enjoyed it, I'm sure.

Back to my favourite *Minder* for two episodes and then another serial came along: the second series of *Fairly Secret Army,* in seven parts. Written by David Nobbs and an opportunity to work with Geoffrey Palmer and Liz Fraser and Jeremy Sinden and Diane Fletcher AND John Nettleton – the place was bursting with talent. Another bonus was the music, by Michael Nyman, a most eminent contemporary composer. For this series he had produced a wonderfully bombastic military march. It is fascinating to hear how a composer can call up a combination of musical instruments and notes which bring vivid pictures of character and atmosphere to the mind's eye. This music makes you laugh out loud at the utterly bogus pretensions of the characters and their total absorption in themselves. Dusty Miller was lighting, an old friend from *Minder*, and Andrew Montgomery was first assistant, also from *Minder* and, in earlier days, *QED.*

THE TUNDRA

Life is full of surprises. Owl TV of Toronto asked me to go over there to talk about a film they were planning. It was an opportune moment to go, because *Flame Trees* was showing there for the second time and was very well received indeed. Owl was the producer of a regular children's TV programme and a long list of children's books and magazines, now ambitious to produce a feature film. The executive producer was Annabel Slaight, delightful company, briskly efficient and couldn't have been nicer.

The subject was a novel called *Whiteout* by one James Houston, who had also written the script. He had published a number of books, mostly about Canadian Indians and the Inuit. He had spent twenty years or more in the tiny village of Cape Dorset on Baffin Island, running the school, the hospital – running the whole community, in fact. He was the principal mover in bringing Inuit art, mostly in the form of soapstone carvings, out of the tundra into Canada and the United States. He mounted the first exhibition of this work in Quebec. He brought two of the Inuit artists with him and one day they disappeared. He thought, perhaps they have sloped off to the shops. A shop-by-shop search was organised. At last they were found. They were suffering so much in the unaccustomed heat of Quebec they had sought shelter in the cold store at the back of a butcher's shop.

We all agreed to meet again in the following spring, to go to Baffin Island where the story was set. This was about a mid-teenaged boy, born and brought up in

Toronto. His widowed mother can't control him so she posts him off to live for a year with his uncle, who is a tough, crusty Scotsman, the manager of the Hudson's Bay Company store, in a remote village close to the Arctic Circle. The boy has to attend school there, together with the local Inuit children. The schoolmaster offers an entirely different treatment of the boy from the uncle's. The situation develops as the boy tries to escape, falls in love with an Inuit girl and so on. The focus then turns on which of the two attitudes to the boy, the uncle's or the teacher's, will prove to be most beneficial, if at all.

The locations at Cape Dorset were ideal. There were six or seven of us in the recce party and we all crowded into the only hotel – The Inn, as it was called. Nobody lives in igloos any longer. This inn had nine bedrooms and regularly accommodated 21 people. The allocation of rooms must be a ticklish problem at times. James Houston and I shared a room and I snored. Not the best behaviour.

Returning to the inn one evening after tramping miles in six feet of snow or whizzing round on a ski-bike – all thoroughly exhilarating, I was in the hall, removing boots, thick socks, Berghaus jacket, jerseys, scarves, hats and waterproof trousers. A woman came up to me. She had arrived at the inn a couple of days previously. She was a birdwatcher and she had come all the way from Connecticut to do it. She was charming. She had just discovered from one of my companions that I directed *The Flame Trees of Thika* and she loved it. An unsolicited testimonial if ever there was one and very nice too. Not the sort of meeting you expect in the Arctic Circle. It is worth remembering how these movies get around and what a wide audience there is, even including Connecticut twitchers.

While assessing the locations we had long discussions about the script and it was decided that I should write a new version. Back in London I set to work. It was received with enthusiasm by Annabel and Timothy Burrill, who had joined the team. Annabel now had to take the plunge. If the film was to be made next year, then all the necessary timber to build the sets, huts, bungalows and so on would have to be put on site before the fall of the present year, when ships would be frozen out until next spring. Boldly the decision was made and furthermore some construction work was done. The sets would look all the better for standing over the winter. We had already had casting sessions in Toronto and had pencilled in some names. In London, I spoke to Billy Connolly about the uncle. He was keen and would have been great. The other important part was the schoolmaster; I approached Alfred Molina about this. He too was interested and was perfect for it. However, by the end of that year we realised that the finance was not to be found and the project was abandoned. It was a pity, after so much good work by so many good people, over eighteen months or more.

Roll up sleeves, return to active service with *Minder*, including the final episode of that series, which was a double-length one. Not a simple job, this one. A lot of work was required to complete the last third of the script and the writer was unavailable. Also, we again had, as the central character, a megalomaniac who has raised a private army, this time a rich man living in a vast country house, complete with stables and all. Worse, Dennis Waterman had an almost non-existent part to play. We could so easily have put in a stable girl for him to chase and bring in further complications in the plots of the other characters. We got some of it right but it was not a resounding success.

In 1990 Eric Ambler celebrated his 80th birthday. He was now living in England again after a long stay in Switzerland. I sent him a birthday card and we had a couple of jolly meetings over fish and chips and other favourites. Eric suggested that I might write a script of his book, *Doctor Frigo*. I jumped at the chance, but it was a daunting prospect. The book is presented as a first person diary, written by a Frenchman. It is a brilliant piece of work by Eric, because it reads exactly as a not quite perfect translation into English, so that the sense of its French origin is preserved. He had set himself a difficult task and like all his work it is meticulously done. Eric once said that it was his favourite of all of his books and it is easy to see why it may be so. Another problem is that, being a diary, all the events and actions are exclusively those of the writer. Therefore the screenwriter must supply scenes involving the other characters. These may be deduced from the information in the diary, but one might be telegraphing some surprises lying in wait for the central character. We went through three drafts of a full script, but I was never able to persuade a producer to take it up. The truth is that the script was never as good as the book. It may be that the book is simply not suitable for a film.

Having described my previous disappointments with European film festivals, always excepting Brussels, the time has come to tell an altogether different story. A complete contrast was to come at Dinard, in 1993. This is a proper film festival, not just fantasy movies. The entire programme is always devoted to British films. Apparently the director of the festival, Marc Ruscart, himself a film director, was discussing the programming with the publisher and critic François Guérif. He suggested some of my work, as being varied over a wide range of different subjects. So, apart from the pictures in competition, they put on a retrospective of seven of my films. I am most grateful to them; it was a great honour. There is a reason for mentioning one of the films in particular. *A Night to Remember* had a particularly striking effect. It was now more than 35-years-old, in black and white. The audience were nearly all younger than the film. Some may have seen it on television, as I had, but no one had seen it on a big screen – and neither had I, since I made it. The effect was to impress everyone with the profound differences in presentation given by TV and cinema screens and especially the heightened emotional impact of seeing it with an audience.

Also in connection with *A Night to Remember* another surprise turned up. Bill McQuitty told me that his old friend Arthur C Clarke, author of *2001* and many many other books, had just published a new novel, *The Ghost From the Grand Banks*. The premise was most amusing to us. The year is 2007. There is great public interest and entertainment in watching the films of the previous century, but the snag is that the audiences can't bear the sight of people smoking. It makes them feel sick. So, a top-notch computer consultant is busy removing all signs of this disgusting habit from the movies. The one he is working on at the moment happens to be *A Night to Remember*. It is a simple job for him because there is so little smoking in it. The book then develops into the rivalry between two consortiums, each trying to raise one half of the wreck of *Titanic*. Needless to say, they fail, to general relief.

I wrote a treatment, which I am bound to say, is good; sent it to Arthur, who lives in Colombo; he liked it too. He came on a visit to London at that time, so we were able to talk about it. It has a smashing part for Sean Connery, by the way. Nobody wanted to back it, or nobody that I approached wanted to. They may have been daunted by scenes at the wreck, four miles under the ocean, but these would be done without water: it's pitch dark and nothing moves, not even a fish.

One consequence of the visit to Dinard was that I was asked to serve as chairman of the jury at the Festival at Nantes in the following year. This again is for proper films and the special angle is that it is dedicated to pictures from three continents, which excludes North America, Australasia and Europe. Here is a chance to see truly exotic works from Africa, South America and anywhere East of Suez, which will never play at your local Odeon. Some of the pictures were most impressive, in particular the one from China, *For Fun*, which won the top prize. As at Dinard, the organisation and the hospitality at Nantes were superb.

Recently, much to my surprise, I was asked again to Sitges. Apparently they had conducted a poll of critics and fans, asking them to nominate films they would most like to see again and *Dr Jekyll & Sister Hyde* was one of them. They also staged an amusing general interview with Robert Wise – he of *The Sound of Music* and many more – and me. We fielded the questions and passed the ball to each other rather well I thought. Being roughly contemporaries and of long experience we politely punctured a few of the more high-falutin' balloons. It was all very good humoured. I suspect this sort of thing was not really what the audience expected or may have wanted, but there you are, most of the practitioners of the art are reluctant to appear pompous or arty-farty in public. Perhaps we don't want to betray trade secrets. Ours is a magic box of tricks and if the public gets to know how all the tricks are done, the magic will vanish and their enlightenment and entertainment will go with it.

So I'll shut up.

IS THAT ALL ?

Yes. Well, I think so. Of course, I do see that ... er ... coming to an abrupt conclusion ... without drawing some conclusions, as t'were, isn't enough.

First of all, this is a book that grew as it went along, with the ambition of interesting the general reader who is a keen filmgoer, by describing the predicaments encountered in directing more than 30 films and nearly a hundred television episodes, over a period of 50 years or so. The book also tries to offer some hints for 17-year-old gophers, which – given the enormous changes which have taken place during that time – may now look old-fashioned. But whatever changes have come about in techniques, or in style, or in fashion, the basic principles abide. So I conclude that there is no need to be hidebound by them, but they are worth some consideration; they can save you a lot of time. And, most important, you will discover how to bend the rules.

Those coming to film now have the benefit of a huge backlog of work, showing the vast range of expression that has been developed over the years by many and varied hands. It is essential to acquire some experience of this library, without soaking one's self in The History of Cinematic Art. You need to see examples of what can be achieved, but the materials you will be working with are ready to hand in the life that is all around you. True, if making a period picture you have to adapt to the culture of that time and place, but humanity doesn't change all that much.

One more question: where do film directors come from? Writers, producers, cameramen, editors, assistant directors, actors, actresses, theatre directors, television directors and commercials directors have all given it a shot, with varying degrees of success. One continuity girl, Muriel Box, also writer and producer, turned in some good work. Of all these categories, which is the most likely to succeed? Writers are too often too literary, few producers ever try their luck, cameramen are too technically-minded – but Nicolas Roeg is the exception that proves the rule – editors, again too technical. Assistant directors should be likely to do well but often don't, the thespians are usually too thespian and we have at least three distinguished gentlemen of the theatre who can't direct films for toffee. The television people offer the most likely to make it, but the big screen is a different cup of tea altogether and is not easy to master. The truth is, a film director can appear from anywhere. So there is no conclusion to be drawn here either. But there is one matter of fundamental importance to which the deepest thought must be given:

When the first-time director has the script and the megaphone in his hand, he must obliterate from his mind all bias that his previous professional experience may have on him. If he was an editor, well and good: he will have no difficulty with that side of life, but he must stop thinking as an editor. His approach to the film must be as a director, using to the full all the values of the other departments.

Another tip is, once the proper experience has been gained, don't go to the cinema too much; you may end up imitating other directors' pictures.

Fare thee well.

AFTERWORD

It's been over 50 years since Roy Baker and I first became friends. I had just been demobbed from the American Army, and Roy, fresh from the British Army, was just about to direct Eric Ambler's *The October Man* – Eric's first picture as a producer-screenwriter. Eric introduced us and I pride myself on having been able to maintain a friendship with both through all their struggles, which are well-outlined in *The Director's Cut*. Through all this time, Roy has been one of those wonderful friends that you just pick up with after years of absence without always filling in the gaps. For that reason, *The Director's Cut* is a very valuable book to me, as it brought me up to date on all of the things which I missed hearing about from my friend.

It is a fascinating examination of the ins and outs of that period of British film production from the end of the Second World War, more properly called the J Arthur Rank era. It is a period which has often been overlooked by film historians in their haste to focus only on Laurence Olivier, David Lean and Carol Reed. What historians refuse to either look at or understand is that the Rank Organisation was active in all areas of the industry. They were production, distribution and owners of the largest chain of theaters in the UK. They stood poised to create a real business, yet were frightened by the pre-War experience of Alexander Korda. Fashioned by thirties and forties Hollywood thinking and plagued by the labor difficulties of the time, Rank chose not to position itself for the future. Showbusiness is not for the fainthearted.

I can remember a dinner meeting with Roy and Alan Sillitoe, even before his novel *Saturday Night and Sunday Morning* was published. Roy had read the galleys and desperately wanted to make it. He saw that British audiences were hungering for a new kind of picture and this could be it. He was rejected by the Rank poohbahs on the grounds that no one would want to see such a subject. This was too different. The book and the movie were international commercial and critical successes and Albert Finney became a star. A new era of modern British cinema had begun.

Roy was disappointed not only about this lost opportunity for himself, but that the times were changing and the so-called structure of the industry would not keep up with them. Rank failed to create an industry, even though the legacy has left us with some wonderful films, among them Roy's *Morning Departure* and *A Night to Remember*.

In my opinion, Roy Baker's body of work not only stands tall but also has long needed appreciation. His work in Hollywood showed an ability to bring a fresh approach to directing Marilyn Monroe in the early days of her career. Her portrayal as a troubled baby-sitter in *Don't Bother to Knock* is often considered her first memorable starring role.

Roy was never one to stand still. When the era of 'The Angry Young Men' began and changes did bring a huge new era of independent production for Britain, filmed television followed. Roy Baker became Roy Ward Baker, the master of suspense and horror films. Many of these marvellous films are today cult classics still pleasing audiences all over the world. His TV work, from the brilliant and sensitive *Flame Trees of Thika* to the ever-popular *Minder* series, are part of a legacy.

Roy's ability to chronicle all of this in the most self-effacing manner and often with humour has always been and still is typical of him. Perhaps, that's another reason why I enjoyed *The Director's Cut* so much.

One final note. I recently read a statement from James Cameron, a writer-director not always known for self-effacement. In essence, he said that if he hadn't seen *A Night to Remember* there never would have been *Titanic*.

Samuel Goldwyn Jr
Los Angeles, 2000

DEBITS AND CREDITS

KEY
ep – executive producer
p – producer
sp – screenplay
ph – director of photography
ad – art director
m – music

FILM
NB Films are listed by year of production. Production companies are given in brackets alongside titles.

1943-1945 ARMY KINEMATOGRAPH SERVICE, RAOC, WEMBLEY STUDIOS

HOME GUARD GUARD TOWN FIGHTING SERIES (1943)
1   Weapons and Equipment
2   Scaling Obstacles
3   Squad Movement
4   A Defended House
5   A Street Obstacle
6   Squad Clearing a House
7   Clearing a Street
8   Platoon Assault on a House

ACCORDING TO OUR RECORDS... (1943/44)
sp	Jack House	Mary Clare
ph	John Wilcox	Sydney Tafler
ad	Millsip Nicol	Geoffrey Keen
m	John Bath	Ian Fleming
RAF	Symphony Orchestra	Henry Oscar

TECHNIQUE OF INSTRUCTION IN THE ARMY (1944)
1   Foundations
2   Framework
3   Methods

WHAT'S THE NEXT JOB? (1944)
sp	Jack House	Moore Marriott
ph	John Wilcox	Lesley Brook
ad	Lawrence Broadhouse	Peter Cotes
m	William Alwyn	Brenda Bruce

WARNER'S WARNINGS (1945)
Security Flashes   Jack Warner

A LETTER FROM HOME (1945)

Children in School   Elsie & Doris Waters
Girl Guides/Boy Scouts
Pre-Fab Housing/Gardens
Football/Harvest Festival
Two Fish and Fourpenn'orth

READ ALL ABOUT IT (1945)

sp   Jack House   John Slater
ph   John Wilcox   Alfie Bass
ad   Lawrence Broadhouse   Barbara Lott
m   John Bath   John Laurie

THINK IT OVER (1945)

sp   Thomas Browne   Faith Brook
ph   John Wilcox   Richard Attenborough
ad   Lawrence Broadhouse   Jack Raine

1946 **THE OCTOBER MAN** (Two Cities)

p   Eric Ambler   John Mills
sp   Eric Ambler   Joan Greenwood
ph   Erwin Hillier   Edward Chapman
ad   Vetchinsky   Kay Walsh
m   William Alwyn   Joyce Carey
                                                      Catherine Lacey

1948 **THE WEAKER SEX** (Two Cities)

p   Paul Soskin   Ursula Jeans
sp   Esther McCracken   Cecil Parker
      from her play *No Medals*   Joan Hopkins
ph   Erwin Hillier   Derek Bond
ad   Vetchinsky   Thora Hird
m   Arthur Wilkinson   Bill Owen

1948 **PAPER ORCHID** (Columbia British)

p   William Collier   Hugh Williams
sp   Val Guest   Hy Hazell
      from the novel by Arthur la Bern   Sidney James
ph   Basil Emmott
m   Robert Farnon

1949 **MORNING DEPARTURE (US: OPERATION DISASTER)** (Rank)

p   Leslie Parkyn & Jay Lewis   John Mills
sp   William Fairchild   Nigel Patrick
      from the play by Kenneth Woollard   Richard Attenborough
ph   Desmond Dickinson   Kenneth More
ad   Vetchinsky   James Hayter
m   William Alwyn   George Cole
                                                      Victor Maddern

1950 **HIGHLY DANGEROUS** (Rank)

p	Anthony Darnborough	Margaret Lockwood
sp	Eric Ambler	Dane Clark
	from his book *The Dark Frontier*	Marius Goring
ph	Reginald Wyer	Anton Diffring
		Naunton Wayne
		Anthony Newley

1951 **THE HOUSE ON THE SQUARE (US: I'LL NEVER FORGET YOU)**
(20th Century-Fox)

p	Sol C Siegel	Tyrone Power
sp	Ranald MacDougall	Ann Blyth
	from the film *Berkeley Square* and play by	Michael Rennie
	John L Balderston & JC Squire based on	Dennis Price
	Henry James' *A Sense of the Past*	Raymond Huntley
ph	Georges Perinal	Irene Browne
ad	CP Norman	Robert Atkins
m	William Alwyn	Beatrice Campbell

1952 **DON'T BOTHER TO KNOCK** (20th Century-Fox)

p	Julian Blaustein	Richard Widmark
sp	Daniel Taradash	Marilyn Monroe
	from novel *Mischief*	Anne Bancroft
	by Charlotte Armstrong	Donna Corcoran
ph	Lucien Ballard	Jeanne Cagney
ad	Richard Irvine	Jim Backus
m	Alfred Newman	Elisha Cook Jr

1952 **NIGHT WITHOUT SLEEP** (20th Century-Fox)

p	Robert Bassler	Linda Darnell
sp	Frank Partos & Elick Moll	Gary Merrill
	from novel by Elick Moll	Hildegarde Knef
ph	Lucien Ballard	Hugh Beaumont
ad	Addison Hehr	Mae Marsh
m	Alfred Newman	

1953 **INFERNO** (20th Century-Fox)

p	William Bloom	Robert Ryan
sp	Francis Cockrell	Rhonda Fleming
ph	Lucien Ballard	William Lundigan
ad	Lew Creber	Larry Keating
m	Alfred Newman	Henry Hull

1954 **PASSAGE HOME** (Rank)

p	Julian Wintle	Peter Finch
sp	William Fairchild	Anthony Steel
	from novel by Richard Armstrong	Diane Cilento
ph	Geoffrey Unsworth	Cyril Cusack
ad	Vetchinsky	Geoffrey Keen
		Kenneth Griffith

1955 JACQUELINE (Rank)
p   George H Brown
sp   Patrick Kirwan & Liam O'Flaherty
     from the novel *A Grand Man* by
     Catherine Cookson
ph   Geoffrey Unsworth
ad   Jack Maxsted

John Gregson
Kathleen Ryan
Jacqueline Ryan
Noël Purcell
Cyril Cusack
Tony Wright

1956 TIGER IN THE SMOKE (Rank)
p   Leslie Parkyn
sp   Anthony Pelissier
     from the novel by
     Margery Allingham
ph   Geoffrey Unsworth
ad   Jack Maxsted
m   Malcolm Arnold

Donald Sinden
Muriel Pavlow
Tony Wright
Bernard Miles
Alec Clunes
Laurence Naismith
Gerald Harper

1957 THE ONE THAT GOT AWAY (Rank)
p   Julian Wintle
sp   Howard Clewes
     from the book by
     Kendall Burt & James Leasor
ph   Eric Cross
ad   Edward Carrick

Hardy Kruger
Michael Goodliffe
Alec McCowen
Terence Alexander
John Van Eyssen
Stratford Johns

1958 A NIGHT TO REMEMBER (Rank)
p   William McQuitty
sp   Eric Ambler
     from the book
     by Walter Lord
     and contemporary documents
ph   Geoffrey Unsworth
ad   Vetchinsky

Kenneth More
Laurence Naismith
Michael Goodliffe
Kenneth Griffith
David McCallum
Honor Blackman
Frank Lawton
Alec McCowan
Gerald Harper
Anthony Bushell
Geoffrey Bayldon

NY Critics' Circle Ten Best 1959
Golden Globe
'Christopher' for Direction

1960 THE SINGER NOT THE SONG (Rank)
p   Roy Baker
sp   Nigel Balchin
     from the novel
     by Audrey Erskine Lindop
ph   Otto Heller
ad   Vetchinsky
m   Phil Green

Dirk Bogarde
John Mills
Myléne Demongeot
Laurence Naismith
John Bentley
Leslie French
Eric Pohlmann

1961 FLAME IN THE STREETS (Rank)
p   Roy Baker
sp   Ted Willis
     from his play *Hot Summer Night*
ph   Christopher Challis

John Mills
Sylvia Syms
Johnny Sekka
Brenda de Banzie

ad   Vetchinsky
m   Phil Green

1962 **THE VALIANT** (United Artists)
p   Jon Penington
sp Keith Waterhouse & Willis Hall
    from the play *L'Equipage au Complet*
    by Robert Mallet
ph Wilkie Cooper

John Mills
Ettore Manni
Roberto Risso
Robert Shaw
Liam Redmond
Dinsdale Lansden

1962 **TWO LEFT FEET** (British Lion/RBP)
p   Leslie Gilliatt
sp Roy Baker & John Hopkins
    from novel *In My Solitude*
    by David Stuart Leslie
ph Wilkie Cooper
ad Maurice Carter
m   Phil Green

Michael Crawford
Nyree Dawn Porter
Julia Foster
David Hemmings
Bernard Lee

1967 **QUATERMASS AND THE PIT (US: FIVE MILLION YEARS TO EARTH)** (Hammer)
p   Anthony Nelson Keys
sp Nigel Kneale
ph Arthur Grant
ad Bernard Robinson

James Donald
Andrew Keir
Barbara Shelley
Julian Glover

1967 **THE ANNIVERSARY** (Hammer)
p   Jimmy Sangster
sp Jimmy Sangster
    from the play by William McIlwraith
ph Harry Waxman
ad Reece Pemberton

Bette Davis
Sheila Hancock
Jack Hedley
James Cossins
Elaine Taylor

1968 **private i (US: THE SPY KILLER)** (ABC-TV)
p   Jimmy Sangster
sp Jimmy Sangster
ph Arthur Grant
ad Scott MacGregor

Robert Horton
Sebastian Cabot
Jill St John

1968 **FOREIGN EXCHANGE** (ABC-TV)
p   Jimmy Sangster
sp Jimmy Sangster
ph Arthur Grant
ad Scott MacGregor

Robert Horton
Sebastian Cabot
Jill St John

1969 **MOON ZERO TWO** (Hammer)
p   Michael Carreras
sp Michael Carreras
    from a story by Gavin Lyall, Frank Hardman
    and Martin Davison
ph Paul Beeson

James Olson
Catherina Von Schell
Warren Mitchell
Adrienne Corri
Ori Levi

ad Scott MacGregor   Dudley Forster
m   Don Ellis   Bernard Bresslaw

1970 **THE VAMPIRE LOVERS** (Hammer)

p   Harry Fine & Michael Style   Ingrid Pitt
sp Tudor Gates   Pippa Steel
    from *Carmilla*   Madeline Smith
    by J Sheridan Le Fanu   Peter Cushing
ph Moray Grant   George Cole
ad Scott MacGregor   Dawn Addams
                          Kate O'Mara
                          Douglas Wilmer

1970 **SCARS OF DRACULA** (Hammer)

p   Aida Young   Christopher Lee
sp John Elder   Dennis Waterman
ph Moray Grant   Jenny Hanley
ad Scott MacGregor   Christopher Matthews
                          Patrick Troughton
                          Michael Gwynn

1971 **DR JEKYLL & SISTER HYDE** (Hammer)

p   Albert Fennell & Brian Clemens   Ralph Bates
sp Brian Clemens   Martine Beswicke
ph Norman Warwick   Gerald Sim
ad Robert Jones   Lewis Fiander

1972 **ASYLUM** (Amicus)

p   Max J Rosenberg & Milton Subotsky   Peter Cushing
sp Robert Bloch   Britt Ekland
ph Denys Coop   Robert Powell
ad Tony Curtis   Patrick Magee
                          Charlotte Rampling
                          Herbert Lom
Grand Prix   Barry Morse
Convention Française du   Barbara Parkins
Cinema Fantastique 1973   Sylvia Syms
                          Richard Todd

1972 **~~AND NOW THE SCREAMING STARTS!** (Amicus)

p   Max J Rosenberg & Milton Subotsky   Peter Cushing
sp Roger Marshall   Herbert Lom
    from the novel *Fengriffin*   Patrick Magee
    by David Case   Stephanie Beacham
ph Denys Coop   Ian Ogilvy
ad Tony Curtis   Geoffrey Whitehead

1972 **THE VAULT OF HORROR** (Amicus)

p   Max J Rosenberg & Milton Subotsky   Dawn Addams
sp Milton Subotsky   Tom Baker

		Michael Craig
	from the strip cartoons	Michael Craig
	by Bill Gaines	Glynis Johns
ph	Denys Coop	Edward Judd
ad	Tony Curtis	Curt Jurgens

1973 THE LEGEND OF THE 7 GOLDEN VAMPIRES (Hammer/Shaw)

p	Don Houghton	Peter Cushing
sp	Don Houghton	David Chiang
ph	John Wilcox	Julie Ege
ad	Johnson Sao	Robin Stewart
		Shih Szu

1980 THE MONSTER CLUB (Sword & Sorcery)

p	Milton Subotsky	Vincent Price
sp	Edward & Valerie Abrahams	John Carradine
	from the novel by R Chetwynd-Hayes	Donald Pleasence
ph	Peter Jessop	Stuart Whitman
ad	Tony Curtis	Richard Johnson
		Barbara Kellerman
		Britt Ekland
		Simon Ward

1983 Screenplay: **JANE THE QUENE**

1984 THE MASKS OF DEATH (Tyburn)

p	Kevin Francis	Peter Cushing
sp	NJ Crisp	John Mills
	from story by John Elder	Anne Baxter
ph	Brendan J Stafford	Ray Milland
ad	Geoffrey Tozer	Anton Diffring
m	Malcolm Williamson	Gordon Jackson

1986 Treatment: **LOVERS ON THE NILE**

1986/87 Screenplay: **WHITEOUT** (Owl Productions)

1988 Screenplay: **DOCTOR FRIGO**

1990 Treatment: **GHOST FROM THE GRAND BANKS**

TELEVISION

NB Episodes are listed in production order. Where they can be reliably established, original transmission dates are given in brackets alongside episode titles. Where programmes did not receive simultaneous network transmissions, a specific region is specified.

1961 ZERO ONE (MGM/BBC)
starring Nigel Patrick, Bill Smith

Million Dollar Life (19 December 1962)
sp David T Chantler

And Maya Makes Three (29 May 63)
sp   Michael Pertwee

1963   **THE SAINT** (1963-66 New World/ITC, 1966-68 Bamore/ITC)
starring Roger Moore
transmission dates given for ATV region

Teresa (10 October 1963)   Lana Morris
sp   John Kruse   Eric Pohlmann

Luella (23 January 1964)   David Hedison
sp   John Kruse and Harry W Junkin   Sue Lloyd

The Good Medicine (6 February 1964)   Suzanne Lloyd
sp   Norman Borisoff   Barbara Murrey

The Scorpion (29 October 1964)   Nyree Dawn Porter
sp   Paul Erickson   Dudley Sutton

1964   **The Set-Up** (14 January 1965)   Penelope Horner
sp   Paddy Manning O'Brine   John Stone

The Inescapable Word (28 January 1965)   Ann Bell
sp   Terry Nation   James Maxwell

The Frightened Inn-Keeper (18 February 1966)   Michael Gwynn
sp   Norman Hudis   Suzanne Neve

1966   **The Helpful Pirate** (28 October 1966)   Erika Remberg
sp   Roy Russell   Paul Maxwell

The Queen's Ransom (30 September 1966)   Dawn Addams
sp   Leigh Vance

The Fiction Makers   Sylvia Syms
(part one 8 December 1968, part two 15 December 1968)
sp   John Kruse

Little Girl Lost (2 December 1966)   June Ritchie
sp   Leigh Vance

Flight Plan (23 December 1966)   William Gaunt
sp   Alfred Shaughnessy,   Fiona Lewis
        from a story by
        Anthony Squire

The Persistent Patriots (6 January 1967)   Edward Woodward
sp   Michael Pertwee   Jan Waters

The Art Collectors (27 January 1967)   Ann Bell
sp   Michael Pertwee   Peter Bowles

Simon and Delilah (24 March 1967)   Ronald Radd
sp C Scott Forbes   Lois Maxwell

1968 **Legacy For The Saint** (13 October 1968)   Ivor Dean
sp Michael Winder   Alan MacNaughton

The Time to Die (10 November 1968)   Suzanne Lloyd
sp Terry Nation   Maurice Good

1964 **THE HUMAN JUNGLE** (Independent Artists/ABC)
starring Herbert Lom, Michael Johnson, Sally Smith and Mary Yeomans
transmission dates given for ATV region

Conscience on a Rack (27 March 1965)   Flora Robson
sp William McIlwraith

Solo Performance (13 March 1965)   Margaret Lockwood
sp William McIlwraith   James Villiers

Enemy Outside (8 May 1965)   Tony Tanner
sp William McIlwraith   Lloyd Reckford

Heartbeats in a Tin Box (15 May 1965)   Judith Scott
sp Robert Stewart   Ray McAnally
                                          Catherine Lacey
                                        Susan George

Dual Control (17 April 1965)   Dennis Price
sp Anne Francis   Peggy Cummins
                                            Annette André

The Quick and the Dead (3 April 1965) Richard Johnson
sp John Kruse   Robert Beatty
                                            Joanne Dainton

Skeleton in the Cupboard (24 April 1965) Sonia Dresdel
sp William McIlwraith   Nora Nicholson
                                          Roger Livesey

The Man Who Fell Apart (10 April 1965) Rita Tushingham
sp John Kruse   Alan Dobie

1964 **GIDEON'S WAY** (New World/ITC)
starring John Gregson and Alexander Davion
transmission dates given for ATV region

The White Rat (13 May 1965)   Virginia Maskell
sp Harry W Junkin   Ray McAnally

The Firebug (1 April 1965)   George Cole
sp David Chantler

Subway To Revenge (27 May 1965)   Anne Lawson
sp   Norman Hudis   Donald Churchill

1965   **THE AVENGERS** (Telemen/ABC)
starring Patrick Macnee and Diana Rigg
transmission dates given for ABC region

Too Many Christmas Trees (25 December 1965)   Mervyn Johns
sp   Tony Williamson   Edwin Richfield

Room Without A View (8 January 1965)   Paul Whitsun-Jones
sp   Roger Marshall   Peter Jeffrey

Two's A Crowd (18 December 1965)   Warren Mitchell
sp   Philip Levene   Julian Glover

Silent Dust (1 January 1966)   William Franklin
sp   Roger Marshall   Jack Watson

The Town of No Return (2 October 1965)   Alan MacNaughtan
sp   Brian Clemens   Patrick Newall

The Thirteenth Hole (29 January 1966)   Patrick Allen
sp   Tony Williamson   Hugh Manning

The Girl from Auntie (22 January 1966)   Liz Fraser
sp   Roger Marshall   Alfred Burke

1968   **THE AVENGERS** (ABC/Thames)
starring Patrack Macnee and Linda Thorson
transmission date given for Thames region

Split! (23 October 1968)   Nigel Davenport
sp   Brian Clemens   Julian Glover

1966   **THE BARON** (Filmakers/ITC)
starring Steve Forrest and Sue Lloyd
transmission dates given for ATV region

There's Someone Close Behind You
(28 December 1966)   Richard Wyler
sp   Terry Nation & Dennis Spooner   Jerome Willis

The Long, Long Day (22 March 1967)   Peter Arne
sp   Tony O'Grady   Dallia Penn

Night of the Hunter (22 February 1967)   Derek Godfrey
sp   Terry Nation   Katharine Blake

The Man Outside (5 April 1967)   David Bauer
sp   Terry Nation   Paul Maxwell

1968   **THE CHAMPIONS** (Scoton/ITC)
starring Stuart Damon, Alexandra Bastedo, William Gaunt and Anthony Nichols
transmission dates given for ATV region

Nutcracker (2 April 1969)	William Squire
sp Philip Broadley	

Autokill (30 April 1969)	Eric Pohlmann
sp Brian Clemens	Paul Eddington

1968 **RANDALL & HOPKIRK (DECEASED)** (Scoton/ITC)
starring Mike Pratt, Kenneth Cope and Annette André
transmission dates given for ATV region

But What A Sweet Little Room (28 November 1969)	Michael Goodliffe
sp Ralph Smart	Norman Bird

Who Killed Cock Robin? (5 December 1969)	Cyril Luckham
sp Tony Williamson	Jane Merrow

1968   **DEPARTMENT S** (Scoton/ITC)
starring Peter Wyngarde, Joel Fabiani, Rosemary Nicols and Dennis Alaba Peters
transmission date given for ATV region

The Pied Piper of Hambledown (30 March 1969)	Richard Vernon
sp Donald James	Gina Warwick

1968   **JOURNEY TO THE UNKNOWN** (Hammer/20th Century-Fox)
transmission date given for London Weekend Television region

The Indian Spirit Guide (16 November 1968)	Julie Harris
sp Robert Bloch	Tom Adams

1970   **THE PERSUADERS!** (Tribune/ITC)
starring Tony Curtis and Roger Moore
transmission dates given for ATV region

Read and Destroy (28 January 1972)	Joss Ackland
sp Peter Yeldham	Nigel Green
	Kate O'Mara

The Gold Napoleon (24 September 1971)	Susan George
sp Val Guest	Alfred Marks
	Laurence Naismith

Someone Like Me (29 October 1971)	Reginald Marsh
sp Terry Nation	Anne De Vigier
	Bernard Lee

The Ozerov Inheritance (11 February 1972)	Gladys Cooper
sp Harry W Junkin	Prunella Ransome
	Gary Raymond

1971 **JASON KING** (Scoton/ITC)
      starring Peter Wyngarde
      transmission dates given for ATV region

      Wanna Buy A Television Series? (15 September 1971) David Bauer
      sp Dennis Spooner   Derek Francis
                                                            Anna Palk

      A Royal Flush (24 March 1972)   Elaine Taylor
      sp Philip Broadley   Penelope Horner
                                                            Georgina Simpson

      Zenia (14 April 1972)   Patricia English
      sp Philip Broadley   Michael Goodliffe
                                                            Angela Douglas

      That Isn't Me, It's Somebody Else (28 April 1972) George Murcell
      sp Dennis Spooner   Patrick Troughton
                                                            Toby Robins

1972 **THE PROTECTORS** (Group Three/ITC)
      starring Robert Vaughn, Nyree Dawn Porter and Tony Anholt
      transmission date given for ATV region

      The Big Hit (26 January 1973)   Derek Smith
      sp Donald James

1977 **THE RETURN OF THE SAINT** (Tribune/RAI/ITC)
      starring Ian Ogilvy

      Yesterday's Hero (22 October 1978)   Ian Hendry
      sp John Kruse, from a story by Roger Parkes   Annette André

      Tower Bridge Is Falling Down (10 December 1978) John Woodvine
      sp Leon Griffiths   Alfie Bass

1978 **DANGER UXB** (Euston Films/Thames)
      starring Anthony Andrews, Maurice Roëves and Judy Geeson
      with Ian Cuthbertson, Jeremy Sinden and Deborah Watling

      Just Like A Woman (22 January 1979)
      sp Jeremy Paul

      The Quiet Weekend (12 February 1979)
      sp Jeremy Paul

      Butterfly Winter (12 March 1979)
      sp Jeremy Paul

1979 **SHERLOCK HOLMES AND DOCTOR WATSON** (Polish television)
      starring Geoffrey Whitehead and Donald Pickering

A Case of High Security   Derek Bond
sp   Robin Bishop   Julian Fellowes

The Case of the Body in the Case   Geoffrey Bayldon
sp   Tudor Gates   George Mikell

The Case of the Deadly Tower   Catherine Schell
sp   Joe Morhaim   Geoffrey Bayldon

The Case of Smith and Smythe   Bernard Bresslaw
sp   Joe Morhaim, Sheldon Reynolds   Tommy Godfrey

The Case of the Luckless Gambler   Derren Nesbitt
sp   Joe Morhaim   Tommy Godfrey

1979   **MINDER** (Euston Films/Thames)
Starring George Cole and Dennis Waterman, with Glynn Edwards, Patrick Malahide
and Peter Childs

The Smaller They Are... (12 November 1979)   David Jackson
sp   Leon Griffiths   Hans Meyer

Aces High – And Sometimes Very Low
(3 December 1979)   Anthony Valentine
sp   Leon Griffiths   Anthony Scott

The Dessert Song (7 January 1980)   Peter Bland
sp   Andrew Payne   Diane Keen

1980   **Whose Wife Is It Anyway?** (18 September 1980)   David Daker
sp   Tony Hoare   Molly Veness

1981   **Why Pay Tax** (10 March 1982)   Kika Markham
sp   Leon Griffiths   Nigel Davenport

Broken Arrow (17 March 1982)   Sean Mathias
sp   George Day   Michael Graham Cox

1984   **Second Hand Pose** (10 October 1984)   Bill Murray
sp   Tony Hoare   Eileen Nicholas

Around the Corner (26 December 1984)   Colin Farrell
sp Tony Hoare   Brian Capron

1985   **Return of the Invincible Man**
(18 September 1985)   John Bluthal
sp   Leon Griffiths   Pat Roach

Waiting For Goddard (9 October 1985)   Ronald Fraser
sp   Leon Griffiths   Kenneth Cope

1988 **It's A Sorry Lorry, Morrie** (2 January 1989)   Ronald Fraser
    sp Tony Hoare   Roy Kinnear

    The Last Video Show (23 January 1989)   Ian McShane
    sp Andrew Payne   Rula Lenska

    An Officer and a Car Salesman (26 December 1988) Richard Briars
    sp Tony Hoare   Diana Quick

1979 **THE FLAME TREES OF THIKA** (Euston Films/Thames)

    The Promised Land (1 September 1981)
    Hyenas Will Eat Anything (8 September 1981)
    Happy New Year (15 September 1981)
    Friends in High Places (22 September 1981)
    A Real Sportsman (29 September 1981)
    Safari (6 October 1981)
    The Drums of War (13 October 1981)

    p   John Hawkesworth &   Hayley Mills
        Christopher Neame   David Robb
    sp John Hawkesworth   Nicholas Jones
        from the book by Elspeth Huxley   Sharon Mughan
    ph Ian Wilson   Ben Cross
    ad Roy Stannard   Holly Aird
    m   Ken Howard & Alan Blaikley   John Nettleton

1982 **Q.E.D.** (Consolidated Productions)
    Starring Sam Waterston, George Innes, AC Weary, Julian Glover and Caroline Langrishe
    Transmission dates given for Central region

    The Infernal Device (7 February 1984)   Ian Ogilvy
    sp Wallace Ware

    The Limehouse Connection (27 March 1984)   Burt Kwouk
    sp William Frug

1982 **THE IRISH RM** (Channel 4/Ulster)
    Starring Peter Bowles, with Bryan Murray, Lise-Ann McLaughlin, Anna Manahan,
    Brendan Conroy, Diane Fletcher, Niall Toibin, Sarah Badel, Alan Stanford, William
    Boyde, John Wells and Dinsdale Landen
    Transmission dates given for Channel 4

1983 **A Horse! A Horse!** (12 July 1984)
    sp Rosemary Ann Sisson

    Oweneen The Sprat (2 August 1984)
    sp Alfred Shaughnessy

    The Aussolas Martin Cat (16 August 1984)
    sp Rosemary Ann Sisson

1984   **The Muse in Skebawn** (2 June 1985)
sp Hugh Leonard

Major Apollo Riggs (9 June 1985)
sp Julia Jones

A Friend Of Her Youth (16 June 1985)
sp Bill Craig

In the Curranhilly Country (23 June 1985)
sp Alfred Shaughnessy

Lisheen Races (30 June 1985)
sp Bill Craig

The Devil You Know (7 July 1985)
sp Hugh Leonard

1985   **FAIRLY SECRET ARMY** (Video Arts/Channel 4)
starring Geoffrey Palmer and Diane Fletcher, with Diana Weston, Jeremy Child, John
Nettleton, Michael Robbins, Liz Fraser, Gary Cady, Richard Ridings and Jeremy Sinden
sp David Nobbs

I've Got A Job For You (1 September 1986)
Odd Chaps, Women (8 September 1986)
This Could Be Extremely Dangerous, Sir (15 September 1986)
One Mistake, Whole Caboosh Plughole (22 September 1986)
Ever Tried Making Love To A Marxist? (29 September 1986)
You're Going To Be A Hero, Harry (6 October 1986)
Treacherous Chaps, Causes (13 October 1986)

1989   **SARACEN** (Central)
Starring Christian Burgess, Jimmy Clarke and Ingrid Lacey

Tooth and Claw (14 October 1989)   Michael Byrne
sp Chris Kelly   John Bennett

1990   **THE GOOD GUYS** (Havahall Pictures/LWT)
Starring Nigel Havers and Keith Barron

The Boys From Briarshill   Sara Crowe
sp Jeremy Burnham   Hilary Gish

Relative Values (31 January 1992)   Sheila Gish
sp John Flanagan, Andrew McCulloch   Elizabeth Hurley

1992   **Dog Days** (19 February 1993)   Joanna David
sp Christopher Matthew   Stratford Johns

1991 Screenplay: **IN THE BEES AND HONEY** (Episodes one and two) (Miracle Productions)

INDEX